About the Author

Diane Allwood Egerton was born in Winnipeg, Manitoba in 1954. She graduated from the University of Western Ontario (gold medal for language and literature) in 1976. During the year of 1976-7 she completed her MA at the University of Toronto and went on to study publications procedures at Harvard University.

In 1977 Diane obtained her rst employment in the production/editorial epartment at the University of Toronto Press. When she left UTP in 1982 she began working as a freelance editor and writer. Her clients included The Porcupine's Quill, *Maclean's* magazine, the Art Gallery of Ontario, Doubleday Canada and numerous other organisations. She also wrote regularly for the *London Free Press*, the *Canadian Book Review Annual*, *Quill & Quire*, and Toronto-based music journal *Fugue.* In subsequent years she wrote biographies of Canadian notables for Gale Publishing, Detroit.

While Diane was the acquisitions editor of T*he Devil's Artisan: the Canadian Review of the Printing Arts* (The Porcupine's Quill), she wrote a number of biographies and review articles on Canadian printmaking. It was only in 1997 that she focused her interest on her Irish heritage (her grandparents were from County Tyrone, County Fermanagh and County Longford). In that year she published an illustrated article on the Ulster sculptor and illustrator Sophia Rosamund Praeger. Positive response to that article led to her researching a grant from the Belfast Natural History and Philosophical Society in 1998 to help reproduce many of Mabel Annesley's wood-engraved images. Fortuitously, Mabel Annesley's archive at McMaster University in Hamilton, Ontario is very close to Stratford, Ontario, where Diane and her husband live.

Concurrently with the publication of *Artist and Aristocrat*, her biography of Mabel Annesley, Diane's attention has turned to the English-born Irish illustrator, Elizabeth Rivers, known for her illustrations for the books of Seán Ó Faoláin, Frank O'Connor and Daniel Corkery, as well as for the Yeats sisters at the Cuala Press.

Front Cover: Untitled, wood engraving,
198 x 122 (no. 5 of 25).
Back Cover: Mabel as a debutante

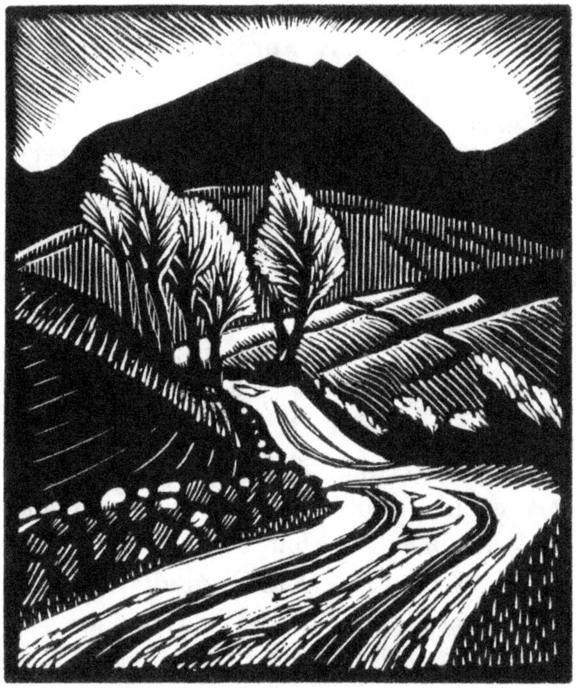

By Bryansford,
90 × 77, *County Down songs,* p. 8.

Dedication

To my husband, Mark, whose steady, loyal presence made it possible to complete this book, and in memory of my father, James Egerton, whose Ulster parentage bred my interest.

Artist and aristocrat

The life and work of Lady Mabel Annesley, 1881–1959

Diane Allwood Egerton

ULSTER HISTORICAL FOUNDATION

Ulster Historical Foundation is pleased to acknowledge support for this publication provided by the Belfast Natural History and Philosophical Society, the Esmé Mitchell Trust, the Mrs Gerald Annesley and Mrs Margaret Ogilvie. All contributions are gratefully acknowledged.

First Published 2010
by the Ulster Historical Foundation
Charity Ref. No. XN48460
E-mail: enquiry@uhf.org.uk
Web: www.ancestryireland.com
www.booksireland.org.uk

ISBN: 978-1903688-98-4

Printed by W&G Baird
Design by Cheah Design

CONTENTS

ABBREVIATIONS

Atsib	*As the sight is bent*
BRAMU	Bertrand Russell Archive at McMaster University

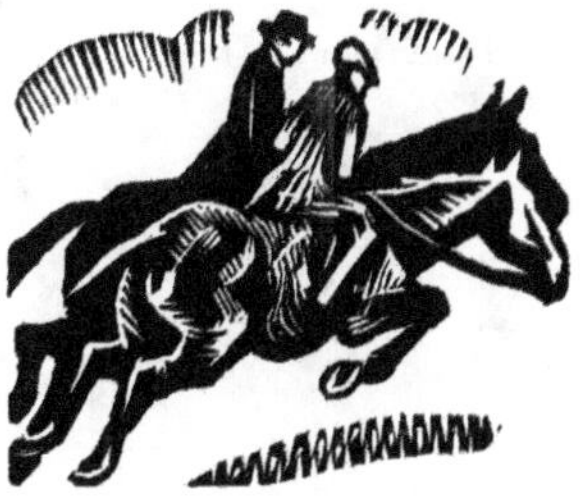

Rides, 35 × 40, *As the sight is bent*, p. 33.

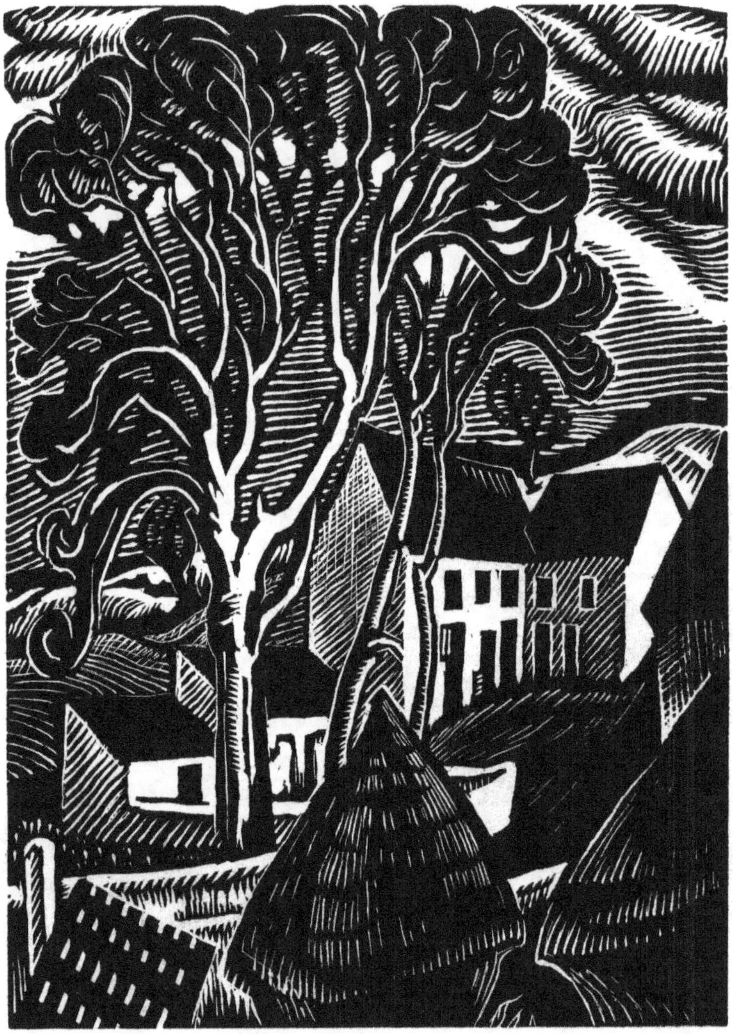

Ash trees beside a farm,
wood engraving, 135 × 100 (no. 14 of 25).

Mabel Annesley

ACKNOWLEDGEMENTS

I am grateful to the following individuals: to Marjorie Allwood for her generous financial assistance, to Martin Andrews for his encouragement and suggestions, to Martyn Anglesea for professional help. To Noel and Caroline Annesley I offer many thanks for the time and hospitality they so graciously extended. To Lil Annesley, for so kindly welcoming me and my husband into her home, and for providing great personal and financial support, thanks are also due. Thanks also to Robert Brandeis, Linda Ballard, Nicola Gordon Bowe, Hazel Curry and Olivia Fitzpatrick for their professional assistance. Many thanks to Andrew Forson for showing us around the castle at Castlewellan; to James Ingle, Paul Larmour, Brian Kennedy, Ruth Lamb, Alicia McAuley, David Morris, Jill Morrison and Christine Mosser for their help in pointing the way in the research, design and editing of the book; and to Tony Mackle, Greta McIlveen, Margaret McNulty and Charles Nugent for their kind encouragement. Many thanks to Mabel's granddaughter, Margaret Ogilvie, for sharing her research material, for her enthusiasm for the project, for her extended hospitality and for her financial support. Thanks also to Fred Rankin, Norman Russell, Patricia Saunders, Joanna Selborne, Randall Speller and Sheila Turcon. Special thanks to Phyllis Urch, who edited several versions of the manuscript, and to Brian Walker for his generous commitment of time and for encouraging the overall project from the beginning.

Deepest good wishes to Fintan Mullan and Angélique Day for their indispensable help in seeing the manuscript published; thanks also to the Esmé Mitchell Trust, the Ulster Historical Foundation and the Belfast Natural History and Philosophical Society for moral and financial support.

Thanks are due to the law firm of Crawford and Lockhart on behalf of Mrs Mary E. Annesley, for permission to use copyrighted material, and to the following institutions for permission to consult and reproduce engravings and unpublished manuscripts in their collections: the British Museum; Ross's of Belfast; the Bertrand Russell Archives, McMaster University, Canada; Queen's University Library, Belfast; Central St Martins College of Art and Design, London; the Victoria and Albert Museum; the Whitworth Gallery, Manchester; the John Rylands Library, Manchester; the Ulster Museum; the Museum of New Zealand Te Papa Tongarewa; the Suter Art Gallery, New Zealand; and the Belfast Central Library (Newspaper Library).

FOREWORD: MABEL MARGUERITE ANNESLEY

It is always a great pleasure for me to remember my grandmother and to think about the days we spent together in Ireland, living in the great silver-grey granite castle that we both loved so dearly and where we both had been born. Castlewellan still stands today, majestically gazing down over parkland to the lake, the wooded hills beyond and the glorious Mourne Mountains sweeping up from the sea just six miles away.

How very fortunate we were to have lived in such a wonderful place. It is my grandmother's homecoming and her years there after the war that I remember so vividly. That was the time when I got to know her.

For some years previously she had lived in New Zealand. As I grew up we had written letters to each other but we had not met since I was a small child. I could not picture her at the time and I doubt that she knew what I looked like either. Nonetheless, her letters were always precious and carefully kept in a little brass box. Through them I felt and thought that I knew her.

When she came home, our actual meeting took place in the Oriental Hotel in London and was a revelation. She was unexpectedly small and seemed so shy. We sat among the oriental décor and drank cups of tea. Gradually I realized that a new chapter in my life was beginning and that she would certainly become a great influence as well as somebody very dear. Suddenly there was much to talk about and to discover. By chance, we had both studied at the same art school in London, albeit some 20 years apart. I too had taken classes in wood engraving, so I could well understand her distress and frustration at being unable to obtain woodblocks during those years when she first arrived in New Zealand. Not daunted, she had taken up the linoleum from the floor of her rented accommodation and set to work. Probably it had not made her a very popular tenant but she had produced some very beautiful, simple and strong cuts.

Many years later I searched for the little wooden house where she had lived in Nelson but without success. Sadly, the place where I thought it had been was now a busy petrol station, but I did find other old wooden houses, which were being carefully preserved and cherished, so I could picture her there. In Takaka, where she moved subsequently, she was still remembered for driving her invalid carriage up and over Takaka Hill. In those days the road was rough, extremely steep and extremely perilous, and her invalid carriage was worked by hand. This demonstrates her determination and the courage that stood her in good stead – for she suffered much ill health and knew much sorrow during her life.

Her New Zealand days were happy and gave her great scope and inspiration for her work. Although she was alone and on the other side of the world, her neighbours were friendly and kind and it was a new landscape to enjoy and to record. Then came her return to Ireland and Castlewellan, which is where I best like to picture her now: lying on a sofa, wrapped in a huge Arabian rug, reading – always reading. Books would arrive by post from the London Library and she would smile and snuggle down cosily with them, for by that stage her hands had become totally crippled by arthritis and her working days were over.

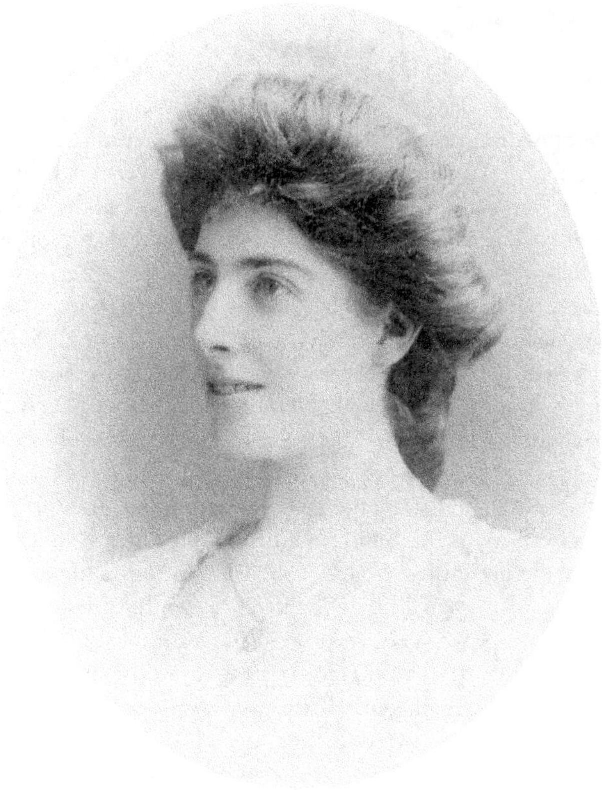

Mabel Annesley in her early years

In the cellars her printing press, which dated from the 1660s, lay idle. It was very handsome and of considerable weight but also working and usable – a boon for an art-student granddaughter to borrow. The downside, because the cellars were cold, dark and damp, was that it had to be used *in situ*. Next to the press was the inconvenience of a great stuffed python, similarly large and unmovable, its head raised in spitting position – a postwar abandonment, which was truly menacing by torch light. However, it could be sat on and, when it was, the press was a joy to use. I wonder what has become of the press and the python now – for, sadly, the last of the Annesley family's Castlewellan days were to be short.

Perhaps this book will introduce Lady Mabel's work to a new audience and younger generations will find it, and her life, of interest. If she had lived to see that she would have been so very pleased and so very proud.

Her wonderful cuts are her legacy to us all and include some superb engravings, which bring the County Down of her time to life again today.

Margaret Ogilvie
Pitmuies
November 2010

INTRODUCTION

In 1977, John Hewitt wrote that the state of being Irish was not primarily a question of blood and birth but a condition of involvement in Ireland's situation and of 'being moulded by it'. At the same time he commented that being an Ulsterman did not mean having a certain accent or being born in a certain place. Rather, it meant claiming an involvement in the life and landscape of Ulster – 'and finding therein the material for [one's] art'.[1] Hewitt might very well have been speaking of Mabel Annesley. Although she was born in London, England, and died in Long Melford, England, Mabel was most certainly an Ulsterwoman, through choice and involvement. And, as any Ulsterwoman would, Mabel worked day and night to embody her nationality in her artistic work. Her sister Constance, also a writer, commented on the 'immense concentration' Mabel applied to her work, and on how she would sit for hours gazing at her woodblocks. When printed, these showed an astonishing artistic gift, supplemented by a critical eye that did not allow for uncertainty or imperfection.[2]

As landlord and overseer of the family estate near Newcastle, County Down, Mabel is remembered fondly by her former tenants. 'She was gracious and courageous,' remarks Andrew Forson, director of the Christian Conference Centre that the estate has become. 'They would doff their caps when she went by: she was a real lady.'[3] She was, in her time, considered one of the foremost wood engravers among those early twentieth-century British artists who drew on the work of Thomas Bewick to revive that art form. Joanna Selborne, whose volume, *British wood-engraved book illustration, 1904–1940: a break with tradition*, is the leading reference work on the subject, comments most succinctly that Mabel was a brave woman. She suffered personal hardship in her early married life, then discovered wood engraving. Sadly, her career was cut short through ill health but she did produce a small quantity of 'highly original and inventive work' in the space of ten years.[4]

As a scholarly subject Mabel is intriguing because of factual errors regarding her life. Mabel Annesley was born in London, not in Newcastle, County Down, as some Irish sources affirm. She died in England, not in New Zealand. She suffered from severe arthritis but she did not lose her right hand, as some have claimed.[5]

Today, very few people know anything of Mabel Annesley. In her day, however, she earned considerable acclaim as an artist for her engraved book illustrations and prints. As a woman she showed exemplary courage in overcoming physical infirmity and in single-handedly saving her family's County Down estate from financial disaster.

Though the total number of books she illustrated is just four, Mabel did in fact produce a fairly significant number of individual prints from woodblocks and linoleum. Some of the prints were produced for private-press publications in England and Ireland; others illustrate Mabel's elegant autobiography, *As the sight is bent.*

A reader of the preface to her autobiography will find clear, concise words that never say too much, with a calm, reserved emotion beneath the modulated phrases. Mabel saw herself first as an artist and sights and symbols intrigued her. Her childhood was filled with images of 'small tenant farmers living in small whitewashed houses; and small shopkeepers living in small market squares', of 'bowler-hatted crowds every twelfth of July, thundering die-hard

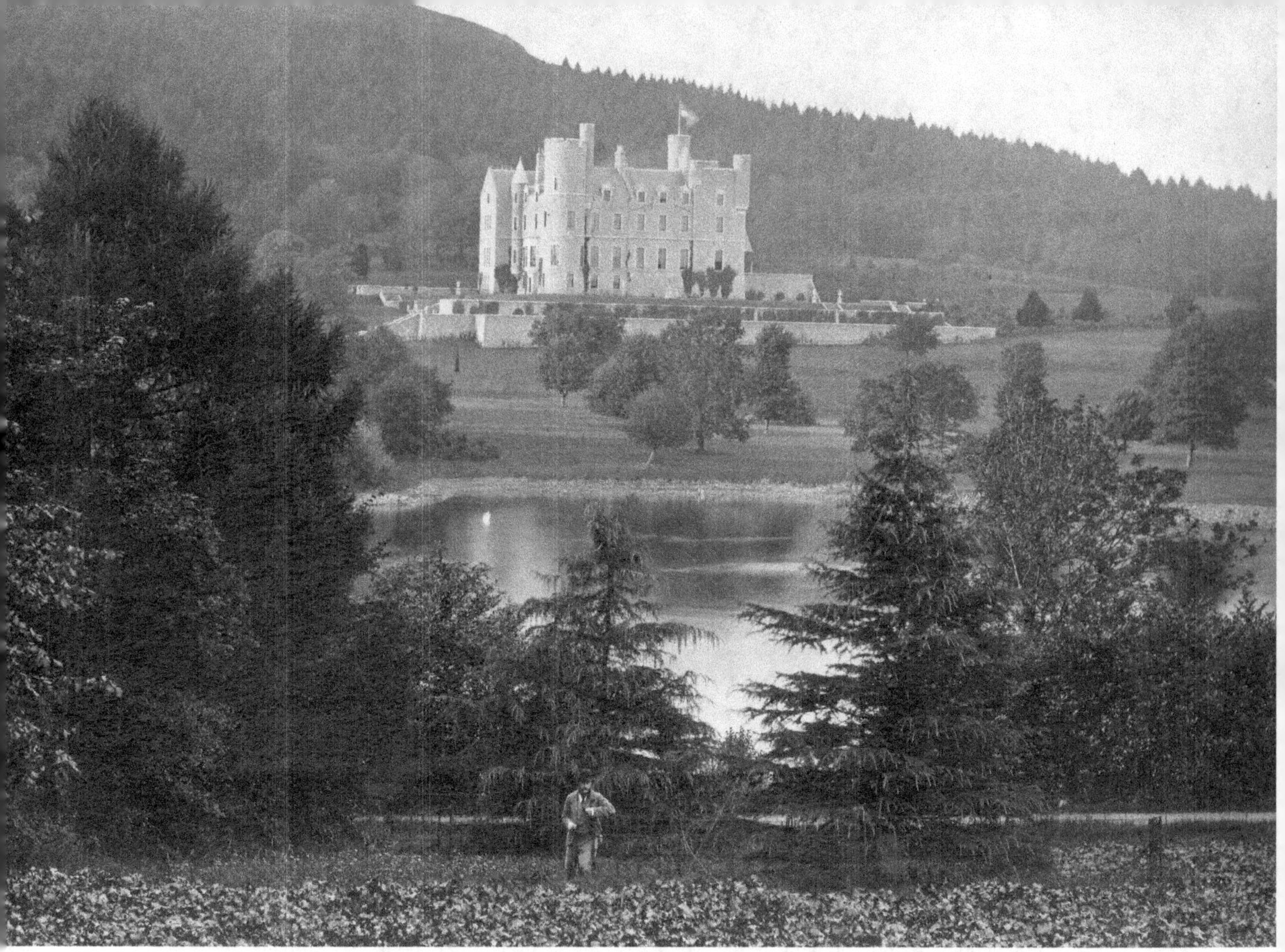

Castlewellan

Unionist principles on the Orange drums'. And then there was the landlord class, her own, which 'inhabited large and solidly built mansions encompassed by broad and boggy acres: mansions filled to the attics with Chippendale furniture; priceless, ill-kept silver; and astonishingly gaudy woolwork'.[6]

Mabel's autobiography is dominated by a strong sense of place, within an Anglo-Irish context. The very centre of her being was focused on the family estate, or the Big House, as was the case with the writer Elizabeth Bowen. Bowen's home, close to Cork, was built on a river. Like Mabel Annesley's, it boasted a magnificent garden:

> The not long past of these houses has been very intense: no Irish people – Irish or Anglo-Irish – live a day unconsciously. Lives in these houses, for generations, have been lived at high-pitch, only muted down by the weather, in psychological closeness to one another, and under the strong rule of the family myth.[7]

The Big House in Ireland rapidly became a symbol of wealth, authority and power, of an invisible dividing line between the native Irish and the transplanted Anglo-Irish gentry. But for the artist Mabel Annesley, who was born into a late Victorian paternalistic society and died ten years before the latest Troubles began, the similarities between landlord and tenant, native and planter, would have seemed much greater than they do today. As an aristocrat whose strongest loyalty still lay with Great Britain, which provided education for aristocratic sons and husbands for aristocratic daughters, Mabel was part of a small group with cultural links stretching beyond the boundaries of Ireland, into a more extensive aristocratic system.[8] She was a member of an Anglo-Irish type not often noticed by historians – the man or woman whose love of place transcended divisions based on religion, politics or place of origin.[9]

Confident in her birth, secure enough to share the land with fellow Irish people, natives and planters alike, Lady Mabel's outlook was similar to that of George Russell, the Ulsterman who commented that the Protestant Irish in Ulster did not want uniformity in culture or ideals, but a balance of diversities in wider tolerance. The moment complete uniformity was achieved, national life would become stagnant: 'we are glad to think we shall never achieve that uniformity which is the dream of commonplace minds'.[10] Like Elizabeth Bowen and Jonathan Swift before her, Mabel Annesley was poised 'between Ireland and England',[11] choosing to live her final years in England but never saying that she was English. She would probably have said she was an Ulsterwoman, and if that was not understood she would most certainly have said she was Anglo-Irish, with the emphasis on Irish. Most of her engravings and illustrations have an Irish theme. When she left Ireland she yearned to be in her home country with as much heartfelt anguish as her Catholic compatriots. Even as she clung to Irish Protestantism, her own sense of religion had been, since childhood, a sense of 'a cold, bare, echoing evangelical dogma'.[12] Her religion sprang from a love of art that embraced the Irish countryside, 'filtering through woodland, over water, across mountains' with new perceptions that worshipped the 'abstract and spiritual value of *things seen*'. For the final word on nationality and belonging, Mabel would surely have turned not to books or historians, but to the sure, true words of her own tenants on the Annesley land of Castlewellan: 'I wrought always here'.[13]

1 John Hewitt and Mike Catto, *Art in Ulster* (Belfast, 1977), p. 146.
2 Constance Malleson, *After ten years* (London, 1931), p. 15.
3 Andrew Forson, pers. comm., 2000.
4 Joanna Selborne, *British wood-engraved book illustration 1904–1940: a break with tradition* (Oxford, 1998), p. 182.
5 Chris Petteys, *Dictionary of women artists: an international dictionary of women artists born before 1900* (Boston, 1985).
6 Mabel Annesley, *As the sight is bent: an unfinished autobiography* (London, 1964) (henceforth cited as *Atsib*), p. 5.
7 Elizabeth Bowen, *Bowen's Court* (New York, 1942), p. 19.
8 A. Shanks, 'Northern Irish gentry culture', in Myrtle Hill and Sarah Barber (eds), *Aspects of Irish Studies* (Belfast, 1990), p. 85.
9 R.F. Foster, 'Varieties of Irishness', in Maurna Crozier (ed.), *Cultural traditions in Northern Ireland* (Belfast, 1989), p. 11.
10 Terence Brown, *Ireland: a social and cultural history, 1922–1985* (London, 1981), p. 133.
11 Victoria Glendinning, *Jonathan Swift* (London, 1998), p. 4.
12 *Atsib*, p. 5.
13 Ibid., p. 33.

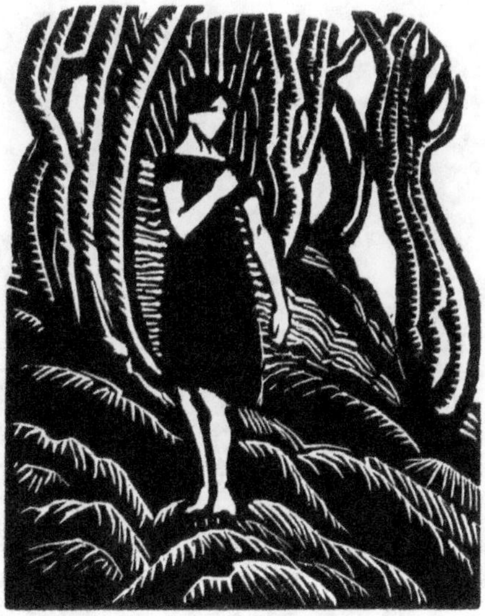

Untitled, 70 × 58,
Songs from Robert Burns, p. 51.

1
Beginnings

For a printmaker, choosing black-and-white wood engraving means rejecting colour and embracing a technically complex art form. Using difficult-to-master tools such as gravers and spitstickers, lint gouges and lining gouges, the wood engraver must cut and gouge within the parameters of an end-grain piece of maple or boxwood. Unlike the woodcutter or linocutter, the wood engraver can achieve an extremely clear image, unbound by the grains of wood that limit the former, and working with a much harder and more durable surface for printing than the latter. The final choice of how the artist will make his or her relief print, however, though certainly influenced by the quality achievable, can be due as much to chance as to anything else.

Mabel might also have been drawn to the art of black-and-white wood engraving because her childhood was full of that other black-and-white art, photography, so skilfully practised by her father. Hugh Annesley is considered one of Ireland's earliest photographers of distinction. His first album of the 1850s includes photographs of Castlewellan, Newcastle, the Mournes, the Mediterranean and India. He is also remembered for his gentle, humane portraits of the employees who worked on his Castlewellan estate. Far from ignoring the lined or rosy faces of gardener or cook, housemaid or smithy, Hugh Annesley was drawn

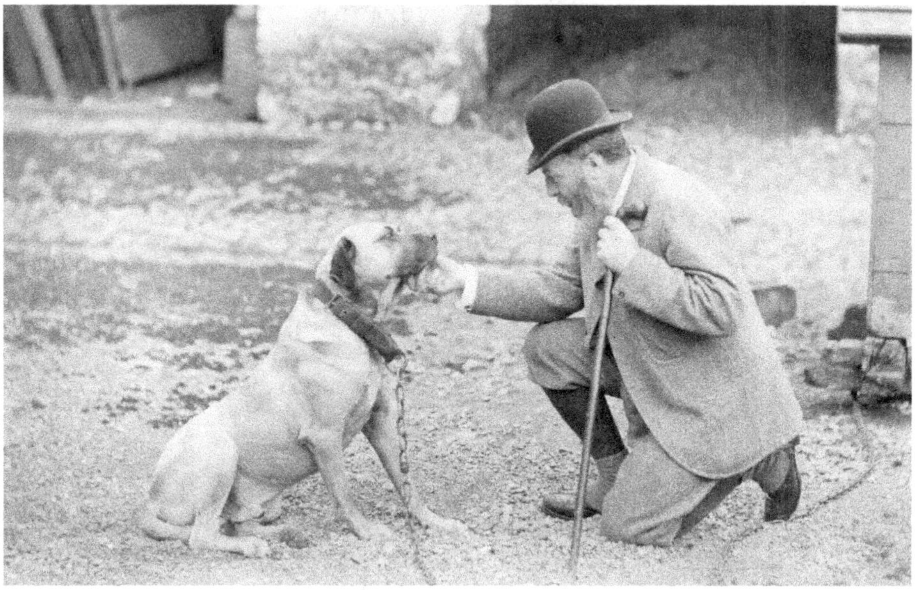

Hugh Annesley

to their unique and spirited character. Mabel Annesley observed them and, when her time came to manage the Annesley estate, emulated her father's sense of compassion and warmth towards them.

As might be expected, Hugh Annesley also produced charming photographs of his first child, Mabel. One photograph, taken in 1906, now in the collection of Margaret Ogilvie, shows the young woman at the age of 25. In it we see a handsome face, with masses of dark hair, arched brows and an aquiline nose. She lies wrapped in a large fur coat, reading. In the background a painter's easel is silhouetted; the window (or is it a painting?) is framed in dark wood. Lying on a makeshift cot, she appears to be the epitome of aristocratic ease, but what even the careful eye does not see is that the pile of books at her side is from a lending library in London. Only the informed will note that the young woman's hands are fearfully crippled with arthritis; moreover, her supine position may be due to a broken pelvis which occurred after the birth of her only son, Gerald, the year before.

In spite of such difficulties, however, Mabel Annesley's early married years were very happy. It was only after her father, husband and brother died, all within a few years of each other, that she was faced with the necessity of abandoning life in England and returning to Castlewellan to muster the soil into a paying estate. That she did so was as much due to her quiet charm and clear knowledge of her abilities as to her place among the Anglo-Irish aristocracy of Ulster.

Mabel Marguerite Annesley was born in London on 25 February 1881, the first daughter of the first marriage of the fifth earl of Annesley, Hugh. Hugh Annesley was the product of a long line of Annesleys. The first earl of Annesley was Francis Charles (the title created in 1789). Francis Charles was the son of William Annesley, who was created first Baron Annesley. Baron Annesley's father was Francis Annesley of Thorganby, Yorkshire, who was posted to Ireland in 1699 as commissioner of inquiry into forfeited estates. As commissioner, Francis 'was quick to paint a lurid picture of neglect, corruption [and] favouritism'.[1] Francis's oldest son, William, aquired the estate in 1741 and in 1758 he was awarded the peerage for his work in reclaiming the land around Castlewellan and for laying out and building the town that stands at the castle gates. The town was originally called Castlewilliam, but 'william' was slurred to 'wellan' by the native Irish accent. Rumour had it that Lord Annesley, a colonel of the regiment, threatened to resign his commission because of the number of Catholics in the ranks. He disapproved of some of his men attending mass and complained that in the Mourne district, over which he presided, the regiment boasted 'a cunning set of Presbyterians mixed with a set of Papists'.[2]

William, Baron Annesley had a way with the ladies. Historian Anthony Malcomson tells the story of William being struck with the appearance of Sophia Connor, wife of his brother's gardener. He eloped with her and later married her, illegally. Following the death of her 'husband', Sophia tried to prove the legitimacy of her son. Though she attempted to claim her son's right to the Annesley earldom, Sophia settled for £400, but complained that this did not permit her to 'resume her splendid appearance in Paris where she kept her barouche [and] her box at the opera, and moved in the finest circles'.[3]

Early letters of Mary Delany, the friend and correspondent of Jonathan Swift, indicate that the Annesleys were aware of their material wealth but honest in their dealings.[4] The

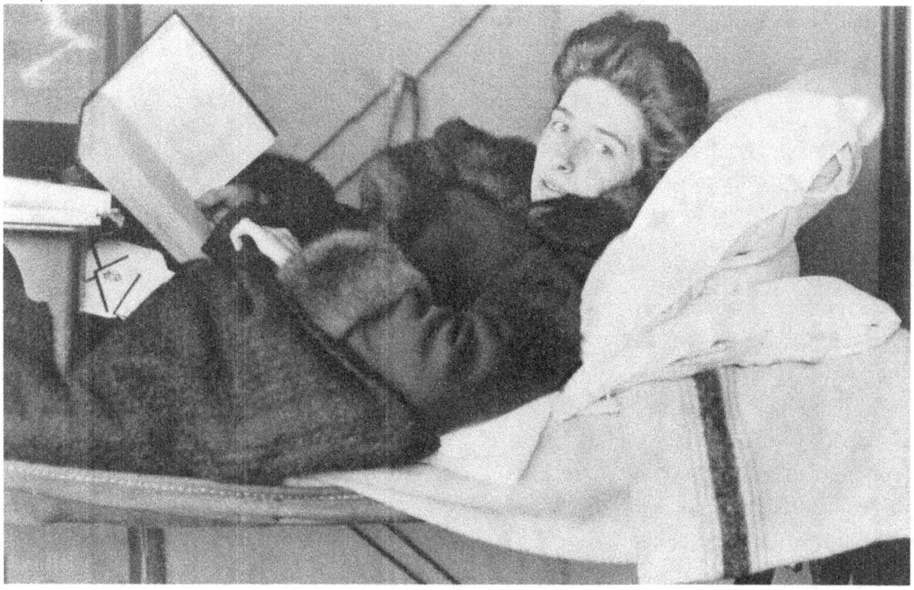

Mabel

women of the Annesley family were noted as unrefined in their feelings, with 'a jolly sort of family love for one another'.[5] Mary Delany's description of the 'cottage' where the family lived in 1751 declared that its situation 'had much of the majestic about it' – with mountains, wild woods and rocks and an extensive view of the ocean.[6] The Annesley estate, associated with the farm (which Mabel later fondly depicted in her engravings), consisted of three large courts. The first, which was arched around a kind of piazza, had houses for the carriages, with the granaries above. The second held barns, stables and housing for cattle, with a hayloft above. The third held two barns, floored with oak. The whole apparatus was very 'neat, strong and clever'.[7]

The youngest son of Francis Annesley of Thorganby was Richard and he succeeded William as the second earl. Richard had read for the bar and kept notebooks that indicate he was cursed with a persecution mania and a general mental disturbance. This led to enforced retirement.[8] Richard was succeeded by his son William Richard, the third earl, who died in 1838. Under William Richard, in the years preceding the Famine, the family built two schools, which were attended by children from 'Episcopalian, Presbyterian and Catholic families'.[9]

In the early 1800s, about 150 families effectively 'owned County Down'.[10] As one of those 150, the Annesleys considered it necessary to show their wealth with the building of a Big House or castle. Much of the land that had been held in partnership in the early nineteenth century was consolidated and the estate enlarged, regardless of tenancy. Like other regionally important families, the Annesleys maintained a lifestyle of 'status assertion, social obligation and mutual recognition, founded on the possession of inherited wealth'.[11]

With the death of William Richard, third earl of Annesley, and during the minority of the next earl, the estate was overseen by Hugh Moore, the brother of the third earl's widow. His notebooks cover problems of dispossessing pauper tenants and finding subscriptions for the Protestant Church. The third earl's widow, Priscilla Cecilia, was devoted to her sacred duties, as this excerpt from the autobiography of Constance Malleson, Mabel Annesley's half-sister, reveals:

> On Sundays she would stand all day on the lawn distributing bibles and religious tracts to the unfortunate trippers who flocked through the park to have a jolly time and to enjoy the beauty of the place.[12]

As a result of this religious fervour, all six of Priscilla Cecilia's sons were imbued with the strictest of principles. However, according to Constance Malleson, only Mabel's father, Hugh, turned out to display any of the virtues with which his mother had wished to inculcate her children. The fourth earl, also William Richard, managed to run through roughly £120,000, leaving a much-mortgaged estate to his brother, Hugh, in 1874.

Hugh, Mabel's father, had a horror of debt and immediately began instituting strict economies in order to save the estate. His first task was to begin working on the estate gardens; this continued until his death in 1908. He tried to develop the estate's collection of plants from all over the temperate world.[13] By purchasing rare shrubs, making new roads and enlarging lakes, Hugh made Castlewellan one of the beauty spots of Ireland – and, some think, of the world. Especially notable were the conifers and the rhododendrons which, viewed from the windows, provided a brilliant show of colour in the late autumn and early spring.

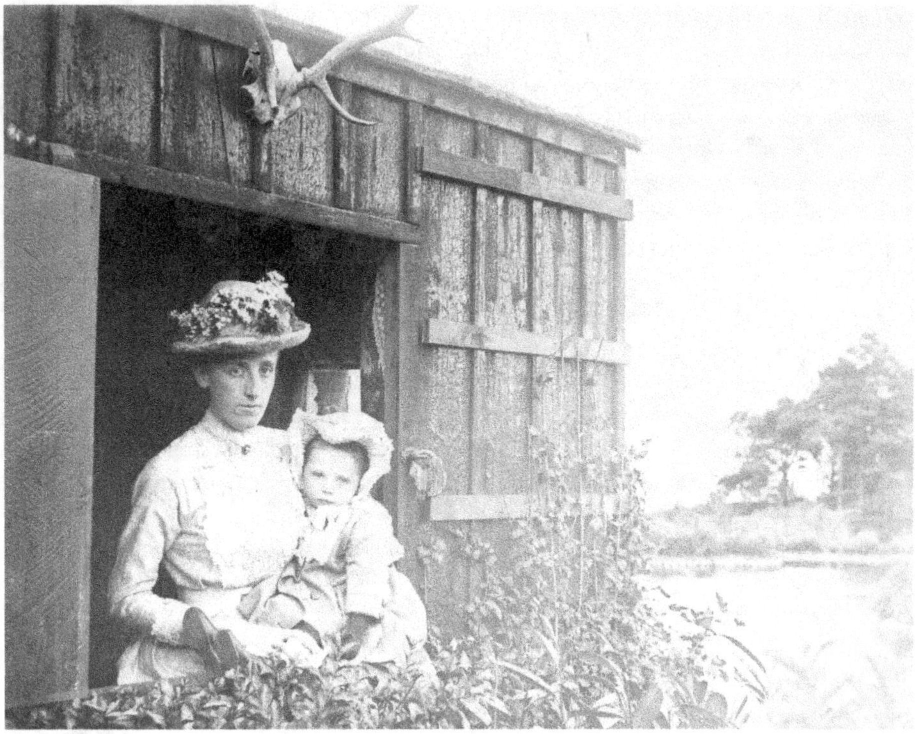

Tea House in Deer Park (August 1883): Mabel Countess Annesley (Mabel's mother) and Mabel

When he was not occupied in his garden, Hugh Annesley was busy with his tripod. Among his many photographs are several of Mabel as a small child. The photographs of the little girl, like the one taken when she was 25, are the work of a craftsman and artisan as much as of a doting father. Several early photographs show Mabel (or Daisy, as her parents called her) with a gentle, pensive look, in what appears to be the garb of an infant cossack (February 1884). In the same year, we see her twirling to get away from her nursemaid. An 1886 picture shows an impish five-year-old at the reins of a patient donkey, weighed down with children and with the pannier baskets that Lady Mabel speaks of so lovingly in *As the sight is bent*.

From earlier still, we have one of the few pictures of the young Mabel in her mother's arms. Mabel was only ten years old when her mother, Mabel Wilhelmina, died. During those first ten years she appears to have been a happy, lively little girl. She also appears to have inherited considerable artistic talent through her mother. Mabel's mother was the granddaughter of Sir Francis Grant, portrait painter and gentleman. Grant (1803–78) was, according to Sir Walter Scott, dedicated to fox-hunting and other sports, but not 'to any species of gambling'. He had also a strong passion for painting and possessed a very fine collection of art.[14] Although Grant was not trained as an artist, he was an attentive copier of the masters, and by 31 years of age he was exhibiting at the Royal Academy, to become the fashionable portrait painter of the day. His work is in many of the Big Houses of Great Britain, as well as in the permanent collections of the National Portrait Gallery and of the National Gallery of Scotland. He painted several portraits of his granddaughter, Mabel Wilhelmina. When he died on 5 October 1878 he was accorded the high honour (which his relatives refused) of burial in St Paul's Cathedral. Curiously, in addition to his great artistic heritage, Sir Francis Grant left behind a member of his household (a pageboy, in fact) by the name of Parr – a terrifying character, who took the job of butler at Castlewellan. According to Constance, 'Parr was large, be-whiskered and pompous.'[15] He was utterly devoted to Mabel, and it was said that on Mabel's wedding day Parr was to be seen with tears pouring down his face, 'his whole body shaking like a jelly'.[16]

Like Sir Francis Grant, Lady Mabel received very little artistic training as a child. In the early 1890s she attended the Frank Calderon School of Animal Painting in London. Her later wood engravings of pigs, horses, donkeys, goats and cattle, not to mention the household dog, all attest to her love for animals. Growing up in the sheltered environment of a baronial castle following her mother's death in 1891, Mabel was drawn to turn an inward eye to matters of the spirit. Though the photographs taken of her in her teens and early twenties show a rather brooding, solemn girl, the beauty of the Mourne Mountains and the sense of security in her home were evidently enough to nurture her aesthetic sense until her marriage in 1904.

Much of the security of the surroundings in which Mabel was raised lay specifically in her home, a Big House designed by the fashionable architect of the day, William Burn. The house, completed in 1855, was built from locally quarried granite, the same granite used for the Albert Memorial in London. The windows and doors are surrounded by ashlar, with a blue Bangor-slate roof. The sweeping approach to the castle is from the east and above the arched doorway is a coat of arms inscribed with the words 'Virtutis Amore' ('By Love of Virtue'), the family motto. Even today, as a conference centre, the castle is impressive. Indeed, William Crowe commented that he brought viewers to the village of Castlewellan in order to show the demesne acquired from the Annesley family. In his opinion, the *châteaux* on the Loire and in other parts of France were far behind the beauty of Castlewellan Castle in Ireland's 'rain-soaked country'.[17]

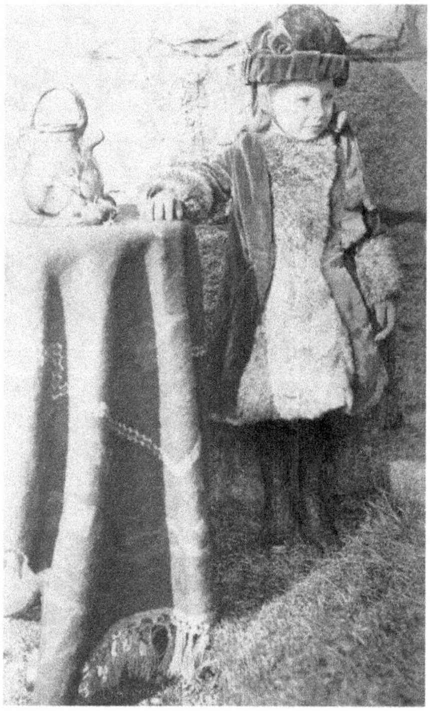

Mabel

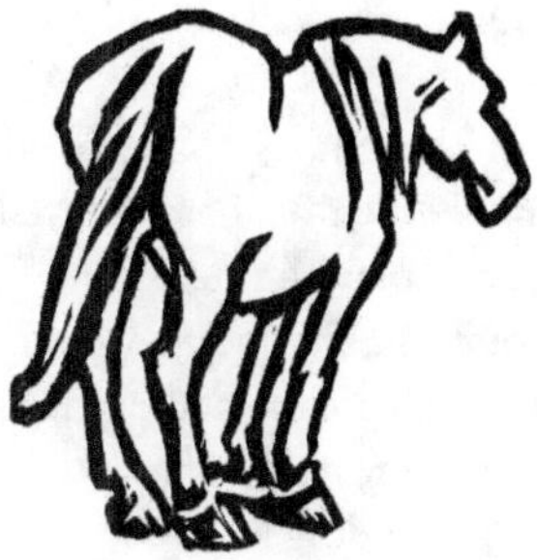

Connemara pony, 37.5 × 37.5, *As the sight is bent*, p. 56.

As with many of the Big Houses built before and at the same time, Castlewellan Castle has become part and parcel of Irish history. Its high walls separated the native population from the English planters, giving birth to two discrete worlds, both alien and close to each other. For Mabel Annesley, the house at Castlewellan became a touchstone of sanity and beauty, one that was to be there for her entire life. The house helped her to deal with the deep unhappiness arising from her relationship with her stepmother, Hugh's second wife, Priscilla.

Hugh Annesley's first wife, Mabel Wilhelmina Frances Markham, was an Englishwoman related to the Rutlands of Belvoir. She suffered very poor health throughout her life and, although she conceived several children during her short marriage to Hugh, only Francis and Mabel survived. In 1892 Hugh married his second wife – Priscilla Cecilia – a beautiful, sociable stepmother who 'frightened' Mabel. She always demanded a response, but Mabel never knew what kind. Priscilla bought Mabel smart clothes, which she wore in secret agony. She told her to 'make conversation' and consequently Mabel used conversation 'as a shield'.[18] While Mabel's tendency towards depression may have been inherited from her father, her melancholy was probably due in great part to her mother's early death. Without her mother to protect her, Mabel suddenly found herself part of a new family formation where the half-sisters were the babies and her stepmother was 35 years her father's junior. Only her father remained unchanged, with his quilted satin smoking jacket and beautiful white gleaming hair. He had a fine brow and a patrician nose, with a rosy complexion and clear blue eyes. Though he looked tranquil and lovable, he was, according to his youngest daughter Constance, both tyrannical and obstinate.[19]

Mabel received drawing lessons once a week from her governess, the 'dragon', and she always had the 'outline of the Mourne Mountains' to return to for inspiration.[20] In the eyes of her sister Constance, Mabel was always up to some devilment: putting her father's best horses over breakneck stone walls, fishing, climbing trees, or bird-nesting. Most important of those activities was horse-riding, which Mabel speaks of lovingly in her autobiography, and in which the local papers of the time reveal her active interest. *The Northern Whig* of the 1890s records that she was a guest at the annual lawn meet of the County Down Staghounds at Mount Stewart, where Lord and Lady Londonderry welcomed local aristocracy like 'Lady Beatrice Butler, the Earl and Countess Annesley and Lady Mabel Annesley'.[21]

By this time Mabel was 18 and ready to 'come out', reluctant and unsatisfactory debutante though she was. During those debutante days Mabel would frequent the Viceregal Lodge in Dublin (now Áras an Uachtaráin), and it was there that she became familiar with another young artist, Winston Churchill. In later years, when asked about Churchill, Mabel adhered to her original opinion. Churchill's reputation as an artist, she felt, was due to his being a great man. 'But I may be prejudiced against Winston,' she was quoted as saying. 'I have never

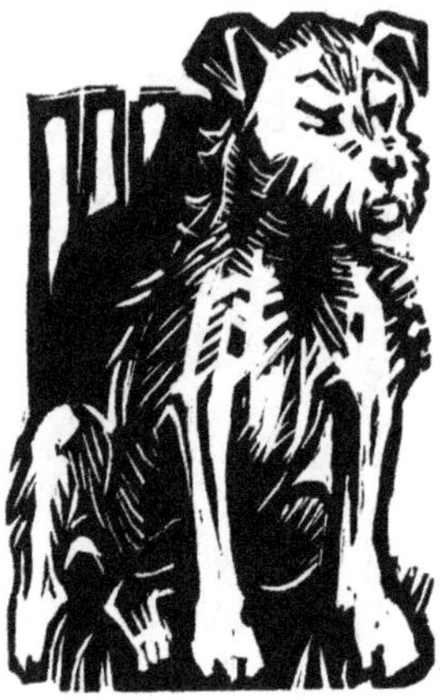

Puck-a-loo, 55 × 35,
As the sight is bent, p. 78.

really forgiven him for defeating me in the finals of a ping-pong tournament.'[22]

Somehow, in the midst of the endless partying that defined the social life of young women of that age, Mabel managed to strike up a friendship with the young flag lieutenant to Admiral Prince Louis of Battenberg. After three years of persuasion, Mabel's father assented to her marriage to Gerald Sowerby, a commoner with a great deal of love to give, if not money. Four years after her wedding in 1904, Mabel's father died of pneumonia. Her brother Francis succeeded him as sixth earl of Annesley. He would be the last of the Annesleys of Castlewellan to hold that title.

Throughout the tumult of birth, death and marriage in Mabel's life a small circle of artists was growing up around her in Ulster. While women were still under-represented in Ireland's gallery of artists – 'the art world [...] was an arena where a woman artist must battle against the odds if she were to survive, let alone flourish'[23] – both men and women artists in the tiny province of Ulster were only just beginning to make the pages of the newspapers. On 3 February 1880 the establishment of Mr Magill, Donegall Place, Belfast, boasted an exhibition of painting on porcelain, terra cotta and wood.[24] It was a time of great industrial expansion in Ulster but little attention was being paid to the arts. Ulster artists were barely able to survive and depended on art schools and dealers to show their work. One reviewer for *The Northern Whig* wrote that the works done by the students of the Government School of Art were most pleasing and valuable, showing the amount of artistic talent among the younger portion of Belfast's townfolk.[25] A few years later John Vinycomb delivered a lecture on the history and development of the Belfast Art Society.[26] In the same issue of *The Northern Whig* it was reported that the annual meeting of the Belfast Art Society was drawing attention to pictures on view in Dublin. On 13 June of that year the same paper indicated that Belfast was chiefly interested in the decorative arts; there appeared to be a growing desire for more artistic decoration of the home. A few months later *The Northern Whig* again commented that the Belfast Art Society was making a sketching excursion to Kellswater and every month each member would give a criticism of sketches. 'Art is not dead in Ireland yet,' pronounced the writer.[27]

Around this time Mabel Annesley was beginning to paint as well as sketch. One of her first known works, in the possession of her granddaughter, Margaret Ogilvie, shows a group of riders against a backdrop of hills. The theme is familiar, but the medium – a rare oil – is not, and it seems that Mabel turned to watercolour shortly before her marriage. *The arts in Ulster: a symposium* described her as 'a boldly decorative watercolourist',[28] while Ann Stewart lists in her reference work *Irish art societies and sketching clubs: index of exhibitors 1870–1980* that from the years 1900 to 1922 Annesley produced watercolours that included *Newcastle shore*, *Shimna River* and *At the top of the hill* (1900); and *The pool in the wind* and *Evening on the hills* (1901).[29] Most of the watercolours that Mabel completed are now in the hands of

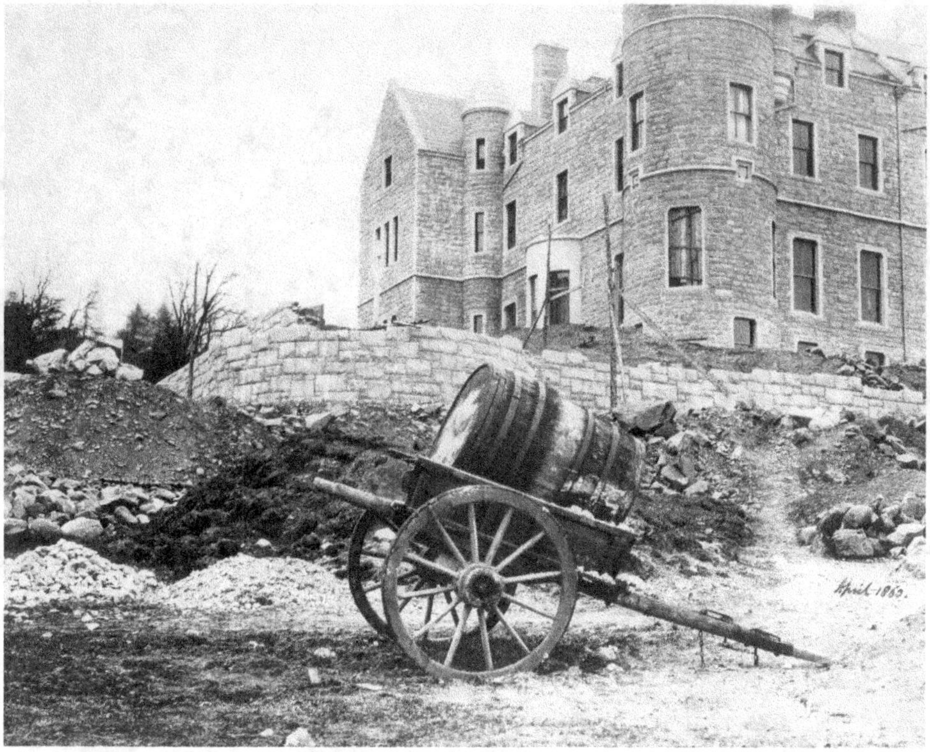

Building the terrace (1860) (Castlewellan)

private collectors; following her husband's death she turned to wood engraving for her solace. Very few of her watercolours can be found in institutional collections today, probably because most were far inferior to her wood engravings. A few of these watercolours, such as *Council flats*, which was reproduced in *Irish life and landscapes*, show a delicacy of feeling and a firm grasp on reality that partially explain her frequent appearance as a painter in artistic exhibitions.[30] Another explanation may lie in the fact that, as a member of the established Anglo-Irish gentry, she was extremely well connected.

After her son's birth in 1905 Mabel was confined to bed with crippling back pain. During this time, though she could not use her talents as an artist, she began to develop the theories and writing skills which would culminate in her autobiography, *As the sight is bent*. As she wrote in that work:

> I could think even if I could not draw. I began to ask myself questions: the questions that always surround the making of even simple pictures. Looking at the mountains I began to feel my way towards building up to a distance: towards a succession of planes. From the window I could see a change in the wind turn the hills from sapphire to opal.[31]

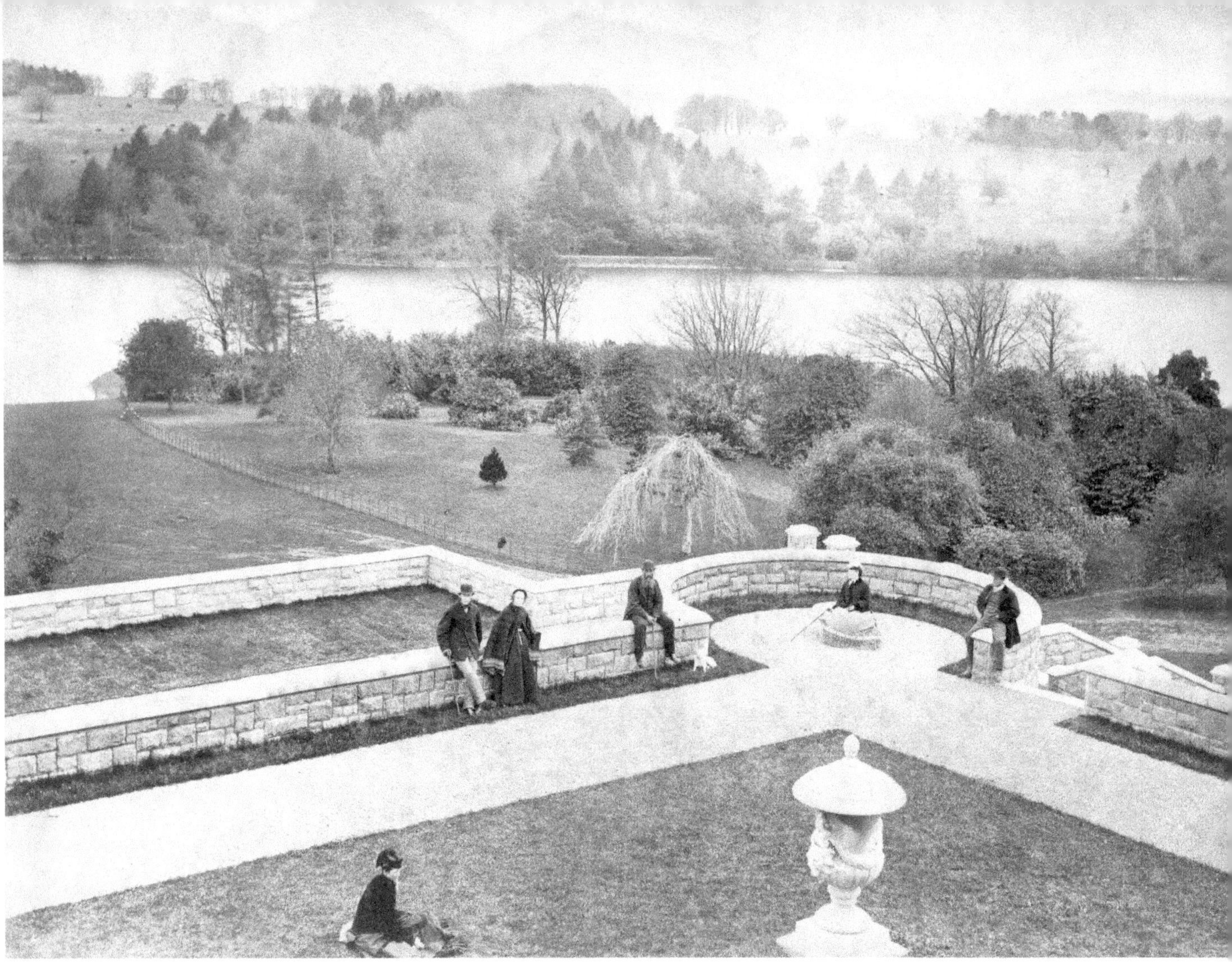

Castlewellan terrace, the lake, the Mournes

These were the thoughts of an artist accustomed to using colour. After a trip to Malta with her husband around 1905, she showed watercolours at 'a London gallery', receiving favourable notice in *The Saturday Review* as well as the financial reward that permitted her to buy the fur coat that she wore for many years, regardless of location or climate.

Happy in her marriage ('I got a good deal more out of marriage than I gave'),[32] she might easily have broken down completely with her husband's sudden death from appendicitis in 1913, only five years after the death of her constant and generous father and a year before the death in action of her younger brother Francis. Mabel does not write a great deal about any of these men, although they were, for a time, the pillars of her existence. Gerald Sowerby was an inveterate traveller who was ideally suited to the life of a flag lieutenant. Mabel rather mournfully commented:

> It was one of the drawbacks in the life of the sailor's wife that, as soon as one attached oneself to a house, one was almost immediately moved. People are like plants: some transplant easily, others suffer. I always attach myself to places, and my roots break and bleed when tugged up.[33]

Gerald, on the other hand, appeared to embrace each new place with the fervour of a natural military man. Even before meeting Mabel he wrote in his logbook about a trip to New Zealand and Australia. New Zealand's North Island, he wrote, was pretty mountainous. There were pigeons and pigs, a good deal of maize and large plantations of coconut trees. Coffee was grown a little way inland, while in the centre of the island there were quantities of wild duck 'which make good shooting if you can get near to them'.[34] Husband and wife shared an attention to detail and natural flow of language, and it was indeed a tragedy when the marriage ended after only ten years. With a simple poignancy, Mabel reduced his death to a few words – an image in black and white:

> In December I wore black clothes with soft white collars stitched in. I went back to Ireland. The men working by the roadside, instead of waving the old cheerful greeting, stood bareheaded for a moment as I passed.[35]

In an unpublished manuscript, Mabel wrote less obliquely about her loss. She wrote that after Gerald Sowerby's death the winter at Myrtle (the house built in Newcastle by Hugh Annesley for his convalescing daughter following Gerald Annesley's birth) seemed dark and interminable. The following spring came late, and Mabel would sit for many hours over the fire, with eyes that were blind to the beauty of hill, sea or sky. It was a sunny, windy June before she was able to climb into the little car her husband had christened Belinda. Descending an unknown road, she pulled up to ask her way. A tall lad and a girl were standing together and the lad replied, 'Why this road goes to every place – to Newry, Rostrevor, to Kilkeel and Annalong. To Ameriky.' That afternoon, continuing along the road that led to 'every place', the power 'to see' returned. She went to Brittany to paint, getting back a few days before the outbreak of the Great War.[36]

One year to the day after the death of her husband, Mabel's brother Francis was announced missing in action, and the autumn of 1914 emerged as yet another season to mourn. This time it was for the passing of a loved one who, apart from her son, was Mabel's closest relative. Mabel commented in her autobiography, 'He was so alive and so vital that few believed – even in the autumn of 1914 – that he had been lost.'[37] Francis's obituary in *The Northern Whig* described him as a golfer, motorist and all-round athlete, who had travelled to almost every corner of the world. Francis Annesley was 31 years of age when he died, but he had not pursued a distinct profession until the outbreak of the First World War. From infancy he had suffered a serious stutter. Lydia de Burgh, who later painted his portrait from a photograph, said he was 'small and looked fun [...] but his eyes did not match' – he had lost one eye in a wild party when at Cambridge.[38] Quite different from his quiet, subtly humorous older sister, Francis was an avid sportsman and party-goer. His liveliness of character, as time would show, was inherited by his only nephew, Gerald.

[1] Lindsay Proudfoot and W. Nolan (eds), *Down: history and society: interdisciplinary essays on the history of an Irish county* (Dublin, 1997) , p. 275.
[2] Ibid., p. 274.
[3] A.P.W. Malcomson, 'Introduction' (PRONI, Annesley papers, D/1854).
[4] Delany, Mary, *Letters from Georgian Ireland: the correspondence of Mary Delany 1731–68* (Angélique Day, ed., Belfast, 1991), p. 54.
[5] Ibid., p. 61.
[6] Ibid., p. 214.
[7] Malcomson, 'Introduction'.
[8] Ibid.
[9] Proudfoot and Nolan, *Down: history and society*, p. 534.
[10] Ibid., p. 234.
[11] Ibid.
[12] Malleson, *After ten years*, p. 12.
[13] Ibid., p. 14.
[14] Unknown, 'Sir Francis Grant' in L. Stephen and S. Lee (eds), *Dictionary of national biography* ('G' vol., London, 1885–1901).
[15] Malleson, *After ten years*, pp. 18–19.
[16] Ibid., p. 26.
[17] G. Fehlmann, 'An historical survey' in Jacqueline Genet (ed.), *The Big House in Ireland: reality and representation* (Dingle, County Kerry and Savage, Maryland, 1991), p. 15.
[18] *Atsib*, p. 14.
[19] Malleson, *After ten years*, p. 17.
[20] *Atsib*, p. 17.
[21] *The Northern Whig*, 25 January 1899.
[22] 'Irish artist hasn't forgiven Churchill', 16 June 1950 (Museum of New Zealand Te Papa Tongarewa, vertical file).
[23] John O'Grady, *The life and work of Sarah Purser* (Dublin, 1996), p. 31.
[24] *The Northern Whig*, 3 February 1880.
[25] Ibid., 24 March 1880.
[26] Ibid., 7 March 1899.
[27] Ibid., 15 September 1899.
[28] Sam Hanna Bell, Nesca A. Robb and John Hewitt (eds), *The arts in Ulster: a symposium* (London, 1951), p. 90.
[29] Ann M. Stewart, *Irish art societies and sketching clubs: index of exhibitors 1870–1980* (vol. i, Dublin, 1997), p. 21.
[30] J. Crampton Walker, *Irish life and landscape* (Dublin, 1927).
[31] *Atsib*, p. 19.
[32] Ibid., p. 21.
[33] Ibid.
[34] Logbook of Gerald Sowerby, 22 February 1894–14 January 1896 (PRONI, D/1854/8/7–18/91–3/MIC 532, reel 38).
[35] *Atsib*, p. 22.
[36] Margaret Ogilvie to Eileen Black, 5 February 1980 (privately held).
[37] *Atsib*, p. 23.
[38] Lydia de Burgh, *Another way of life* (Downpatrick, 1999), p. 72.

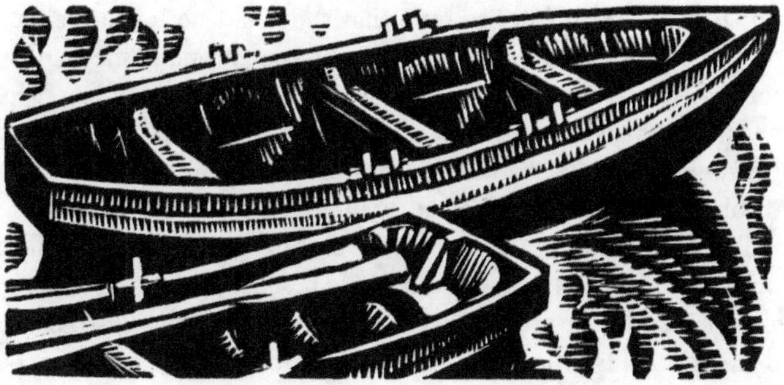

Fishing boats, 40 × 90, *As the sight is bent*, p. 79.

2

Book illustration

In 1921 Mabel Annesley was still producing watercolours for the Belfast Art Society, works that reflected her abiding love for the Mourne Mountains, for the animals that inhabited that landscape and for the creatures and scenery that she saw on her travels.[1] Even at this early time, however, her interest in the black-and-white medium was developing.[2] Despite her obligations as owner of Castlewellan (not without a battle in court, as she vividly described in her autobiography) and overseer of the Annesley lands, she did find time to continue to paint and draw and to turn her thoughts to a new art – book illustration. She was also the mother of a rather impetuous child, whom she taught to stay on a horse, noting wryly, 'It was about all that I ever did teach him [...] As early as he was able, he went his own way.'[3]

Her granddaughter, Margaret Ogilvie, wrote to Eileen Black in 1980 that Mabel had managed with only a small pension to take over an estate encumbered by death duty, reverting to her maiden name and changing her son's name to Annesley for the sake of continuity. It had always astonished Margaret that, with so many problems to deal with, Mabel was still able 'to achieve so much in the field of art'.[4]

Ensconced in the familiar Irish landscape, Mabel commented that whoever found country life dull, especially Irish country life, must be inclined to dullness themselves. Her difficulty, given the amount of work to be done on the estate, was to find time to think about the weird and whimsical tales and the angular, labouring figures seen in the 'stark, hilly landscape'.[5]

After studying the Old Masters, the Impressionists and the Post-Impressionists, along with her native landscape, Mabel began to develop her own theory of art. On examining the hills, the trees and whatever else attracted her, she 'wanted to be simple, not complex. [She] wanted to summarize, not explain. At forty, [she] began to woodcut.'[6] At another point, she commented that before the First World War she had been prepared 'to slop water-colour about for ever'.[7] But the war hit her so hard that she could no longer paint. When it was finally over she bought tools and wood. To learn the craft properly she went to the Central London School of Arts and Crafts (now Central St Martins College of Art and Design). In 1921 she moved into a small room in a boarding house in London, studying each day under Noel Rooke (1881–1953). Rooke had been educated in London and at the Lycée de Chartres in France and throughout his life discussed French as well as English books. He used his knowledge of French artistic developments to compare and analyse different kinds of development in Britain. It seems to have been partly because of this that he was given his first teaching appointment at the age of 24. He was responsible for book illustration at the Central School. Wood-engraved illustration 'was an ideal medium for printing, as it could be locked up with metal type and printed in one operation', and Rooke took special care with this work when he began teaching in 1912.[8]

At the Central School Mabel completed one of her first woodcuts. The simplicity and individuality of her work seems to have attracted the eye of fellow Irishman Richard Rowley. Rowley, whose real name was Richard Valentine Williams, was born in Belfast in 1877 and divided his life between working in the family firm of cotton-handkerchief manufacturers, and writing poetry and publishing books on his Mourne Press. He was an outgoing and witty man who was termed 'a prince of entertainers, the heaven-sent head of a dinner table, the most gallant squire of dames that ever made obeisance over a bubbling glass to beauty'.[9] As a poet Rowley is not well known, yet his verse shows a sympathy for the working man that captures the atmosphere of early twentieth-century Belfast with passion and clarity. In his poem 'The city of refuge' he dreams of building an ideal city far from 'the dark streets used by [one's] daily tread' and away from the slavery of the 'whining wheel' and the 'humming loom'.[10] Paul Henry, a fellow Ulsterman and artist, also wrote about longing to escape from Dublin to the comparative quiet of Belfast. Henry applauded 'The city of refuge' for its inspirational qualities. It gave him a tremendous amount of pleasure.

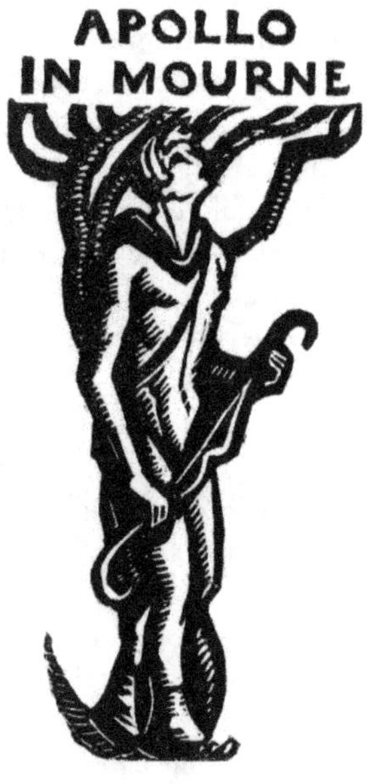

Apollo in Mourne, 75 × 37, half-title to *Apollo in Mourne*.

It is most likely that Rowley knew Mabel Annesley before she began studying at the Central School and that, with their common love of the Mournes, where they both owned houses, they were friends long before Mabel became interested in book illustration. Whatever the case, in 1923 Rowley commissioned Mabel Annesley to illustrate his *County Down songs*.

John Hewitt considered the woodcutting work in *County Down songs* to be 'one of the most successful marriages of picture and word to have come out of the north'.[11] This was a remarkable compliment from someone who considered Ireland's strength to lie in the graphic art of illustration:

> If, as has been suggested, the visual genius of this island is not three dimensional but linear, then, perhaps, this little company, from Hugh Thomson to Elizabeth Shaw, can be taken as true exponents of a natural trait, even though their individual impacts upon us have been diverse and disparate, and not easily to be resolved into a coherent convention.[12]

It appears that Mabel stepped easily into the role of illustrator, taking in her stride the important fact that the book artist is an artistically developed organism, 'whose perception may on occasion be more cognizant than our own'.[13]

Benefitting from the training with Noel Rooke, Mabel Annesley revealed her talents as a subtle and intuitive illustrator in her first book (*County Down songs*). Like her master, she appreciated line, tone and harmonious proportion between lettering and blank paper. A familiarity with such proportion would lead 'to illustration [which] is best practised in wood engraving'.[14]

Mabel's second book for Rowley, published by Duckworth in 1926, is a small but lovely volume: *Apollo in Mourne: poems, plays and stories*. Victor Price remarked in his introduction to the 1978 reprint of *Apollo in Mourne* that Rowley thought highly of it because it is his only work that reconciled 'the high-flown bardic side of his nature with his more naturalistic dialect persona'.[15]

Established as one of the prime artists in the Duckworth stable ('one of the first publishers to revive engraving as a medium of illustration'),[16] Mabel was soon approached by the art director of the Golden Cockerel Press, Robert Gibbings. Gibbings was a prolific and talented author and wood engraver from County Cork, as well as a notorious ladies' man. According to Gibbings's biographer, Martin Andrews, Mabel's house at Cox Green was very close to Waltham St Lawrence and the Golden Cockerel Press: 'Annesley and RG were obviously friends.'[17] Gibbings's relationship with Mabel's half-sister Constance (see chapter four), may have been more than platonic but, seeing Mabel's character emerge from the pages of her autobiography, letters and essays, we have no reason to believe that there was ever anything but a friendly, professional tie between Gibbings and herself. We learn a great deal about Mabel and Gibbings from Constance, who declared that Gibbings always seemed to be the finest of contemporary English wood engravers (with perhaps the exception of Eric Gill). Besides being a fine artist, she said, he somehow managed to be an extraordinarily lovable person – 'and to look exactly like God the Father with his great beard'. He was an admirer of Mabel's work.[18]

Scholars agree that Constance describes the figure of Gibbings in her novel, *Fear in the heart*. Hilary Barnes, the artist and private-press proprietor in that work, might be based on Robert Gibbings, though the affair portrayed in fiction would most certainly not have occurred between Gibbings and Mabel. The Mabel figure, Auriel, sheds some light on how Constance saw her sister. In the novel, thinking of Jenny (Constance) always makes Auriel feel old. She feels very much the big sister, having been hammered by life but having managed to survive it. Like Mabel, Auriel cares 'more for Lullington [Castlewellan] than for any person or thing on earth. She knew it ought not to be so. People ought to come before places. But she could not feel that instinctively.'[19] Like Mabel, Auriel believes that the secret of well-being lies in hard work, and she deals honestly with the men who work for her and depend upon her. Likewise, the philosophy that the Annesley sisters shared and that Jenny expresses in her artistic beliefs is that determination and staying power go further than almost anything toward 'making a good picture'.[20]

In 1924 Mabel Annesley's wood engraving formed part of the prospectus for the 1925 Golden Cockerel spring list.[21] Later that year her *Songs from Robert Burns* appeared under the Cockerel imprint. Joanna Selborne describes Annesley's technique as creating a woody effect. She writes that 'the dramatic element of Burns's songs is skilfully interpreted, particularly through facial expression and gesture'.[22] It was in this accomplished and striking book that Mabel revealed how she agreed with Gibbings that illustration should be visually integrated and harmonious with the text and not simply a decorative afterthought. Mabel's illustrations for *Songs from Robert Burns* are neat, direct, unsentimental expressions of a vision that reflects the carefully arranged flow of type on the page.

Unlike some of her colleagues in the field of illustration, Mabel Annesley had a number of contacts in the art world, and the brevity of her career in book illustration was due more to ill health than to lack of connections. Nicola Gordon Bowe's beautiful and distinguished biography of Harry Clarke makes us aware of the much more typical difficulty experienced by that illustrator in his early days:

> Clarke had unsuccessfully shown his portfolio to twelve London publishers before he visited George Harrap as his last attempt. 'But for me,' so he said, '[Clarke] would probably have abandoned the idea of illustrating books.'[23]

While Mabel Annesley explored her natural talent for engraved illustration, the eyes of Ireland were turned elsewhere. In 1920 a measure was adopted that proposed to set up two Home Rule parliaments in Ireland: one for the six north-eastern counties and one for the remainder of the country.[24] The early 1920s unfolded as a murderous and strife-filled sequence of years. The character of the Protestant Northern Irish, amongst whom we must include Mabel Annesley, was strong – 'in some ways more British than the British, yet in other ways more Irish than the Irish'.[25] For Mabel, an isolated landlord on a large estate, the internal violence in the province must have been an ever-present worry, symbolised by 'a short barbed wire entanglement going up around the police barracks'.[26]

The first sign of hostility coming close to her staunchly Protestant house occurred on a fine, dark night in May 1922. She sat with her neighbour and friend Miss Kate Fisher, whom she affectionately called Fish, on the bedroom floor when rifle shots rang from the surrounding hills and footsteps sounded on the gravel beneath the bedroom window. 'Every night' thereafter 'houses were burnt down and people shot'. Every night, in tweed skirt and thick shoes, with valuables packed in suitcases ready to throw out of the window, Mabel lay awake. Occasionally she crept out of her room to see if all was well, but the long murky passages frightened her. Whenever she got back to her dark bedroom it always felt friendly and safe. When dawn came and the birds twittered, she slept.[27] Finally, the mounting tension at Castlewellan became evident even to the authorities and a garrison of B Specials was sent in to occupy the Annesley house. For almost two years a platoon of men lived there who were, according to Mabel, distinguished by their valour at night and their humanity by day.

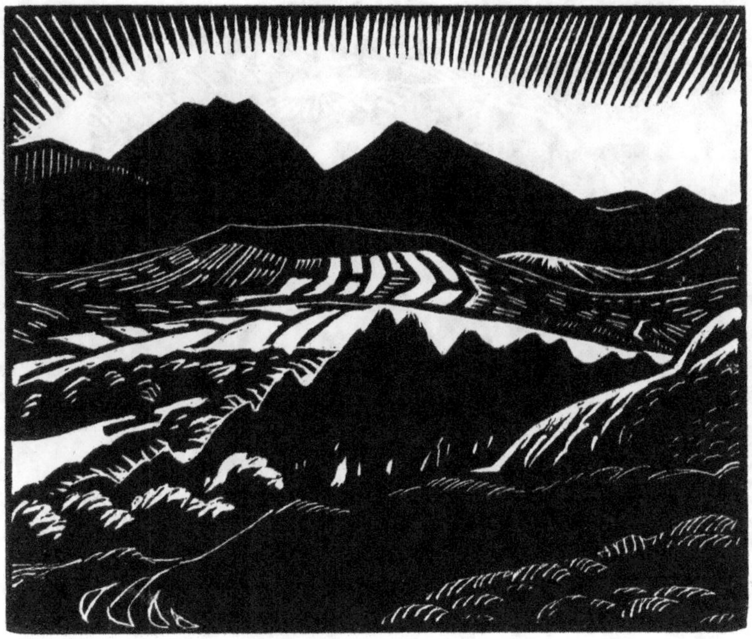

In the kingdom of Mourne, 83 × 101,
frontispiece to *Apollo in Mourne.*

A young Englishman, called in to inspect them, complained that 'Their shirts and Mills bombs and raspberry jam are all mixed up under their mattresses.'[28] By 1924 the worst of the fighting, at least near Castlewellan, was over and something resembling ordinary life resumed. 'Both sides forgave or forgot – more from necessity than virtue; because, if we didn't share our loyalties, we still shared the land.'[29]

Politically, Mabel Annesley was staunchly pro-British. She had grown up in a part of Ireland where the Ulster Volunteer Force was backed by an equally disciplined female force of volunteers; as a solitary woman she was not afraid to voice her political views.[30] As she wrote in the 1930s (a comment not published until after her death):

> My forebears had come to Ireland in Elizabethan days. If I am not English, I – like my forebears – am Protestant and my flag is the Union Jack. I venerate good, blundering, unimaginative Great Britain.[31]

Though her half-sister Clare stood as Labour candidate for Bristol West in 1925, and her son Gerald was to take up the nationalist cause in his political leanings, Mabel never wavered in her devotion to the British side.

At the same time, her work is filled with the close feelings she held for the men who worked for her. Despite her love for Britain, an even stronger love for Ireland emerges from the pages of her autobiography and from many of her engravings. A small vignette of two

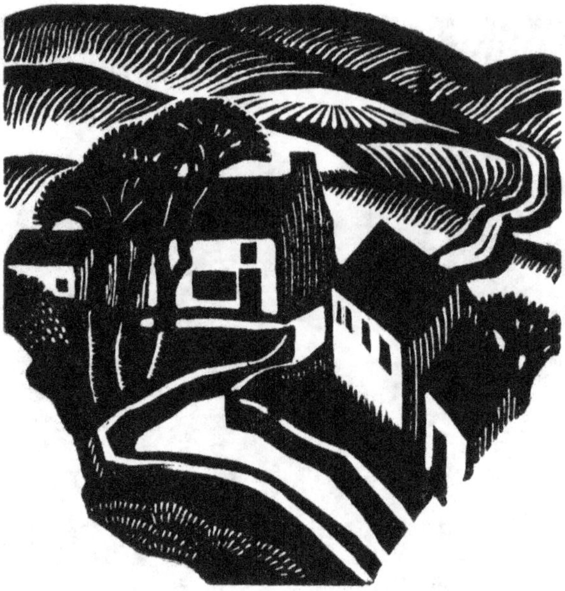

Untitled, 77 × 77, *Apollo in Mourne*, p. 19.

riders shows a native Irishman riding side by side with his gentlemanly master. It is a perfect picture of communality and it highlights with simple dexterity the fact that the Annesley family 'had always been in close touch with the men who worked for us. Their roots and ours had grown together in the same soil.'[32]

By 1926, the year that *Songs from Robert Burns* was published, Mabel was just as passionately committed to her familiar surroundings, but her son Gerald had come of age and taken over the running of the estate. Bolstered by the friendship of Fish, she made the decision to move away from Castlewellan to a neighbouring town. Mabel's father had built her a house, known as Myrtle, by the Shimna River in Newcastle when she was recuperating from the birth of her son in 1905, and it was as neighbours that Fish and Mabel had met – their 'back gates had opened opposite each other into the same green lane'.[33] Fish was well liked by all of Mabel's family, and it is to her that Mabel's sister Constance attributed the regularity of Mabel's routine:

> She [Fish] was a very small, very compact person; always on the go; never idle; never tired (at least never owning to being tired). She had the moral attributes of all the saints in heaven.[34]

In 1925 Mabel and Fish moved from Newcastle to share a house that Mabel had built for them at Rathfriland, County Down – a small whitewashed cottage with a view to the south.[35] There Mabel continued to engrave, adding toymaking and textile printing to her skills. In 1927 her son married Lady Elizabeth Jocelyn, daughter of the eighth earl of Roden, whose lands abutted the Castlewellan estate. In due course they had two children, Margaret and

Patricia. Though Mabel was devoted to her grandchildren, she did not see herself becoming 'a prim, stingy mother-in-law'.[36]

Gerald's first marriage ended in divorce and Mabel found herself returning to Castlewellan in the mid-1930s, embracing her position as head of the Big House and continuing to love her former tenants wholeheartedly. Just as she admired the textured granite of the Big House, she loved the grittiness of the people of Ulster, who were 'elemental, unrelenting, heaven and hell people with an Old Testament religion. They thought about their religion and politics. They took birth and death and marriage in their stride.'[37] Though she had travelled extensively as a young married woman, and would travel even further as an older woman, it seemed that Ulster was where Mabel was truly at home. There she could appreciate the idiosyncracies of the Ulster Scot, who was no longer a Scot, though similarly energetic and hard working. The Ulster Scot was in less of a hurry than the Scot, and took 'less account of time'.[38] The dialect of the countryman of Ulster, in the opinion of Cyril Falls, had 'a general effect of strength without harshness, raciness without extravagance, the sweetness of fine old words that have become embedded in the soil'.[39]

In 1925 Mabel was still involved with the Belfast Art Society, and on 2 September *The Northern Whig* commented on her watercolour *Lough Island Reavy*, saying that it was an admirable study of a quaint farmyard flanked by sun-splashed houses. The atmosphere conveyed in such a small canvas was remarkable and the handling of colour left nothing to be desired. Mabel had been elected vice-president of the Belfast Art Society in 1924 and the following year she offered to lecture on wood engraving and to lend the society her collection of modern French woodcuts. It was her suggestion 'that small loan exhibitions should be more regularly organized by the Society'.[40]

By 1927, however, she had resigned from the society, turning her attention to family problems and to her own ill health – which, in the form of septic arthritis, had made it difficult for her even to hold her engraving tools. Undaunted, she arranged for Lawrence, the blockmaker, to make her some tools with cork handles, 'which were much easier to hold'.[41] Her hands had become quite crippled and there was a period during which she lost the use of her right hand completely. However, with her 'indomitable courage' she taught herself to write and engrave with her left hand.[42] Her spirit was, and remained throughout her life, devoted to Castlewellan, which she handed over to her son. She tried to leave the place herself, 'yet never quite did, always coming back'.[43]

1 *British Friesians* and *Ride! Ride forever ride*, 1921, listed in Ann M. Stewart, *Irish art societies and sketching clubs: index of exhibitors 1870–1980* (vol. i, Dublin, 1997), p. 21; *The camel and the elephant*, 1921; *Brittany market*, 1922, ibid.

2 *Ploughing*, 1922, ibid.

3 *Atsib*, p. 25.

4 Ogilvie to Black, 5 February 1980.

5 *Atsib*, p. 25.

6 Ibid., p. 26.

7 Ibid.

[8] Patricia Jaffé, *Women engravers* (London, 1988), p. 17.
[9] Richard Rowley, *Apollo in Mourne: poems, plays and stories* (Victor Price, ed., Belfast, 1978), p. 2.
[10] Ibid, p. 15.
[11] Hewitt and Catto, *Art in Ulster.*
[12] Ibid.
[13] C. Sandford and O. Rutter, quoted in Selborne, *British wood-engraved book illustration,* p. 15.
[14] Noel Rooke, quoted ibid., p. 57.
[15] Victor Price, 'Introduction' in Rowley, *Apollo in Mourne,* p. 7.
[16] John Jolliffe, *Woolf at the door: Duckworth, 100 years of Bloomsbury behaviour* (London, 1998), p. 40.
[17] Martin Andrews to the author, 13 July 2000 (privately held).
[18] Malleson, *After ten years,* p. 216.
[19] Constance Malleson, *Fear in the heart: a novel* (London, 1936), p. 12.
[20] Ibid., p. 22.
[21] A. Mary Kirkus, *Robert Gibbings: a bibliography* (London, 1962), p. 86.
[22] Selborne, *British wood-engraved book illustration,* p. 182.
[23] Nicola Gordon Bowe, *The life and work of Harry Clarke* (2nd ed., Dublin, 1994), p. 30.
[24] F.S.L. Lyons, *Ireland since the Famine* (London, 1973), p. 413.
[25] E. Evans, quoted in F.S.L. Lyons, *Culture and anarchy in Ireland 1890–1939* (Oxford, 1979), p. 115.
[26] *Atsib,* p. 29.
[27] Ibid.
[28] Ibid., p. 30.
[29] Ibid., p. 31.
[30] Diane Urquhart, 'The female of the species is more deadlier [*sic*] than the male?' in Janice Holmes and Diane Urquhart (eds), *Coming into the light* (Belfast, 1994), p. 102.
[31] *Atsib,* p. 29.
[32] Ibid., p. 33.
[33] Ibid., p. 28.
[34] Malleson, *After ten years,* p. 215.
[35] *Atsib,* p. 34.
[36] Ibid., p. 38.
[37] Ibid., p. 36.
[38] Cyril Falls, *The birth of Ulster* (London, 1936), p. 231.
[39] Ibid., p. 233.
[40] Martyn Anglesea, *The Royal Ulster Academy of Arts* (Belfast, 1981), p. 66.
[41] Selborne, *British wood-engraved book illustration,* p. 182.
[42] Ogilvie to Black, 5 February 1980.
[43] Ibid.

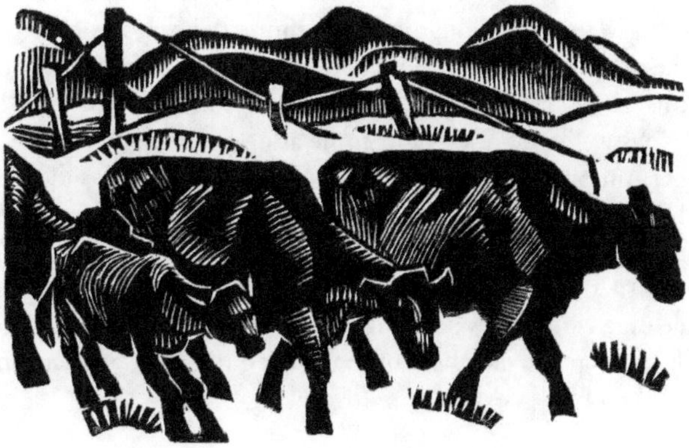

Kerrys, 50 × 80, *As the sight is bent*, p. 67.

3

Engraving

In 1930 an exhibition to promote the artistic life of Ireland was arranged and transported to Brussels. Mabel Annesley is represented in that exhibition by four wood engravings.[1] Co-organised by Thomas Bodkin, the exhibition meant little in the development of Irish art. However, it was the first time that Ireland had made an international impact in the art world. Those represented in the exhibition were considered amongst the most important in their field.

Mabel, writing to her sister Constance from Rathfriland in the early 1930s, was experiencing the usual upheaval associated with moving house. In one letter she complains of missing books from her library. In another she describes the roughness of cottage living – in order to fill their cistern they had to fill buckets of snow 'and melt them on the fire'.[2] The summers, however, were beautiful and she rejoiced in a visit from her friend Margaret Pilkington: 'We ate and sang songs on the terrace till the moon came out and the motor lights flew like fireflies over the country beneath us.'[3] Mabel and Fish were now coming to the decision to leave Ulster behind, at least for a while, and to take up residence in the west of Ireland, in Connemara. One would do well to turn to her autobiography for an extended description of her time in Connemara. The two women stayed first in a hotel and then in a dilapidated house, not far from a house occupied by Oscar Wilde during his childhood. By this time Mabel had put many of the family woes – Gerald's headstrong impetuousness coupled with his difficult marriage – into the distance and was turning to writing, as well as engraving, for creative outlet. She was slowly developing her ideas about the place of art in society. In a letter to Margaret Pilkington she commented that the only way for a modern artist to control the world of mechanics and applied science was by embracing total humility. Instead of thinking about masterpieces, one should think how best 'to learn how to do ordinary useful things well'; the rest would come as one grew up.[4]

In 1924 Mabel Annesley had been elected a member of the London Society of Wood Engravers, and she described that society's beginnings with typical acuteness:

> Round about 1920, the Society of Wood Engravers was formed – Lucien Pissaro [sic] in wide cape with glasses dangling on watered silk ribbon and Gordon Craig of theatre fame, were the old guard of the Society, the Nash brothers, in beautiful lounge suits, the advanced wing.[5]

In an essay written in 1951 she explained how the Great War had affected her so deeply that she could no longer paint, and so bought tools and a woodblock, responding to the pressure on modern artists to design for mass production. It was no longer art for art's sake, but art for everyday life's sake. At this time woodblocks in book production were looked upon as exotic. Thomas Bewick had been almost forgotten. The new movement was more in accord with its forebears of the fifteenth century than with its grandparents, the reproductive engravers of the 1860s.[6]

Mabel went on to say that, with her first commission firmly in her hands, she 'hailed a jaunty car and drove round the slums of Dublin' until she found an old Albion printing press that dated from the Restoration. With this press she began to print engravings for a commission from the Golden Cockerel Press. Its owner, Robert Gibbings, told her that he was going to be her dancing master, so she needn't mind 'if he trod on her toes'.[7] Mabel began to appreciate that wood engraving should never allow ornament for ornament's sake. Engravings, hung with due regard to space, could be 'quite successful, particularly in small houses'.[8]

In producing single engravings for exhibition and sale, Mabel applied her own theories – and revealed considerable artistic capability. It is as an engraver today that she is best known. Her engravings are in the collections of the British Museum, the Victoria and Albert Museum, the Ulster Museum, the Whitworth Gallery, Manchester, Central St Martins College of Art and Design, London, the National Gallery of Canada, the Suter Art Gallery, New Zealand, the National Art Gallery of New Zealand, the Museum of New Zealand Te Papa Tongarewa and the Sarjeant Gallery, New Zealand. A very extensive collection is in the hands of her granddaughter, Patricia Saunders, who received her engravings from her aunt Clare, Mabel's half-sister.

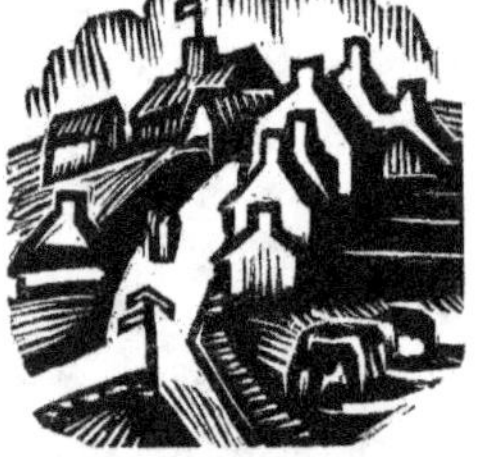

Rathfriland,
32.5 × 32.5,
As the sight is bent, p. 34.

Patricia Saunders's collection reflects well the themes treated by Mabel Annesley in her wood engravings and linocuts. Slieve Donard, thatched cottages with pigs and cattle on hills are only a few of the scenes Mabel described with her engraver's tools. Campbell Dodgson noted that her inspiration came from the mountains of her own County Down but that she was equally drawn to the animals and people that inhabited those mountains. She was remarkable, thought Dodgson, for her understanding of how to make a picture to decorate a small room such as 'most of the world inhabits in days when the burden of taxes is heavy'.[9]

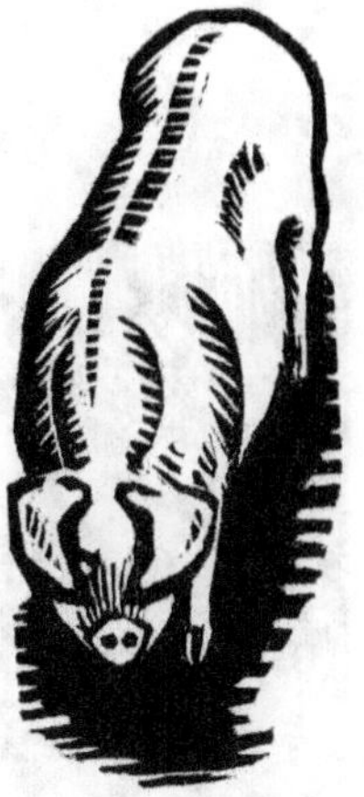

Yon's the rare jewl o' a wee pig, 52 × 26, final page of *Apollo in Mourne.*

In her work for Duckworth and the Golden Cockerel Press, Mabel had absorbed the principles of engraving that involved the use of proper paper, sensitivity to type and beauty of image. The masters Gibbings and Rooke taught her a great deal and she might well have agreed with Christopher Sandford when he wrote, several decades after her blossoming, that wood engravers must always print on the right sort of paper. Some, thought Sandford, would think of an engraved piece of wood as an end in itself. Books could be printed without engravings, but they must have good paper. The Golden Cockerel Press was known for its fine paper. For Sandford, many wood engravers (apart from the older ones) seemed to strive after a superficial cleverness (in tool work) that lost sight of the fact that engraving produces a printable picture. Neither Gibbings nor Mabel ever wallowed in what could be described as a 'petit point to the extent that their engravings ceased to be printable pictures'.[10]

Recent books on wood engraving, displaying Mabel's work and that of later engravers, show the older artist in favourable contrast with the following generation.[11]

In 1930 a special spring edition of *The Studio* was devoted to wood engraving in Great Britain and around the world. It is not surprising to find Mabel Annesley in these pages. The journal noted the paucity of wood engravers who approached wood respectfully, seeing it as a medium to be studied and cultivated 'with as much art and finesse as the copper on which the etcher draws and bites his picture'.[12] *The Studio* then went on to list the wood engravers of the time who showed respect for their medium:

> Lucien Pissaro [sic], Gordon Craig, Sydney Lee, Gwen Raverat, Eric Gill, Robert Gibbings, David Jones, Paul Nash, Eric Ravilious, Clare Leighton, Noel Rooke, Alec Buckels, C.W. Taylor, John F. Greenwood, Margaret Haythorne, John Buckland-Wright, Percy Smith, and Lady Mabel Annesley, with her 'pleasant tales of greenery'.[13]

An earlier (1927) edition of *The Studio*, also devoted to the contemporary woodcut, showed a full-page engraving by Mabel Annesley, which revealed her talents at their most glowing. *The tryst gate* focuses on winding tree trunks and leafy boughs, with a small central gate just to the right of centre. There are no tricks or artful subtleties here, only a keen sense of white and black in balance and an understanding of how foreground relates to background. *The tryst gate* was one of Mabel's most successful engravings because of its simplicity and openness.

Between 1922 and 1939 Mabel exhibited 27 prints with the London Society of Wood Engravers.[14] These were the work of a woman who had mastered a difficult craft in which no

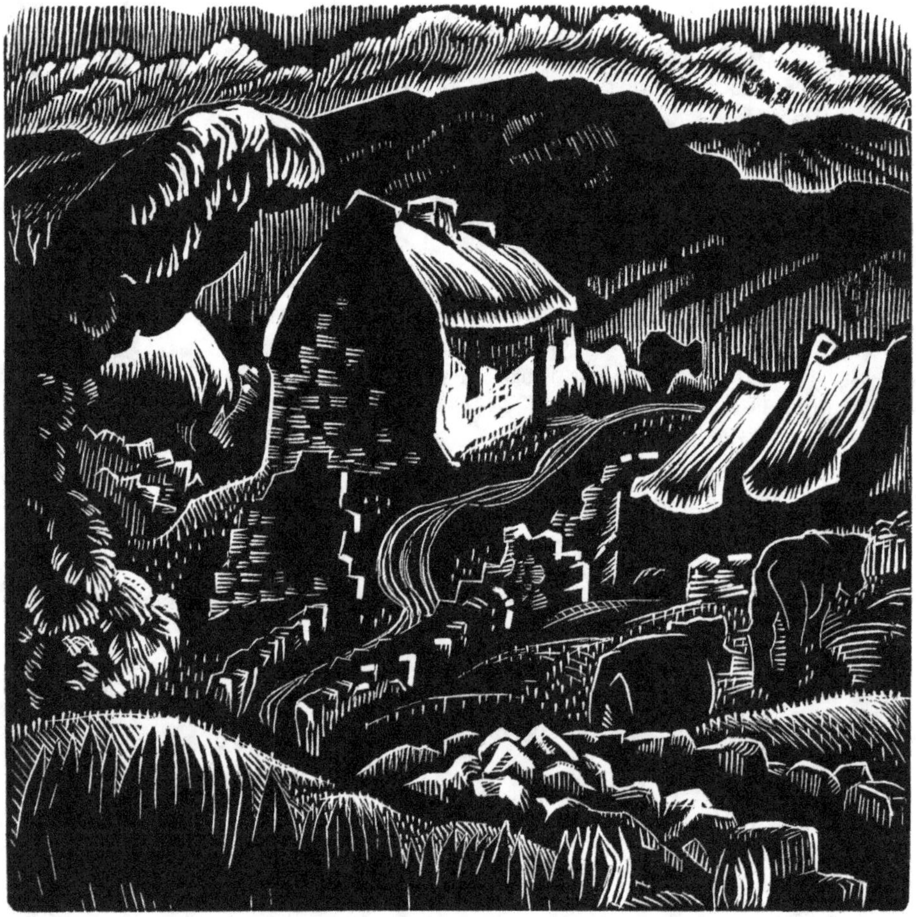

Cabin in Connemara, wood engraving
(Museum of New Zealand Te Papa Tongarewa), 120 × 125.

one could become proficient without much thought and practice. Apart from her own solitary meditations on wood engraving, Mabel was encouraged by the artist William Conor, to whom she often sent her woodcuts 'for his opinion, criticism and advice'.[15]

In 1932 Conor and Mabel designed the costumes which were used in a pageant held at Castleward, Strangford Lough, to commemorate the 1,500th anniversary of the landing of St Patrick at Saul, County Down. The drawings for those costumes, though signed by Conor, show the flowing lines and feel for period costume that Mabel had revealed in her engravings for the Golden Cockerel Press. The costumes brought alive the portrayal of *Patrick as herd boy*, *Michel's elder daughter* and *Captain of the pirates* as well as numerous other characters.[16] An exhibition of Mabel's watercolours, engravings and silverpoints was held at Batsford Gallery, London (*c.* 1933), and in 1932 and 1939 she presented the Belfast Museum and Art Gallery with her collection of contemporary wood engravings, including 18 of her own.[17]

In 1934 Mabel travelled to Germany with her friend and colleague Margaret Pilkington, but much of Pilkington's diary from this trip indicates that Mabel, at the age of 53, was increasingly suffering from ill health. Margaret Pilkington (1891–1974), honorary director of the Whitworth Gallery and secretary and president of the Society of Wood Engravers, would have met Mabel through the latter organisation. It was largely Pilkington's decision to engage in an extensive tour of galleries and museums in northern Europe. This was in February and March of 1934, and Pilkington noted the marching of brown-shirted men as well as the prevalence of the swastika when they were in Stuttgart.[18] In her diary for 25 February 1934 she notes that she and Mabel wandered down the street, ignoring the Schlossplatz and focusing instead on the designs of the modern buildings juxtaposed against the old design, 'yet with consideration of harmony in line or contrast'.[19] On 27 February she noted that they walked through Stuttgart and Mabel took photographs, 'then [they] went home to rest'.[20] Almost a month later Mabel appeared to be overtired and required long periods of rest, while a few days after that, in Sweden, the weather was damp and cheerless, leaving Mabel depressed. On 8 March the two ladies made the delightful journey up to Stockholm. The day was clear and sunny with a sprinkling of snow. There were deep steely blue lakes with blue distances, the deep brown-black of earth and red houses. The contrast was striking. They arrived in Stockholm on a sparkling evening. The water was full of glittering reflections, the air most exhilarating. Pilkington wished they had not booked such a 'plutocratic' hotel, with unattractive rooms at an exorbitant price. Mabel, however, was thrilled and anxious to explore the city. They went for a walk and eventually dined at a small restaurant.[21] A few days later Mabel took photographs in the snow. She then received a letter with bad news. She was very upset though 'as always entirely stoicle [*sic*]'.[22] The bad news, it seemed, was the breakdown of Gerald's first marriage to Lady Elizabeth Jocelyn (it ended in divorce in 1936).

The character of Gerald Annesley has been much discussed by those who knew him well and those who knew him not so well, but it is quite likely that his aunt Biddy (as Constance was known to the family) had a good grasp on the nature of her charming, unconventional nephew. In 1925 Constance told of a visit to Ireland, where Gerald met her at the railway station, surveying the platform with an amused glint in his eyes. She said, 'That glint in his eyes was one of the nicest things about him [...] Gerald had what is called "a way with him".'[23]

It is possible that Mabel's recognition of Gerald's 'way' and a sense of foreboding about the fate of his first marriage contributed to Mabel's decision to move to Connemara in the early 1930s. That removal from the scene, though of no lasting help to the marriage, did allow Mabel to cement her theories of art and to understand her feelings for Ireland as a whole and for her own County Down. Around 1935, Fish, Mabel and their yellow dog left Belfast with 13 'bulging suitcases', proceeding through the 'cultivated, hilly North' to the 'flat dull centre of Ireland'.[24] They arrived in Connemara by bus some days later. There they were treated to the sight of Connemara's Twelve Pins. In Mabel's eyes everything there, at first, seemed small:

> The houses were cabins, the Kerry cows dwarfs, the iron-grey ponies and fluffy dogs stunted. The sheepdogs were undersized. The oats and potatoes grew in diminutive patches, the fields looked like children's gardens. The only man-made objects of generous proportions were the large brown stacks of turf.[25]

Somehow, however, despite the fact that her surroundings seemed 'fantastic, uncouth, exaggerated or distorted', Mabel's spirit opened and she began to put words to paper to describe her own artistic principles. Though the job of landscape painters was, she noted, to arrange and rearrange the glorious disorder of nature, her own interest lay in understanding 'the distinctive features in a new bit of country; to learn the rhythm of the surface of the earth'.[26] It was through an understanding of the uniqueness of whatever landscape she inhabited that she could find what Franz Marc described as 'the bridge into the spirit world'.[27] Everything that Mabel saw she saw with the eyes of the artist. Near the hotel where they first stayed, there were rocks 'that might have inspired El Greco', while the people who walked and talked around her 'might have walked out of El Greco's pictures'. She wondered, sometimes, if El Greco's baroque outlook had been shared by his Spanish models, 'when he exaggerated their slender limbs and their narrow, dome-like foreheads'. She went on:

> When Peter Brueghel burlesqued his low-browed peasants, had he an audience who saw them as he did? And did the Georgians see Rowlandson's grotesques as he did? Do people see only what their minds look for? Is fashion only the direct descendant of herd instinct?'[28]

While Fish, her English-born companion, gardened, Mabel took to hiking in the stormy Connemara mountains and to formulating her theories for engraving and painting. 'Could I search out the reason why one outline had more value than another?' she wrote. 'Could I put my response to "the world I looked at" into words as well as into forms?' It was necessary that she learn to communicate. Without that talent she was no better than 'a little boy with a piece of chalk making a mark for the sake of making it'.[29] Yes, she could paint and engrave, but as she wrestled with her skills as a writer she revealed an ability that lay far beyond 'modest prose'. As well as the eye of the artist, she had the ear of the storyteller. 'When not drawing, I was scribbling: elbow grease my only qualification,' she asserted modestly at one point in her autobiography. At the same time she realised that scribbling came from much more than elbow grease: 'My thoughts were clear as crystal, yet fused and subtle as the tents of the sky itself. It was my hour of vision.'[30]

It was also her time for comprehending human beings, particularly the Irish in the north and south. While the southerners spoke with a slow drawl – 'Would yez please send no more letters, yez have that many writ the Post Office is out of stamps,' – Mabel longed for 'crisp Northern voices and turns of speech'.[31] Watching ragged farmers scattering cow dung, she lamented that she could not live altogether in the west of Ireland. She warmed to a young man from the north who spoke public-school English with the unmistakable overtones of Belfast, and she was alienated by a withered west-coast man who had just fathered a child. Though the 'ragged hills of Galway [became] as familiar [...] as the plum-pudding hills of [her] own country',[32] the people could not lodge themselves in her heart as northerners could. The young man from the north had 'a slightly arrogant nose [that] stood out above his cupped hands. I remembered other slightly arrogant noses and felt suddenly homesick for the raw-boned North.'[33]

Because of difficulties at the hotel where they were staying, Mabel and Fish set off for a cottage of their own, by the shores of Lough Fee, near Kylemore Abbey. Mabel was able to concentrate once more on the civilising place of art in her life: how to construct a picture. Historically a picture had been, before it had been anything else, an architectural decoration on a wall. Whatever the picture was, however, it had come to us through the threads woven by pattern-makers. In the past, rough stone carved by masons had been able to stir crowds to worship. The holiness of Giotto's vision had come through his simple forms. Lucas Cranach had been more than a lewd old painter: his Venus was not only the naked figure of a woman but a great, glowing, symbolic pearl. Mabel wrote, 'Perhaps Laurence Binyon put something of the truth into a few terse words: "Gifts of hand and eye are not enough in art."'[34] For Mabel, 'a sharp graver seemed a mightier weapon than the pen' and, as she developed as a writer and theorist, she clung doggedly to the realisation that if she were to write a book it must surely be a picture book, laden with engraved images.[35]

Though she dreaded the upheaval that came with move after move, the 1930s were a decade of travel for Mabel. Her understanding of life broadened with her study of foreign peoples and landscapes. On her trip to Germany in 1934 she had responded strongly to 'the roar of the crowd as it shouted "Heil Hitler," with the reverberating thump of heavy boots marching slowly and ominously into the dark night'.[36] After a visit to Italy she wrote:

> I had been outraged by modern, middle-class Italy. Recollections of crude Capri pot-boilers, and coloured postcards of Naples came between me and the Italian landscape. See it with eyes of my own I never could; I so badly wanted to see it with the eyes of a Mantegna or a Bellini.[37]

When she travelled to Egypt on a liner, late in the autumn of 1935, she noted with disdain a stout little Aussie – a preposterous little man with overstated patriotism and a sense of humour that was ineffectual. Often, it seemed, her thoughts returned to Ireland in her travels, whether it was through conversation with Anglo-Irish cousins in Cairo, who remarked, 'The students are rioting [...] so you'll find it quite homelike. The police occasionally fire a shot

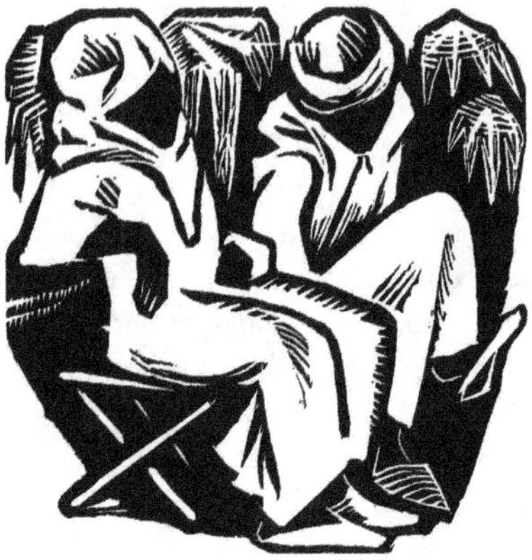
Egypt, 50 × 50, *As the sight is bent*, p. 90.

over their heads!' or through her own observation of Egyptian rifles jigging up and down just as, a few years earlier, 'rifles had jigged up and down along the roads of Northern Ireland'.[38] The Nile boats reminded her of the pointed wings of birds in Connemara and she found herself deciding that the Egyptian, with his own form of Blarney, was not unlike the Irishman (a young Egyptian remarked to her, '"I know you ride horse, you make even donkey look nice with you. Some people look *very* funny on donkey."')[39] In Cyprus she saw courtyards piled with oranges 'exactly as we pile turnips or taters in Co. Down'; and in Cyprus, as in Ireland, differences of religion 'seem to have hindered intermarriage'.[40]

As portents of the Second World War were making themselves felt throughout the world, Mabel continued to keep a close connection with artistic life in Ireland. In 1934 she showed three watercolours with the Ulster Unit at Locksley Hall, Belfast.[41] She was appointed an honorary member of the Royal Ulster Academy – somewhat ironically, given that she had protested so strongly against that organisation's name change from Belfast Art Society. In fact, she had announced that if her name was ever put forward as academician or associate, or anything other than ordinary member, she would be forced to resign. This was because she had never sent a picture to either the Royal Academy in London or the Salon in Paris. She did not want it to be thought that she relied on any qualifications other than those of an ordinary member when she submitted her work to a Royal Ulster Academy exhibition.[42]

In 1938 Mabel took part in an exhibition of the Society of Dublin Painters. She would then have come to know other members of that society. Such artists included Margaret Clarke, Sylvia Cooke-Collis, Frances Kelly, Phyllis Godfrey, Mrs Lennox (Dolly) Robinson, and Edward McGuire.[43] One of those artists, Sylvia Cooke-Collis, was in fact a distant relative of Mabel's, being the daughter of Hilda Phillips, who later married R.A. Grove-Annesley of Castletownroche.[44] Cooke-Collis seemed to keep close account of her northern cousins, and of the troubles in the Gerald Annesley household she remarked that everyone made mistakes. Mabel seemed to make a bad one, she thought, when she handed over so much to Gerald, knowing his character. At times Mabel actually seemed afraid of Gerald. She once said that he'd never been quite right since a pony kicked him as a child.

Cooke-Collis was very loyal to Mabel, asserting that no one could ever call Mabel 'cranky'; she just did not suffer fools gladly. In the mind of Cooke-Collis, Mabel was 'a brilliant, long-suffering darling who suffered a very long life'.[45] One of the best descriptions of Gerald came from his daughter, Margaret Ogilvie, in this conversation with the BBC in Ulster:

> Gerald was a very large man in every way; tall, big, good looking when he was young. He had a fantastic sense of humour, and a rather endearing stammer. He also had a wonderful eye for the ridiculous.[46]

As war loomed and Gerald courted a second wife, Mabel found herself moving yet again, this time to a handsome little house in Belfast, on University Road. She was only a short walk away from her friend William Conor's studio there, and she was able to participate much more easily in the activities of the city. Presumably she could also walk to her own studio on Lombard Street in the centre of Belfast. She continued to work on engravings for her autobiography, and on separate cuts. Curving hills and billowing Irish clouds mark some of these engravings, with cattle crossing a bridge and a dominant church in others. Though churches do make their appearance in several Annesley engravings, Mabel was not a religious woman. Her need for religion was as likely to be satisfied by a belief in Great Britain as by the great vaults of Northern Irish churches. Constance, describing her sister in a passage from Constance's novel, *Fear in the heart*, wrote that Mabel's lack of religion sprang directly from honesty and courage. Her sister, she thought, would have been the very first to castigate herself for conventional church-going. At the same time there was within Mabel a deep conflict that set aristocratic tradition against modern communistic thought.[47]

Honest and courageous, one of Mabel's engravings in the Saunders collection shows the profile of an ageing woman in a bonnet that captures every nuance of pain, age and sobriety with remarkable sensitivity. The engraving might well have issued from a portrait painter, so alive and acute is its technique. Yet Mabel was wed to hills and nature more strongly than to the human face, and the bonneted lady in the Saunders collection appears to be unique among her engravings. Sailboats and farm buildings, sunflowers and birds, the hind end of an old mare, chairs and tables, driving teams of horses and bursting foliage are all well represented in her symmetrical engravings. Some of the street scenes have a European look, perhaps inspired by her many travels.

By 1942, having suffered in the bombing of Belfast and exhausted by disputes with her son at Castlewellan, Mabel Annesley could only think that she wanted to be as far away from Ireland as possible. She set her sights, therefore, on the unlikely shores of New Zealand, where the currency was the pound sterling and the countryside, if unfamiliar, was lush and green.

1 Musée d'Art Ancien (Musées Royaux des Beaux-Arts de Belgique), *Exposition d'art irlandais* (Brussels, 10 May–8 June 1930).

2 Letters to Mummerley [i.e., Mabel], n.d. (BRAMU, Colette collection).

3 Ibid., 9 September (no year given).

4 Mabel Annesley, 'A wood engraver looks back' in Victoria University College, New Zealand, Regional Council of Adult Education, Community Arts Service, *The Lady Mabel Annesley: wood engravings, linocuts, silverpoints* (Wellington, New Zealand, 1951).

5 Ibid.

6 Ibid.

7 Ibid.

8 Bruce Arnold, *Irish art: a concise history* (rev. ed., London, 1977), p. 160.

9 Campbell Dodgson, 'Foreword' in *Contemporary English woodcuts* (London, 1922), p. 1.

10 B. Roberts, John Roberts Press, to C. Sandford, 10 October 1955 (Golden Cockerel Press Archive, McGill University Press, Canada).

[11] Studio One Gallery, Museum of Oxford, *'Shall we join the ladies?': wood engravings* (Oxford, 1979).
[12] C.G. Holme (ed.), 'The new woodcut by M.C. Salaman', *The Studio* (spring 1930), p. 2.
[13] Ibid., p. 26.
[14] T. Balston, 'Introduction' in Robert Gibbings, *The wood engravings of Robert Gibbings: with some recollections by the artist* (Patience Empson, ed., London, 1959).
[15] Judith Wilson, *Conor 1881–1968: the life and work of an Ulster artist* (Belfast, 1981), p. 26.
[16] The fifteen wax-crayon and charcoal mixed drawings by Annesley and Conor have been restored with lottery funding. They now hang in the Public Library, Armagh.
[17] Data printout for Annesley, Mabel, *c.* 1998 (Ulster Museum).
[18] David Blamires, 'Essay', in David Blamires, Patricia Jaffé *et al.*, *Margaret Pilkington, 1891–1974* (Buxton, 1995).
[19] Uncollated MSS (Margaret Pilkington Archive, John Rylands University Library, Manchester).
[20] Around this time Mabel wrote to a friend that she was considering taking up photography as her major medium of artistic expression (BRAMU, Colette collection).
[21] Margaret Pilkington Archive.
[22] Ibid.
[23] Malleson, *After ten years*, pp. 214–15.
[24] *Atsib*, p. 40.
[25] Ibid., p. 46.
[26] Ibid.
[27] Ibid., p. 48.
[28] Ibid., p. 50.
[29] Ibid., p. 52.
[30] Ibid., p. 45.
[31] Ibid., pp. 51, 65.
[32] Ibid., p. 66.
[33] Ibid., p. 72.
[34] Ibid., p. 64.
[35] Ibid.
[36] Ibid., p. 53.
[37] Ibid., p. 81.
[38] Ibid., pp. 86, 87.
[39] Ibid., p. 87, 93.
[40] Ibid., p. 94.
[41] Ulster Unit, *Ulster Unit: exhibition of contemporary art* (Belfast, 18–29 December 1934).
[42] Anglesea, *Royal Ulster Academy*, p. 82.
[43] S.B. Kennedy, *Irish art and modernism 1880–1950* (Belfast, 1991), p. 368.
[44] Theo Snoddy, *Dictionary of Irish artists: 20th century* (Dublin, 1996), p. 79.
[45] S. Cooke-Collis to Colette O'Niel, 20 August 1964 (BRAMU, Colette collection).
[46] *Studio talk*, BBC Radio, Edinburgh, 13 January 1993.
[47] Malleson, *Fear in the heart*, p. 270.

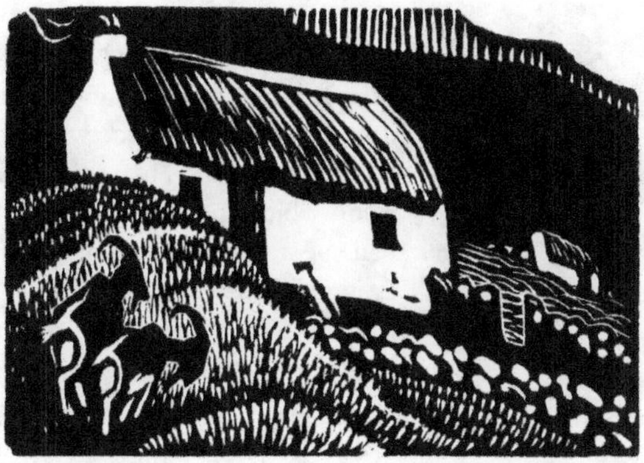

Untitled, 48 × 71, *County Down songs*, p. 13.

4
Family

Writing in 1929 to her youngest sister Constance (or Colette O'Niel, as she was known on stage), Mabel Annesley remembers how their brother Frank (Francis) had commented on the four children of their father, Hugh: 'Clare was born different, but the little 'un is far more like us.' Mabel went on to say:

> Frank had no intellect, but he had an uncanny quickness, he had the intelligence of the uneducated. He was *far* cleverer than any of us. *I* am much the stupidest of the four, but [have] most staying power – what an odd four.[1]

Of the four, Constance, or the 'little 'un', may have been a little odd, like the rest of the Annesleys of that generation. She was, however, very close to her sister Mabel. The two women read each other's work with precise attention, and their ties were so strong that when Constance was a small baby it was only her sister Mabel who could stop her from crying.[2] It is likely because Mabel was reclusive and Constance was extroverted, that each sister learned a great deal from the other. Whatever the case, the strength of character that marked the Lady Mabel was so evident in Constance that the latter could lay claim to a lasting place in history as the one great love of Bertrand Russell's life. Russell, it has been noted, loved Constance 'as deeply as [it] was possible for him to love'.[3]

Constance Mary Annesley was born on 24 October 1895 at Castlewellan, the second daughter of Hugh Annesley's second marriage to his cousin, Priscilla Armitage Moore. As a

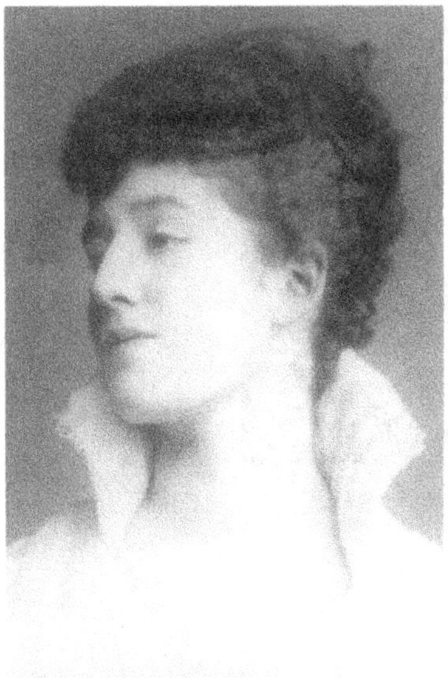

Priscilla (Mabel's stepmother)

baby Constance cried a great deal, and, as noted, her mother would send for Maley, as Mabel was known, to comfort her. Constance was educated at home until her father died; she was then sent to an English boarding school. The school was Downe House in Kent, which she christened 'Damned Hell'. Darwin had spent the last years of his life there and she was assigned his room.[4] After Downe House, Constance went to a finishing school in Dresden and then for several years to a *pensionnat* in Paris to study French literature. There she firmly committed herself to study dramatic art and to work in the theatre.[5]

In 1913 Constance and her mother were invited on a German cruise; when they arrived at Kiel they were introduced to the captain of the Italian man-of-war *Amalfi*, which was anchored amidst the German battleships and the kaiser's yacht. The captain, as it might be imagined, was handsome, dashing and amorous, and it was he who swept the young Constance off her feet, perhaps introducing her for the first time to the pleasures of romance.[6]

By the autumn of that year Constance had enrolled at the Royal Academy of Dramatic Art, encountering there her fellow student, Miles Malleson, later to become a character actor, playwright and translator. His translations of the plays of Molière were noteworthy and he can also be remembered for his roles as hangman in the film *Kind hearts and coronets* (1949) with Alec Guinness, and as Canon Chasuble in the classic film of Oscar Wilde's *The importance of being Earnest* (1952), with Edith Evans, Margaret Rutherford and Michael Redgrave. Malleson and Constance fell in love but, knowing that the Annesley family would never approve, they married secretly on 6 May 1915. We can surmise a great deal about Constance's mother and her hold over her youngest daughter when we learn that Lady Priscilla Annesley demanded that the young couple be married a second time with all of the usual outward show – which they duly did. Though Malleson and Constance lived together as husband and wife after the public ceremony, they both agreed that each would be allowed the liberty to cultivate other relationships.

One of Constance's most important influences was her beautiful socialite mother, Priscilla, the dowager Countess Annesley, whose wide set of friends and ability at correspondence gave her youngest daughter a gracious model to emulate. Priscilla was engaging and courageous, with a warm heart and generosity that brought many people close to her. She was instinctively drawn to humanity in a way that quite clashed with the withdrawn ways of her husband, Hugh. Priscilla cherished a somewhat romantic idea that she could transform the lonely life of her handsome, melancholy husband. To that end she got up at dawn to go duck-shooting with him, learned to ride in order to go with him to outlying parts of the estate, learned to fish in order to go mayfly-dapping in the desolate west, walked out daily with him to inspect work in the already famous gardens and sat with him every evening silently reading until the clock struck the hour of release at ten o'clock.[7] Phyllis Urch, in her unpublished commentary to Constance Malleson's letters to Bertrand Russell, says that Priscilla's was a sort of feudal life where religion counted for little. If daily prayers and Sunday church-going were observed it was probably due to a sense of social obligation, for much the same reasons as one attended feasts for the tenants, distributed food to cottagers, opened bazaars and handed out school prizes. Priscilla Annesley was also often present at stag hunts, and in 1899 she took up the cause of art by opening exhibitions of the Belfast Art Society. It was her feeling that Belfast, as a wealthy and prosperous city, did not give art its proper, prominent place.[8] Mabel's mother, Mabel Wilhelmina, had been noted for her artistic refinement and a rather impish sense of humour, as well as for her involvement in such institutions as the Belfast Ladies' Institute.[9] Likewise, there was a light, even fun-seeking, aspect to Priscilla's life as wife and widow of Hugh Annesley. When Hugh died in 1908 (Mabel was four years into her marriage with Gerald Sowerby) Constance felt the new freedom. She tells us that Priscilla, in widow's weeds, deposited the elder daughter, Clare, at a Dresden finishing school and then took her youngest daughter, Constance, to 'a court ball in Berlin'.[10]

In Berlin, Count Seckendorff, chamberlain to the Empress Frederick, proposed to Priscilla Annesley but she refused him, probably because she was in love with Prince Henry of Prussia. In fact, Priscilla and Henry did become lovers and remained so until his death in 1929.[11]

On 20 September 1916, a few days before the London convention of the No-Conscription Fellowship, Bertrand Russell attended a dinner of left-wingers, including Ramsay MacDonald, the publisher Francis Meynell and Constance, who was a friend of Clifford Allen (later Lord Allen of Hurtwood), whom she had helped found the fellowship. Russell had actually first set eyes on Constance in July 1915; they had been introduced in the police court. He learned that she was one of Clifford Allen's friends and saw for himself that she was generous with her time, a free thinker and a wholehearted pacifist. She was also young and very beautiful. As an actress she had had some success, with two leading parts in succession. However, when the war came she spent all of her days addressing envelopes in the office of the No-Conscription Fellowship. With this knowledge Russell took steps to get to know her better.[12]

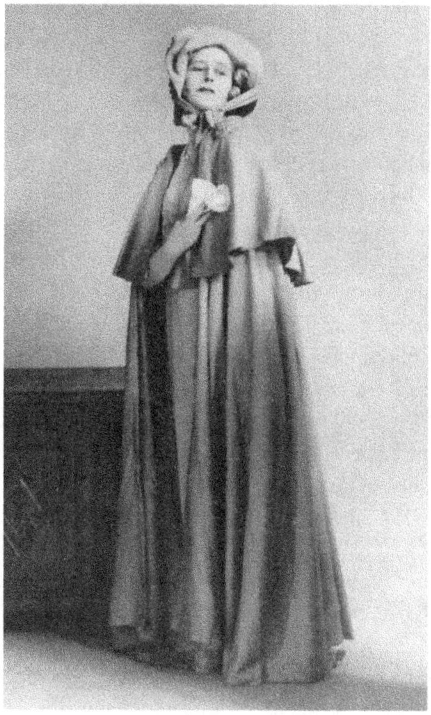
Constance (Mabel's half-sister)

For the young Constance, her first sight of Bertrand Russell in the police court was unforgettable: he had aristocratic features, silver hair and a deeply passionate expression. Conventionally dressed in dark clothes, he

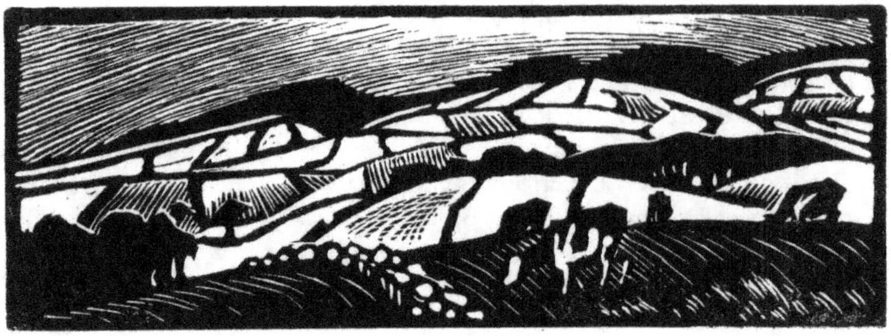

Ab exilio, 40 × 115, *County Down songs*, p. 25.

wore a high, stiff collar. Though he seemed detached in mind and body, 'all the furies of hell had raged in his eyes'.[13] As a result of the strong mutual attraction, Russell accompanied Constance home following a lecture he had given at the Portman Rooms, Baker Street. The two talked together all night and 'in the middle of talk they became lovers'.[14] After their first night together, Russell could not stop thinking of Constance. When he was unable to see her, as was the case in the first few weeks of their love, he would send letters to which she replied, expressing the great sense of freedom and endurance their love inspired. On 28 September 1916 Constance wrote to him, 'Teach me to go out into new and immense worlds: your worlds of thought and infinity.'[15]

By April 1917 Russell appeared to have accepted that Constance was the great love of his life, for he broke off his affair with Lady Ottoline Morrell and turned to his young Irish friend as a possible travelling companion for his proposed sojourn in Russia. Constance, however, who valued her liberty and her career as an actress above all else, refused the invitation, leaving Russell to complain, 'I get so troubled, wondering how your ambitions and mine are ever going to fit with each other.'[16]

In July 1917 the two of them did manage to take a three-week holiday – a blissful interlude when they walked, read, bathed in the River Teme and shamelessly enjoyed Welsh farmhouse cooking.[17] By September Russell had proposed that Constance and he have children together, even if she could not separate from her husband. Constance was not willing to have children and, not wanting to jeopardise her acting career, replied by travelling to Blackpool for the shooting of the film *Hindle wakes*, in which she played the leading part. The director Maurice Elvey was a man whom Constance found tremendously attractive. In fact, she became pregnant by Elvey but chose to abort the child in November 1918. In the fall of 1917, however, Elvey was merely a tormenting sexual competitor in Russell's mind. Infuriated by Constance's apparent infidelity, Russell wrote her a judgemental letter in which he analysed her nature as composed of inharmonious elements. She had one side that loved freedom, hated cruelty and desired a simple formula for making the world perfect. Since this side of her nature lay dormant, her 'soul is filled with a strange ill-understood hunger and despair, of a kind that produces frantic moods and acts of madness in the search for relief'.[18]

Constance described his analysis as one 'which very few women would be likely to forgive',[19] proving by her involvement in the theatre and her writing and editing accomplishments that there was much more to her than 'frantic moods' and 'acts of madness'.[20] The fact that she showed a resolve and commitment to her career as an actress may have enraged the jealous Russell, but it distinguished her as one of the few women in his life who was able to put anything ahead of her relationship with him. If the lack of interest in children and the tendency to match Russell's infidelities with her own do not explain why Constance and Russell never married, then perhaps Ray Monk, Russell's biographer, gives us some insight into their relationship:

> The most natural interpretation of his [Russell's] feelings at this time is that he was still deeply in love with Constance, but feared that he was losing her to the theatre.[21]

Not only was Constance a committed actress, but she also completed two novels and two autobiographical books that reveal her as an unconventional and spirited character. Her first novel, *The coming back*, was published in 1933 and is loosely based on her own life, with the figure of Russell prominent within the story. She shows her life's great love in an objective light, as a man both possessive and jealous. Russell, she wrote, was a man who exhausted others by his intensity, wearing out his friends and 'never giving any real happiness, or finding any'.[22] Mabel, who read most things her sister published, found *The coming back* to be beautiful and flowing – 'The whole thing is not just alive, it is brimming with life.'[23] Constance's second novel, *Fear in the heart*, is based on the life of her sister, Mabel; it was dignified by praise from as distinguished a critic as Sir Harold Nicolson.

Though some would argue that Constance was much better at writing non-fiction than novels (the reception to her autobiography, *After ten years*, was one of appreciation, and her edited version of Lady Mabel's autobiography is still readily available in most libraries), there was little doubt that Constance's psychological insights were as acute as Russell's. In *After ten years*, Constance wrote that Mabel furiously resented Priscilla; she burned with a sense of injustice done to her own mother's memory. Mabel despised pretty clothes; Priscilla loved them. Mabel loved horses and dogs; her stepmother neither liked nor understood them.[24]

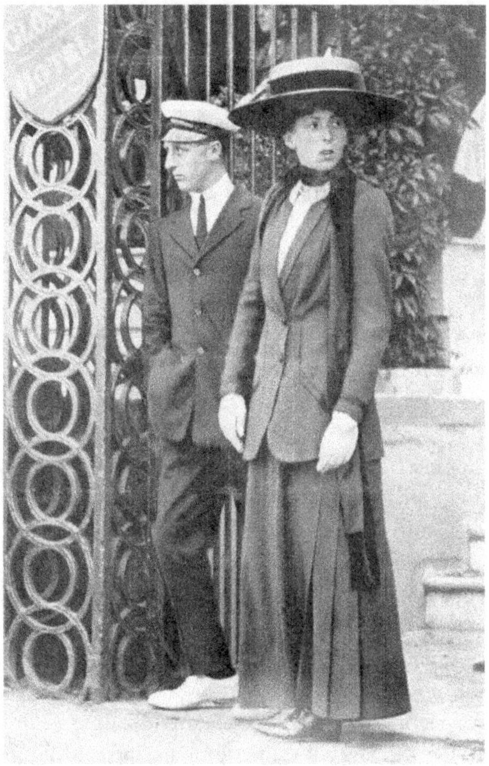

Frank (Mabel's brother) and Mabel (1910)

Constance was much closer to her mother than to her father and she saw the latter as moody, tyrannical and obstinate. She saw her sister Clare as the favourite who got all the special attention, but she worshipped her brother Frank, or 'Brongie', as they called him, who would take her ratting on a Sunday afternoon or along the coast and into the mountains in his racing car.

As for Mabel, Constance considered her 'the object of even greater awe than Brongie'.[25] Mabel was a small woman with beautiful hands, the Annesley aristocratic nose, perfect teeth and eyes that were extremely intelligent and would light up with immense understanding. Her manner was direct and she had Hugh Annesley's strong sense of duty. She 'managed to embody all of the good qualities of the family without any of the bad'.[26] Since 14 years separated them, Constance was only a child when Mabel married, but she remembered her sister on the day of her wedding as 'blissfully happy in all the glory of white satin and orange blossom'.[27] Constance remembered the nationalist attack on Castlewellan, which took place in 1914, when she was an impressionable 19-year-old:

> They turned up at one o'clock in the morning. Sentry challenged them to halt. They opened fire. Sentry replied with his revolver. Within fifteen minutes, two hundred men of the Ulster Volunteer Force had mustered from Kilkeel and Ballina – and a skirmish took place in the park.[28]

Several years later, in 1920, while attending the Central School of Arts and Crafts, Mabel came across her sister by chance at a London theatre. Mabel remembered Constance as a 'rosy child, with enquiring eyes, a wide mouth and bunches of brown bright ringlets'. She later saw a good-looking, pale young woman, 'with a sleek head and a mouth one big smear of lipstick'.[29] Then, when they met at Mabel's flat, Constance wore a preposterous little hat with make-up to match. Mabel's clothes, like herself, 'were very countrified in comparison'.[30] In spite of their differing looks, the two sisters were good friends and Mabel watched over and corresponded with her sister with an indulgence that was almost motherly.

In July 1920 Constance was still involved with Russell. The latter had returned to England from Russia, determined to marry Dora Black, whose chief attraction for him was her desire to have his children. In order to facilitate his divorce from his first wife, Russell was required to provide evidence of a wrong that had been committed – that is, evidence of adulterous conduct. Constance was evidently not aware of Russell's involvement with Dora; in any event, and perhaps too considerately, she interrupted her touring schedule to go to London 'for a night of "official adultery"' before she left Russell for Portsmouth the next morning.[31]

During this period Constance remained, like the rest of the Annesley family, 'well connected'. Ray Monk tells of how, in the early hours of the morning, the First World War suddenly came to an end. An agreement to end hostilities was signed in a railway carriage deep in the French countryside. Though peace was announced to the public at 11 o'clock in the morning, Russell learned the news a few hours earlier than that. Moments after the armistice was signed, Winston Churchill phoned his Aunt Leonie, Lady Leslie. She passed the news on to her friend Lady Annesley, who in turn phoned her daughter, Constance. Constance, of course, immediately called Russell, who was in London that morning. Nothing terribly

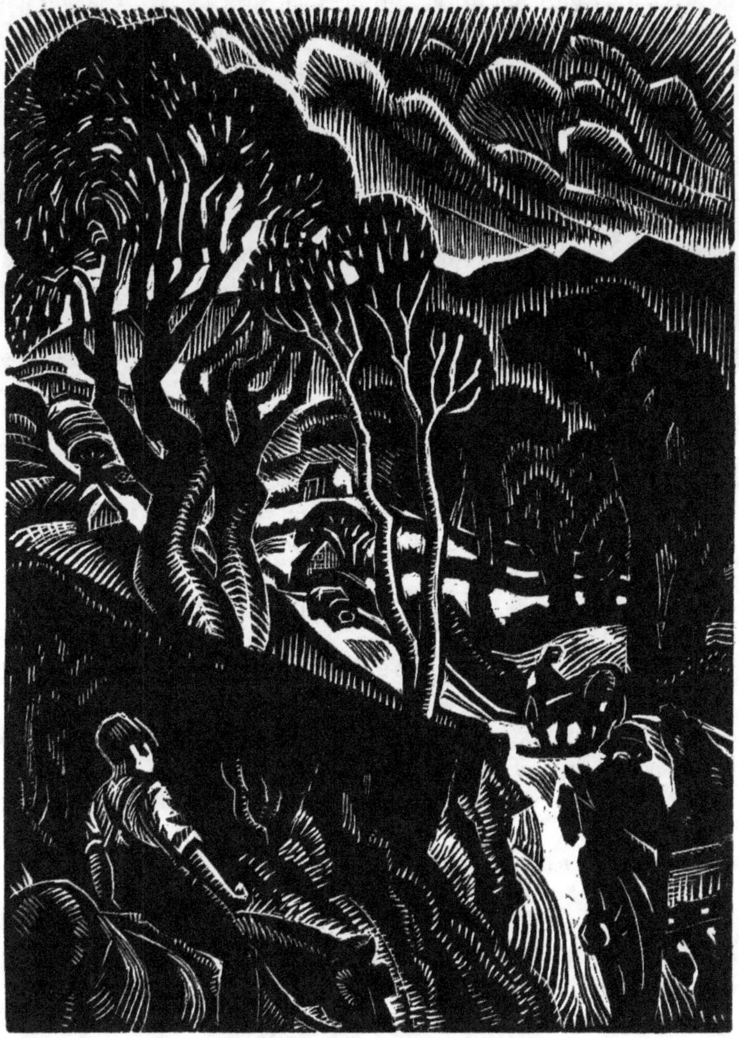

Country road, wood engraving,
135 × 101 (no. 4 of 25).

dramatic was done – no one wept or sang for joy or cursed or moaned. 'It was like the slow lifting of a very heavy load.'[32]

A few years later, on 27 March 1921, Constance was shocked beyond any previous degree of emotion when a Japanese journalist, learning that Russell was severely ill, reported his death. False news of his death was spread around the world and Constance, who was in Paris at the time, wrote, 'The news broke me.' It was a 'neat job: short, sharp and permanent'. Thrown into a deep depression, she contemplated suicide and was filled with a black destructiveness. She 'wanted to destroy all beauty over the whole earth'.[33]

Perhaps a little like Russell, Constance could feel the intensity of whatever relationship she was involved in at the moment to the exclusion of all other emotions. We do know that around the same time as she was reeling from the news of Russell's death she was engaged in what may have been a full-blown affair with Robert Gibbings. There exists a charmingly illustrated letter that Gibbings sent to Constance around this time, which was reprinted in the fine-print journal, *Matrix*, in 1989. Here, it seems, Gibbings is on a courteous, if professional, footing with Constance. He writes, 'Beautiful lady, I was very glad to hear that you are about to leave the jarring sounds, and the empty fashions of London for the peace and simplicity of the country,' and ends the letter, 'perhaps I may at least have a chance of drawing you'.[34] Another letter, written by Gibbings to Constance, hints that his thoughts had often strayed to the beauty of her figure as well as of her face. He writes that, as a result of thinking of her, he feels that the 'poor bloody wrapper' (that is, the jacket) of his recently published book should have been 'more VIRILE, more erect, more teeming and turgid'.[35]

Gibbings makes reference in another letter to the fact that Constance was no longer a city-dweller, but drawn to the countryside. She lived in the country from 1924 (following her divorce from Miles Malleson) until her death in 1975. Moreover, she wrote that, since leaving it in late adolescence, she had always wanted to go back to Ireland. Like Mabel, Constance adored Castlewellan because of the beauty of its hills and lakes, the mountains and the sea. Being there somehow fulfilled her; when she was away she often thought of the mountains, the distant sea and the smell of turf at night along the bog. Most of all she missed the sight of the 'small white farms and the sound of County Down voices'.[36]

Unlike Mabel, however, Constance had no involvement in the affairs of Castlewellan and her visits to Ireland were relatively rare. After leaving London she divided her time between frequent visits to her English friends and travels to the Middle East and Scandinavia. Her love for Sweden was so great that she returned to it often, sometimes for six months at a time. She wrote an evocative, though unpublished, long essay comparing Ireland to Lapland. She found Ulster to be Scottish in feeling. People from the north were hard headed, being neither English nor totally Irish. In many ways she found them quite 20 years behind the English. At the same time they had much of the 'inconsequence of the Irish'. Unlike the southern Irish, she thought, they had an aptitude for work. On her return to Ulster from Lapland, Constance found the soft Irish air to be like a caress after Lapland's sharp electric air. She found the brightness of the Ulster sky at eight o'clock in the morning to be quite surprising. She went on to describe the Ulster country, spread into a wonderful pattern of fields all chopped up into different shapes and enclosed by sharp grey stone walls or dark hedges of brown thorn. The fields were never very far from the sea; gulls, white as fallen stars, sat together in the fields like 'the Pleiades in heaven'. The roads ran like stone walls through the fields and up and over many little hills to the foot of the Mournes; those mountains, the Annesley mountains, rose up from the sea. Each generation of Mourne farmers lived in little white houses. Their land was stolen from 'the whins and the bracken'.[37]

On one of her trips back to Ireland in the 1930s Constance went to stay with her sister Mabel, and the latter sister recorded the following comments:

> Though we both enjoyed exploring a countryside, our methods were different. She ranged over an area of thirty miles. My area was nearer three. In high-heeled shoes, she sped along tarmac roads. I strolled over mountains and picked my way on tussocks over bogland. Loitering round a heathery hill or a sandy bay occupied me for a week. Short-sighted, I enjoyed the soft golden moss under my feet, the pattern made by the close-woven trefoil, bleached sphagnum, or the frilly lichen on boulder stones. I loved the star-like faces of wild lobelia, scarlet pimpernel, pansies and geranium; and I crowed with delight when I met a stiff little group of worldly orchis [*sic*]. Longer sighted than I, she saw the headlands that thrust out to the sea. She looked at a distant hill and in no time she had reached its summit. She always ran where I walked. I fumbled with a pencil to fix my impressions. *She* beat hers out on typewriter. They were clear, limpid impressions.[38]

Constance spent the Second World War in Finland and then in Sweden, but her influence also extended to England during that time and earlier. She was engaged in a variety of good causes, including the Campaign for Mental Health Reform in the UK (in 1935). She, in fact, initiated that campaign, being joined by Havelock Ellis, H.G. Wells, Bertrand Russell, Lord Olivier, Sybil Thorndike, Lord Queensborough, and her mother, Countess Annesley, amongst others.

After the war, Russell rekindled the affair with Constance that had begun almost 30 years previously. In March 1946, after his third wife had moved to Wales because of severe depression, Russell made overtures to Constance, telling her that he would be living alone in Cambridge during term time. Constance responded with some ardour, inviting him to London:

> within a few weeks she believed – and had reason to believe – that their affair would, after a break of nearly thirty years, be resumed. 'Every moment of my visit to you was a joy,' Russell wrote to her on 21 March 1946. 'I wonder how soon, if ever, we shall meet again.'[39]

However, the fire of love between Russell and Constance was not to sustain its heat for long. According to Ray Monk, Russell was tormented by thoughts of losing his youngest son, Conrad, if he should separate permanently from Conrad's mother. Russell left an unpublished manuscript, written to his wife, concerning his passion for Constance. He wrote (rather ungallantly) that Constance had become 'middle-aged, very fat, nearly stone deaf, and without any traces of her former beauty'.[40] Phyllis Urch, Constance's close friend, maintains that Russell completely contradicted himself in that same year, when he told her about Constance,

'I love her beauty; the beauty of her face, I've always loved. I've loved her more than I've ever loved anyone.'[41]

Whatever the truth of the matter, Russell did appear to sustain a deeply emotional – indeed, spiritual – feeling for Constance, as his letters between 1946 and 1950 indicate. He wrote in December 1946 that he longed to see her. In April 1947 he commented that he hoped for the opportunity 'to carry on the rebirth' of their mutual affection.[42] In May 1948 Russell secured an invitation to Sweden that would allow him to visit Constance; he then suggested to her that she buy a cottage near his in Wales. When Constance arrived in Wales the following September, however, Russell confessed that he had been having an affair with a Norwegian woman, Nalle Kielland. He feared that if he resumed relations with Constance his wife might sell their cottage and leave him, taking their son Conrad with her.

By 1950 Constance had given up completely on Russell, settling in her own cottage in Lavenham, Suffolk. In 1952 she wrote to a friend about Russell:

> Before BR knew Nalle almost every letter to [me] ended with 'Thank you for giving me your love.' In 1949, four months after he had left his third wife, he wrote 'Thank you for the warmth that you bring into my life.'

Constance felt, for her own sake, that he ought to marry someone, just to keep him occupied for a few years. Unafraid of his wanting to marry *her*, she feared that if he didn't get involved with someone new he would fall back on her, if only for the relief of being forgiven. Constance also enjoyed the sense of power that their love gave her. That love might be seen as a desire for 'something akin to religion (the orthodox kind being intellectually tabu) [...] if only by proxy' because Russell knew that love of him had been part of her spiritual life since the age of 20.[43]

Constance maintained a lively correspondence with many people over the years, assuring her friends that while living in Lapland she had had only one bath between November and May, and that she found Swedish life rather demanding, moving between four wooden huts in two years.[44] She was blessed with an enduring relationship with her former mother-in-law, Mrs Malleson, whom she regarded as 'a regular old aristocrat'.[45] In one undated letter she talks of a luxurious weekend at Baroness Palmstierna's (Baroness Palmstierna's husband was Swedish minister in London) – 'the Baroness was very amusing about London folk'.[46]

As time went on, contrary to Russell's reassurance to his wife, Constance's appearance maintained a unique, if eccentric, attraction for others. In a portrait painted by William Conor 'she holds in her hands her only piece of jewellery, a large baroque pearl which she wore on a cord around her neck'.[47] And her great-niece, Margaret Ogilvie, recalls her wearing a collection of rings which, being over-large, flew off her hands as she talked and gesticulated. As Russell (who himself later became deaf) so cruelly pointed out, she had suffered from deafness in one ear since an illness in 1921; after the Second World War she became deaf in the other. 'Her head,' she told sympathetic enquirers, 'was always filled with the roar of the sea, a frightful din which shut out all sound from the outside.'[48]

One of the most engaging of Constance's family members was her mother's cousin, Percy French (1854–1920), songwriter, painter, illustrator and actor. French was born in County Roscommon and studied engineering at Trinity College, Dublin, but his real love was for

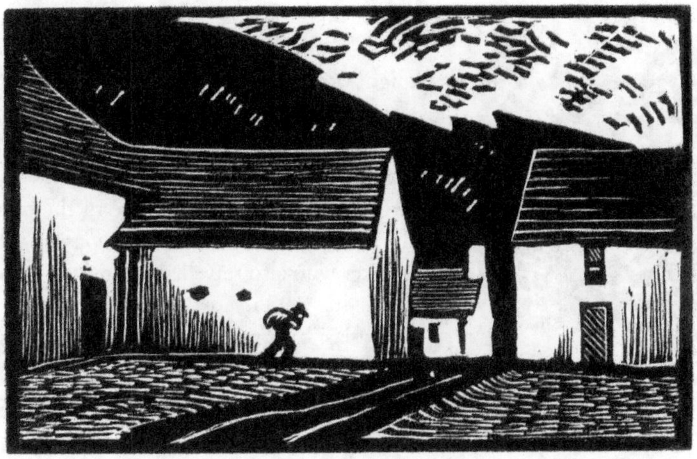

The rooks, 59 × 95, *County Down songs*, p. 36.

sketching, songwriting and watercolours. Between 1891 and 1901 he showed dozens of works at the Royal Hibernian Academy. He was responsible for the libretti of a musical comedy and an opera. However, since he lacked any business sense, his watercolours were either sold very cheaply or given to friends.[49] *The Northern Whig* described French's unusual sense of theatre and song as giving him a reputation as an entertainer in Ireland and Great Britain. His songs were of the proper Irish type, not the stereotypical article where the hero becomes drunk in the first verse, leading him to murder all his relations in the second. There was mirth and drollery in French's songs, but it was in his illustrated ditties that he was at his best.[50]

French's talents were put to good use when he completed numerous watercolours for Priscilla Annesley's personal photograph albums, now in the Bertrand Russell Archives at McMaster University, Hamilton, Ontario, Canada. They include a corner of Priscilla's boudoir, two seascapes, two London street scenes, the Thames at Chelsea and Windsor Castle. In addition to these and other scenes the albums were decorated with flowers, which wound their way across pages, surrounding the photographs and signatures.[51]

Constance took over her mother's albums some time during the 1920s and her career as a stage actress is brought to life in them. There are also photographs of her two tours of Africa in 1928–9, a journey to France with Margaret Pilkington in 1931 and a trip to the Middle East with Sybil Thorndike in 1932. With the death of her mother in 1941, and her sister Mabel's move to New Zealand in 1942, Constance found herself more and more dependent on letters and travel to widen her perspective.

Though she never got over her feelings for 'BR',[52] Constance was able to develop a real affection and concern for her sister, Clare, who lived in London for most of her life. While as a child, Constance had always felt that Clare was given preferential treatment by their mother. But what could have been an antagonistic relationship between Priscilla's two daughters emerged as a rather gentle and understanding sympathy. As a political person herself, Constance most likely admired Clare for her membership in the English Labour Party.

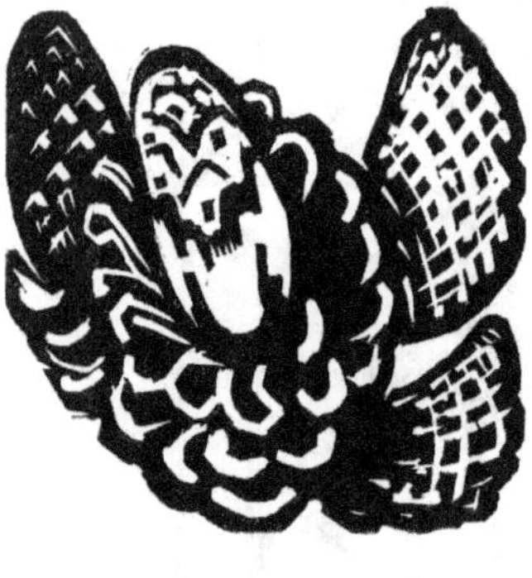

Pine cone, 45 × 45,
As the sight is bent, p. 113.

Clare was a woman of gracious personality and obvious ability and was much taken up with the plight of the poor in London's East End. She joined the Independent Labour Party in the 1930s, believing that the support of an aristocratic figure would give credence to the philosophy of a party that strove to achieve social justice in the period before the Second World War. She was an able public speaker who also travelled extensively – to Germany and, in 1935, to Canada, where she was enthusiastically received.[53] Clare stood for parliament on two occasions – not because she wished to enter it, but because she felt her candidature would make known the cause she had at heart.

Cut from a more serious mould than her sister Constance or her mother, Priscilla, Clare seemed to have inherited from her father that high sense of duty and responsibility that made the latter such a well-liked landlord. Curiously, when Constance edited Mabel's letters for publication in *As the sight is bent*, she eliminated all of Mabel's references to Clare, revealing a certain reserve between the sisters that endured from childhood to old age. The Bertrand Russell Archives possess one short letter from Clare to Constance: 'I gave Maly [Mabel] the little brown straw (sailor) hat. So thankful to find anything she wanted.'[54] The letter confirms that Clare was much guided by personal kindness, although Mabel was (if we are to read the letter correctly) at times a little difficult to please. Neither Constance nor Mabel left many letters to indicate their feelings for their middle sister. One doctor's report sums up the old age of Clare Annesley in this manner:

> unmarried, sleeps all night and most of day. Works whole days and late evening (unpaid) in Caledonian Road. Can't cook at all; drives herself unmercifully. Gives most of her money away to anybody who asks for it. Is religious: always has been.[55]

She remains an intriguing but enigmatic figure in the lives of her sisters Constance and Mabel.

In 1964 Constance suffered a stroke, which left her paralysed on the left side. This, coupled with blood poisoning caused by contact with a species of sumac tree, left her barely able to write letters. The following summarises her account of her stroke on December 14, 1964, and it shows her acute self-understanding, stoicism and courage. She felt herself to be in such physical distress from the stroke that she did not know if she could hold out for the next ten days, until Christmas Eve when she expected a visitor. She decided she would have to construct an SOS. She would have to smash a pane of glass and hurl the SOS into the street before the cleaning lady left work next door. She would then have to use her chin, instead of her dead left arm, to tape the latchkey of the cottage into a tall Bath Olivers tin, together with the SOS. This took eight hours to do. A heavy Denby pottery lid by her bedside smashed the window to perfection, with the broken glass making a splendid clatter. Out went the SOS tin after the Denby lid. Sweating with effort and exhaustion, she then slumped back to await results. After being rescued she felt greatly elated, but she had the grace to wonder 'how many thousands of England's impoverished old women are in a similar plight'.[56]

At the age of 69, Constance was permanently paralysed in her left side, but resolute in her determination to live alone at the cottage in Lavenham, Suffolk. Visited fortnightly by a public-health nurse, she moved around the cottage with the help of a stick, dragging herself up and down stairs with her right arm. Various villagers, who were aware of her circumstances, watched out for her. They could not, however, prevent the inevitable and, in 1973, she fell and broke her hip, remaining alone for four days without food or drink until the police broke in and took her to hospital. Following her release from hospital she went to live in a nursing home in Thurston, near Bury St Edmunds, which she had once described as 'a shoddy, godforsaken town'.[57]

As John Slater points out, Constance was loyal, passionate, impulsive and generous. It was probably the combination of these virtues that made it impossible for her to become Russell's wife.[58] In the early years, Russell had seen her as an antidote to the horrors of war; she was a woman who preserved love in a world of hate. She possessed a quality 'of rock-like immovability which in those days was invaluable'.[59] Later, however, he saw her as an impulsive spirit who could not confine her generosity and passion to him. Russell did seem, however, to command much more of her loyalty than the other men in her life:

> And so she got shunted out of his life for long agonizing periods; her passion was banked but it would spring instantly aflame with the fresh draft brought by a letter from him.[60]

Finally, with Russell's death came a time of tranquility. She could prepare for her own death with acceptance, remembering the man who had once been an almost religious figure in her life. It was, however, with Mabel's death in 1959 and the publication of her autobiography in 1964 that Constance's career as a writer came to fruition. She edited *As the sight is bent*, which remains the most lasting testimony to the Annesley family.

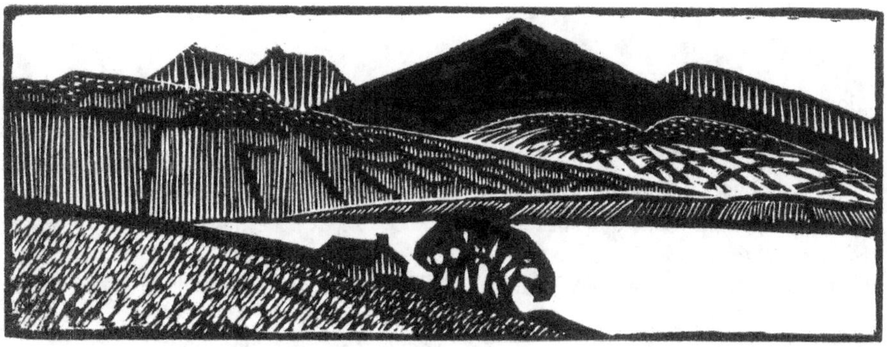

Upon a hill-side, 44 × 121, *County Down songs*, p. 16.

1 Mabel Annesley to Constance Malleson, n.d. (BRAMU, Colette collection).
2 Phyllis Urch, notes, April 2002 (privately held).
3 Ray Monk, *Bertrand Russell: the spirit of solitude, 1872–1921* (London, 1996), p. 567.
4 J. Slater, 'Lady Constance Malleson, "Colette O'Niel"' in *Russell: the Journal of Bertrand Russell Studies*, xx (winter 1975–6), p. 4.
5 Urch, notes.
6 Slater, 'Lady Constance Malleson', p. 4.
7 Phyllis Urch, 'Preface', letters to Bertrand Russell (BRAMU, Colette collection).
8 *The Northern Whig*, 5 October 1899.
9 A. Jordan, 'Opening the gates of learning: the Belfast Ladies' Institute' in Holmes and Urquhart, *Coming into the light*, p. 35.
10 Urch, 'Preface'.
11 Ibid.
12 Bertrand Russell, *The autobiography of Bertrand Russell, volume 2, 1914–1944* (London, 1968), p. 25.
13 Ibid., p. 26.
14 Malleson, *After ten years*, quoted in Slater, 'Lady Constance Malleson', p. 6.
15 Monk, *Spirit of solitude*, p. 502.
16 Ibid., p. 479.
17 Ibid., p. 495.
18 Ibid., p. 508.
19 Ibid.
20 Ibid.
21 Ibid., p. 558.
22 Constance Malleson, *The coming back* (London, 1933), p. 11.
23 Mabel Annesley to Constance Malleson, 20 January (no year given) (BRAMU, Colette collection).
24 Malleson, *After ten years*, p. 13.
25 Ibid., p. 24.
26 Ibid., p. 25.
27 Ibid., p. 26.
28 Ibid., pp. 77–8.
29 *Atsib*, p. 27.
30 Ibid.
31 Monk, *Spirit of solitude*, p. 587.
32 Ibid., p. 542.
33 Ibid., p. 600.
34 Robert Gibbings to Colette O'Niel, *Matrix*, ix (1989).
35 Robert Gibbings to Colette O'Niel, n.d. (BRAMU, Colette collection).
36 Malleson, *After ten years*, p. 71.
37 Constance Malleson, 'Lapland to Ulster', n.d. (BRAMU, Colette collection).
38 *Atsib*, p. 60.
39 Ray Monk, *Bertrand Russell, 1921–70: the ghost of madness* (London, 2000), p. 293.
40 Ibid.

[41] Bertrand Russell to Phyllis Urch, 1946 (privately held).
[42] Monk, *Ghost of madness*, pp. 293–4.
[43] Constance Malleson to Colonel T.G. Gayer-Anderson, 12 July 1952 (BRAMU, Colette collection).
[44] Constance Malleson to Robert Gibbings, 5 June 1943 (BRAMU, Colette collection).
[45] Constance Malleson to Priscilla Annesley, n.d. (BRAMU, Colette collection).
[46] Constance Malleson to Mabel Annesley, n.d. (BRAMU, Colette collection).
[47] Martyn Anglesea, *William Conor: the people's painter* (Belfast, 1999), p. 23.
[48] Slater, 'Lady Constance Malleson'.
[49] Snoddy, *Dictionary of Irish artists*, p. 123.
[50] *The Northern Whig*, 27 October 1899.
[51] S. Turcon, 'French surprise', *McMaster University Library Research News*, vi, no. 1 (spring 1996).
[52] Margaret Ogilvie, pers. comm., May 2000.
[53] Ibid.
[54] Clare Annesley to Constance Malleson, n.d. (BRAMU, Colette collection).
[55] Doctor's report, n.d. (BRAMU, Colette collection).
[56] Slater, 'Lady Constance Malleson', p. 13.
[57] Ibid., p. 14.
[58] Ibid., p. 44.
[59] Russell, *Autobiography* (vol. ii), p. 26.
[60] Slater, 'Lady Constance Malleson', p. 14.

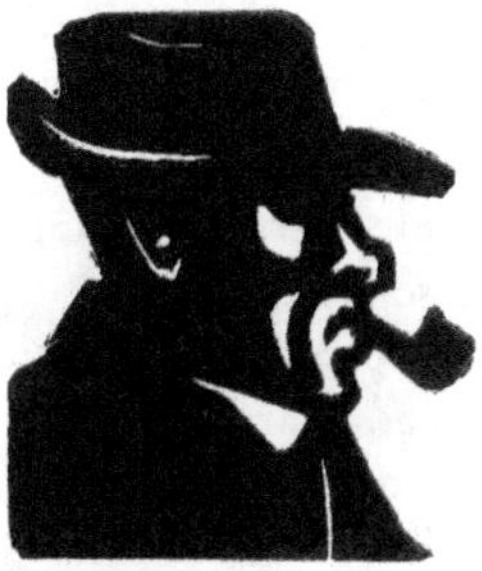

The bachelor-man,
36 × 32, *County Down songs*, p. 14.

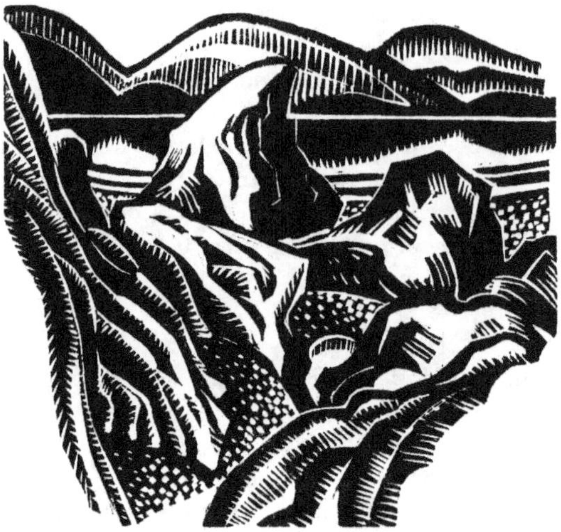

Diamond mountain, 65 × 70, *As the sight is bent*, p. 47.

5
New Zealand

Mabel's departure for New Zealand in 1942 was not an easy one. Not only did she leave Ireland for completely unknown territory, but she also abandoned an artistic and personal reputation that spanned the Irish Sea. Three years earlier, when she had presented a number of engravings to the Belfast Museum and Art Gallery, John Hewitt had acknowledged her position in the art world. He had proclaimed that Annesley's devotion to art was shown not only in her personal practice but also in her eagerness to assist all movements dedicated to art, in her service on commissions and committees and through her resonant public utterances, 'in which she consistently claimed art as an indispensable part of man's best heritage'.[1]

In New Zealand Mabel was a stranger, an ageing woman whose sense of duty led to the unexpected task of picking ergot for the Allied cause. (Ergot is a fungal disease of rye that yields a chemical that can be used in drugs.) England's supply of ergot from Europe was cut off and chemists were badly in need of it. Though the picking was wearisome (it took two long days to collect an ounce), it was a way of getting into good country. In Mabel's opinion her time was not valuable – although, she remarked, when one had to wash and mend and cook and clean, it was quite extraordinary how very fast the time could go.[2]

Even before arriving in New Zealand, however, she had begun to analyse the landscape of Australia and the inevitable comparison with Northern Ireland began. She commented that 'the gum trees strike a silvery grey note of characteristic colour practically everywhere. They are the ash trees of Northern Ireland.' She found the people in Australia loud and rude but friendly, and the food very good and cheap.[3] One explanation for her settling in New Zealand was elucidated by her friend, Miss Gladys Beasley, of Nelson. Hugh Annesley, Mabel's father, once paid a visit to New Zealand – most likely with Nelson in his itinerary. He must have been deeply impressed by New Zealand's native flora, 'later planting a variety of specimens in his gardens at Castlewellan'.[4]

In a letter to Fish, undated, Mabel remarked that every time she went out she liked the place better. Indeed there was much in the landscape of New Zealand to remind her of Castlewellan. She had never seen so many Jersey cows and calves and, of course, sheep. They all walked about in short, green grass. With cherry blossoms around each house, and the houses painted red, green, and rust-orange-maroon, she could not help but think of that maroon that was so loved by builders in Northern Ireland.[5]

Mabel also found the people of New Zealand to be very congenial, with their 'splendid weather-baked faces, stringy and mahogany-coloured'.[6] By 5 October a permanent home had been found at 7 Nile Street in Nelson (the site is now part of a car park). Although the rent was expensive, the little cottage soon became friendly and homely and Mabel was able to forget Castlewellan Castle, at least for a while.

Arnold Wall of the *Nelson Evening Mail* recounted an amusing story which establishes the atmosphere of Mabel's war years in 'the colonies'. During the Second World War a Nelson policeman, patrolling Rabbit Island by bicycle, spotted a lone elderly female sketching the coastline. He pounced upon her, saying, 'Don't ye know that it's agin the law to be drawing the beaches when there's a war on?' The lady explained that she was no spy, but an innocent artist from Ireland. Eventually she satisfied the guardian of New Zealand's shores and the policeman pedalled away, calling back, 'But I know ye're not from Oireland – I come from there meself and ye've not got the accent!'[7]

One of the first things Mabel looked for for her home in Nelson was a wood-engraving press. It is easy to imagine that her letterpress, like the one purchased in Dublin for £10, would have met the standards laid out by Noel Rooke in his letter to her friend Margaret Pilkington. The best kind of press, according to Rooke, was the Albion, which was used at the Central School of Arts and Crafts. The best makers were Oliver and Richards. The great days for the Albion were in the 1860s, when wood-engraved illustration was being revived. A press of that date was likely 'to be a good one if it has been well treated'. Several other halftone presses, such as the Reliance, were even better than the Albion, but they were seldom to be had second hand because they were so much in demand. Halftone presses were different from the Albion, which supported the bars of the platen (the plate which is pressed down towards the bed). Such bars were reinforced in later presses. The chapter on Albion presses in Charles Thomas Jacobi's guide to printing would, according to Rooke, give a better understanding of how they worked.[8]

Even if her new press was satisfactory, the difficulty in finding decent wood for engraving seems to have led Mabel to the related medium of linocutting; she literally pulled up the linoleum from her floor in order to continue cutting relief prints. Around this time she wrote to Margaret Pilkington concerning the difficulty of finding proper engraving tools and materials, saying, 'I'm in touch with all the right people, and know a few ropes.' Nonetheless, she could not find wood and there was a shortage of ink and paper, so she was 'in pieces' and did not work very often.[9] One of the 'right people' she did get in touch with was the aunt of John Buckland Wright. Buckland Wright (1887–1955) was born in New Zealand and died in London. Like Mabel, he did some work for the Golden Cockerel Press as well as much highly esteemed engraving for other limited editions. His aunt was 'a dear old thing' who had brought him up. She had plenty of the eminent Buckland Wright's work to help Mabel feel at home even in the southern hemisphere.

Mabel loved the river that ran through Nelson: it was a grey-green colour like the willows and the flax that bordered it. Close to her house was a hydrangea, and wisteria and lilacs all bloomed together in the hot New Zealand sun. As a confirmed animal lover (she tells us of her first dog in the beginning pages of her autobiography and makes Puck-a-loo, the old yellow terrier that accompanied her during her Connemara travels, seem almost human) she managed to overcome her natural antipathy to cats. Alone in the New Zealand countryside she acquired a serviceable feline, whose job it was to get rid of the rats that climbed from the river into her house.

At first, Mabel worried about her letterpress going through the floor onto the head of 'the old dame who lives below me', but she was soon totally absorbed in her work, at one point having four different pieces at different stages; 'also a fifth if a comic sketch could possibly be counted'.[10] The making of a silverpoint print looking down upon the Maitai Valley occupied much of her time, while she continued to explore the New Zealand countryside, with its slippery grass and deep gullies. When not occupied with her artwork she tried to widen her circle of friends, including the drawing master at the college. Spare moments saw her taking on more war work, gathering wool and knitting quilts for the forces. Presumably none of this was good for her arthritic hands, but she makes little complaint of this in her letters to Fish.

In a letter dated 28 November 1941 she refers to a linocut she was finishing: it was a large image of the big hill that enters Maitai Valley. Called Kaka, the hill stood guard over a convent and a Roman Catholic church. It made 'a fine thing, full of problems'.[11] By December Mabel had learned that Gerald was very happy in his second marriage, but she did pine for more mail from her beloved friends overseas. To fill the hours she even did a little gardening for a lady nearby who owned a rather large house and garden.

Nonetheless, Mabel was very lonely, responding 'typically for the homesick by yearning for letters that don't arrive', then withdrawing.[12] She had been encouraged to seek refuge from the catastrophes in the northern hemisphere by her son, Gerald. His daughter, Margaret Ogilvie, wrote in a 1980 letter to Eileen Black that New Zealand was just 'so far away'. Gerald Annesley had visited it following his divorce and decided his mother would love it. He encouraged her to go to New Zealand when it became possible. He hoped that the climate would help her arthritis. New Zealand also used the pound sterling, although later there were problems over double taxation.[13]

Our impression of Mabel during these early days in New Zealand is of an uncomplaining, dutiful soul, anxious to keep her hours filled with work but ever devoted to printmaking and exploring the surrounding countryside. As soon as one good war cause finished she turned

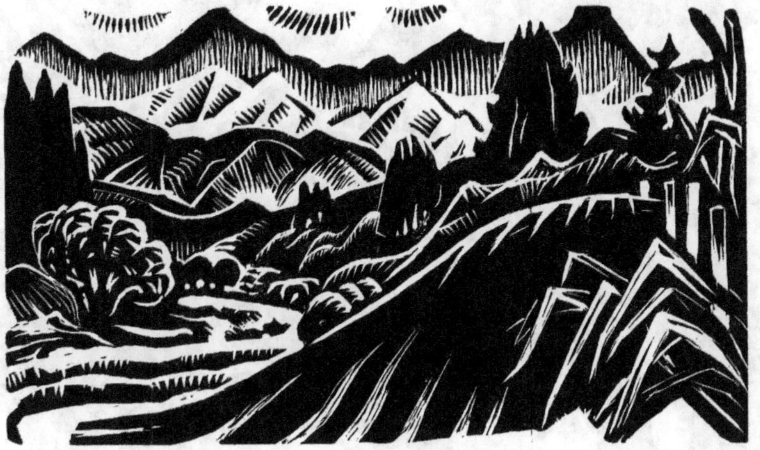

Sheep country, 60 × 100, *As the sight is bent*, p. 121.

to another; after knitting and ergot picking, she turned to child welfare; she was in the clothes department and made whatever was needed. With time to read to 'a dear old thing, [who] though over eighty-six is bright as a bee', Mabel could not deny that she was 'homesick for County Down voices and County Down hills'.[14] On a trip into the bush she discovered a farmer's wife who sold her cream, eggs, milk and peaches; the discovery led her to wonder how many Englishwomen would put up with the loneliness.[15] The subtropical bush that the farmer's wife inhabited was carpeted with fern, and creepers hung everywhere like the twisted cables 'beneath a sea of many ships'.[16] There were many towering trees, with an assortment of lovely smaller shrubs, 'every one of them visual food for an engraver'.[17] She climbed part-way up the immense mountains, almost to the snow-line, and thought again of Ireland: 'Two rivers wind everywhere. Think of them as greater Donard Falls. Think of the mountains as steeper than the Mountains of Mourne.'[18] The birds and the insects were captivating, bringing out the best in her as a writer as well as an engraver. She wrote:

> The wood pigeon was bright green and red and grey, and very big. The bell birds had flute-like notes and fan tails. All the birds were tame, showing interest in humans, rather than fright. On certain days the air was quite full of the humming and buzzing of the winged cicada.

Mabel, having never seen them up close before, 'found the long, back-folded wings' gave the cicada the appearance of 'Walt Disney insects'.[19]

During this period Mabel worked on several of the relief prints that were to feature in an early 1950s exhibition of her art held at the National Art Gallery of New Zealand. Though some of the engravings were from an earlier period, a number of the linocuts must have been completed during the time Mabel lived in New Zealand. *Rogerson River* is from the New Zealand years, as is *Little hills*, which was reproduced in the 1947 *Yearbook of the arts in New*

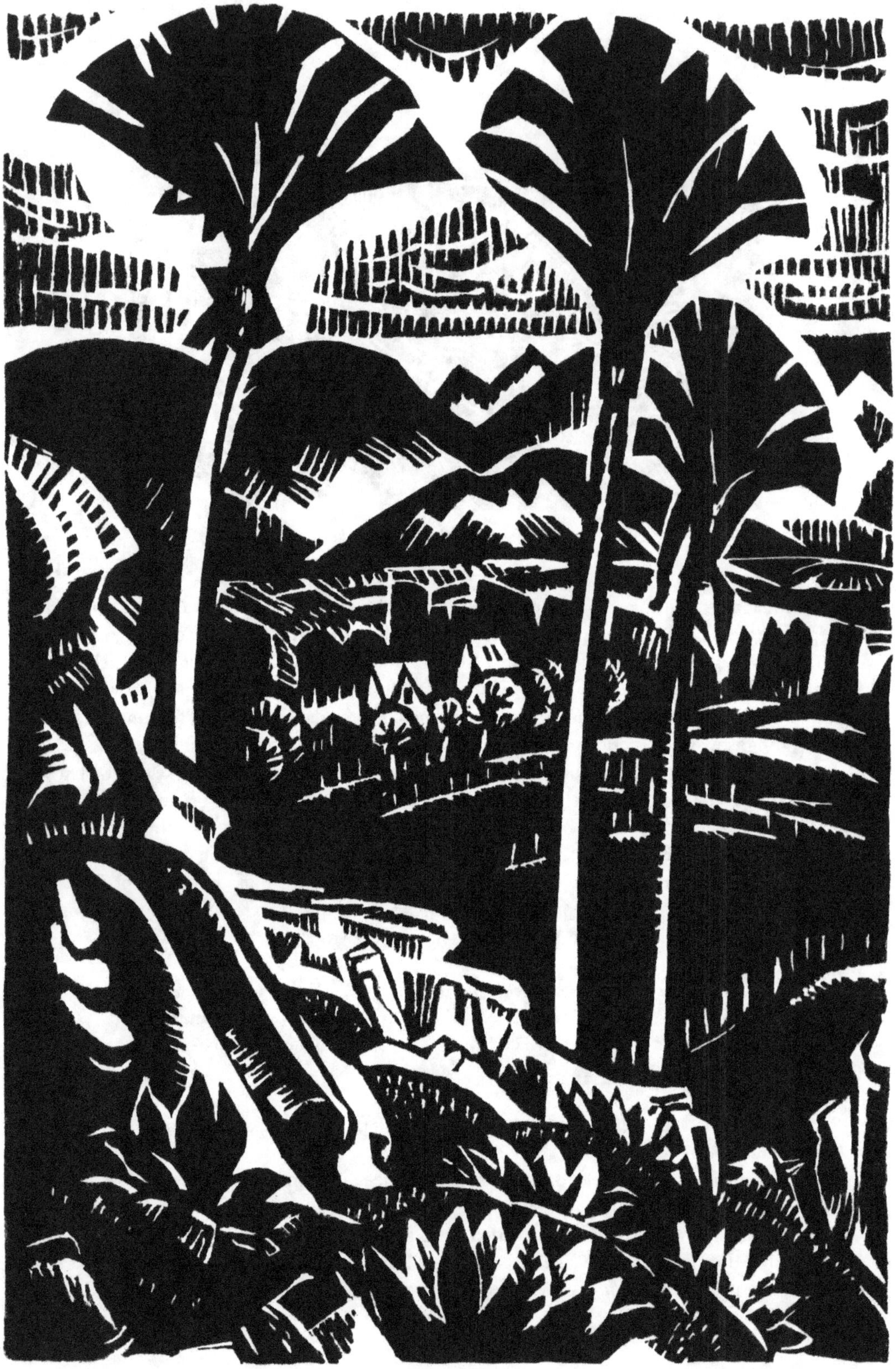

Nikau palms, linocut, *c.* 1940–45 (Museum of New Zealand Te Papa Tongarewa), 210 × 145.

Zealand. Pelorus Pass, which was exhibited in Manchester, New York and Pittsburgh, was a New Zealand linocut that was reproduced in the 1950 *Yearbook of the arts in New Zealand.* Mabel also completed and exhibited the linocuts *Willows, Nikau palms, The fringe, At Pohara* and *The glen* between 1941 and 1953, when she lived for the most part in New Zealand. *Anatoki* is a linocut that depicts the Takaka neighbourhood of one of Mabel's friends. The linocut looks across the Anatoki Range and exaggerates some landscape features in order to emphasise other rhythms that unify the elements of the print.

By the end of the war Mabel was ready to return to Ireland and England. And so, packing her odd collection of worldly goods, she took the liner back to the northern hemisphere. In Tiverton, County Devon, she found a place to live and wrote to Margaret Pilkington that she had tried by mail to obtain printer's ink, 'the town of Tiverton producing nothing'. Having only small bits of paper, it was just luck if she could make a decent print. She knew for certain, however, that she would have to give up sending watercolours, as she would never get the canvases into Tiverton. There were no buses or trains serving the village, so she had to carry everything on her back. The country around Tiverton was lovely but her cottage was primitive and cold.[20]

Around the same time, she sent a postcard to Pilkington, anguishing over the fact that the block she was working on had vanished. She was lucky to have three linocuts and a framed but small watercolour. Pilkington, she thought, might not think the works worth hanging; Mabel pleaded with her to use her own judgement when she came to exhibit them. Without anyone to help pack the watercolour, and with some difficulty finding materials for the linocuts, Mabel was not in a position to show much to her friend at the Whitworth. 'Anyhow,' she went on to say, 'many thanks for the school of Patinir.'[21]

The house in Devon where Mabel lived was an ugly, stone, small house, the only kind she could get when she came back from New Zealand. The only light available came from oil lamps; the only water had to be pumped from the top of a hill. Without servants or carpets, it seemed that its chief attraction lay in its furniture, which belonged to the 'dead officer, son of the nearest lady of the manor'.[22] The house was decorated with a Coptic Christ, which Mabel had found in pieces in Cairo and carefully reassembled, on one wall, and a magnificent Paul Nash on the other.[23]

By 1949, perhaps because of her health, or perhaps because of Gerald's financial and marital troubles, Mabel made up her mind to return to New Zealand, this time to a tiny house on Packard Road, Takaka, on Golden Bay. *Pinus insignis* was a linocut completed during this period. It drew some criticism from her New Zealand contemporaries, who considered pine trees to be 'unsuitable' subjects for artwork. Campbell Ewing, who organised a retrospective exhibition of Mabel's art in New Zealand in 1981, felt that Mabel probably would not have worried about her popularity among fellow New Zealand artists like Cedric Savage, Betty Wishart and Enga Washbourn. Ewing maintained that Mabel's prints, particularly those of the Golden Bay area, were 'interesting to residents there because of the way she portrays the landscape's ambiguities'.[24]

Although she had not been heavily involved with the gardens at Castlewellan ('Mabel Annesley was not a specialist gardener, though she loved the place'),[25] she found herself growing fruit, vegetables and flowers in New Zealand, and even acquiring a second cat, whom she called Tiger. Her friend Fish had grown very old, so Mabel turned to her granddaughter, Margaret Ogilvie, for epistolary companionship. The letters to Ogilvie during this period were edited by Mabel's sister Constance, to be included in *As the sight is bent*, but since Ogilvie was kind enough to allow access to the unedited version every effort will be made to quote from the original.

Mabel's artistic taste was widely varied and well informed. She wrote that she always liked the German things in the National Gallery, Dublin, and also the Turner watercolours and the Goyas. Of the contemporary printmakers, Paul Nash seemed to have the most to say. She owned a beautiful picture in ink and watercolour by Nash. For her, the modern collection in Belfast was worth a visit, though she did not think much of the Laverys there. She wrote to her granddaughter that she must read Milton, Spenser, Keats and T.S. Eliot. By listening to some modern music, Mabel thought that Margaret might get close to the framework of all the different arts, and how they lie together – 'music, design, poetry, must all be built into order of some sort, out of words or shapes or sounds'.[26]

She wrote that her sister Biddy (Constance) was an artist in her own right – whether it was acting or writing, she worked like a navvy. Sometimes that meant that she did, and no doubt would do again, the 'most crack brain things'.[27] Though Constance was totally dependable and always there for her family, she showed that she had all of the brains 'and as little sense as the rest of the family'.[28]

Mabel often thought of her old Restoration press in Ireland and a certain nostalgia crept into her letters. She remembered her old fur coat, which she had bought with the proceeds of her very first commission at the beginning of the century. She wondered if it was still at Castlewellan, at the same time thinking of a *falconeri* bush that she herself had planted there but had never actually seen as a mature specimen.

Ever devoted to her work, she continuously mused upon her own and others' artistic production: she was exhibiting a one-person show in Wellington, finding that her taste in contemporary artists embraced the work of Paul Nash, Frances Hodgkins, and David Jones. From her red house in Takaka, she wrote to her friend Margaret Pilkington about fellow artist Robert Gibbings: Gibbings had arrived, with his secretary, about two months previously – 'trumpets etc. sounded, but since then silence'.[29] Her letters are full of intimacy and little details concerning her great love of art – of Altdorfer, Cranach and the statuary under the main galleries at the Louvre.

Many of the letters, however, contain little hints to her granddaughter Margaret Ogilvie not to get too involved with family politics and to maintain good feelings for Mary MacDonald, Gerald's second wife. Mabel believed that Mary had been a good and loving stepmother: 'she was an altogether splendid person in every way'.[30] Alas for Mabel, Mary left her husband when their younger son, Richard, was six years old. Later, Gerald was to be smitten by the charms of his housekeeper, Lil – slender and auburn haired. They married and had twin sons, who later died tragically young.

By the early 1950s, in her seventies, Mabel reported on a show of her work that was going on tour for three months – '45 items on catalogue and I'm nearly dead of the effort'.[31] In describing the work that Mabel completed for this exhibition, Stewart MacLennan, director of the National Art Gallery of New Zealand, commented that Mabel was part of the group

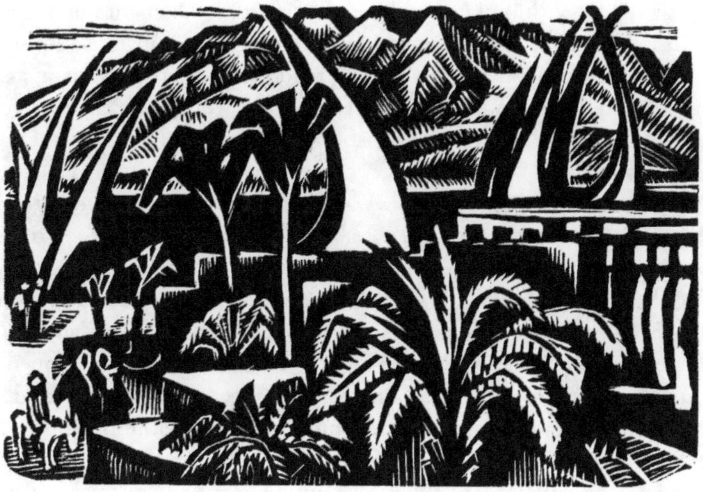

Crete, 65 × 95, *As the sight is bent*, p. 85.

who helped revive wood engraving in Britain. Paul and John Nash, David Jones, Robert Gibbings, Eric Gill, Gwen Raverat, Clare Leighton and Noel Rooke were some of the others. Apart from Mabel's craftsmanship, she was gifted in handling black and white. Her particular talent showed 'that natural but elusive wit that finds expression only in the print'.[32]

As Mabel grew older, she became physically less and less able and she worried about the failure of her son's second marriage. Writing to her sister Constance, she reported that she was in a perpetual state of upset concerning family matters, the condition of her own back and the New Zealand weather, which was plagued by 'floods and frosts and every sort of detestable and unusual wet and cold'.[33] She was so lonely for the company of her son that she responded to his invitation to return to Castlewellan by booking a passage at once. She wrote, 'The only utter heart-break is leaving my poor old Tom Cat.'[34]

Mabel continued to write to her granddaughter Margaret Ogilvie with encouraging tips about art and typography (Ogilvie also studied at the Central London School of Arts and Crafts), on one occasion enclosing the gift of an emerald and diamond ring and, later, a book by Gertrude Hermes, with whom Ogilvie had studied. She commented that design was so wonderful that you could never be finished with it. Though people and schools might come to a dead end, others would inevitably spring up to replace them. You must, she commented, translate nature, not merely copy it: 'You must never let the vision of nature out of your mind.'[35] Looking forward to 1953 and a proposed six-month stay in Ireland, she felt that the idea of a summer at Castlewellan was almost too good to be true. Once home in Britain she made plans to contact the Irish artist Louis le Brocquy and the English illustrator Ethelbert White. Part of the preparation for her plunge back into the northern hemisphere was to read three-month-old weekly editions of *The Times*, sent to her by her granddaughter. She had been asked to acquire pictures for the New Zealand gallery in Nelson but feared that she was 'so old and deaf and forget[ful] of everything nowadays' that she might not make the best of her journey to England. She also seemed to dread leaving the comparative sunshine of New Zealand for the fogs of London and envied her granddaughter a trip to Spain, asserting that no other country had the colour and outline of Spain. She would have enjoyed working with Spanish people, she said – they had an air about them, 'even the ass [seeming] to have a rakishness all his own'.[36]

Sadly, Mabel's return to the British Isles was marred by an unhappy venture while acting on behalf of the Suter Art Gallery of New Zealand. She was given permission to buy pictures on behalf of the gallery, valuing £125. After conscientiously informing the board by letter and photograph of her proposed purchases she was assured of their confidence in her judgement. However, when the paintings arrived, the gallery rejected her choices. Mabel's appreciation of contemporary art did not meet with the Suter Art Gallery's; they condemned two of her purchases outright and criticised others. Some of her choices for the Suter included prints by John Keith Vaughan, Graham Sutherland, John Piper, John Minton, Robert MacBryde, Robert Colquhoun and Henry Moore – prints that were successfully exhibited in a 1953 Wellington show, 'Contemporary British lithographs'. However, her choice of Paul Nash and Frances Hodgkins for the Suter led to a vote of no confidence. Not surprisingly, she was very upset by this and resigned from the Suter Art Gallery in December 1952. In November 1953 she returned permanently to Britain.[37]

In retrospect, Mabel Annesley's time in New Zealand after the war was not a great success. With two shows there and some appreciative commentary from New Zealand journalists (who uncovered a scarcely cited show of Mabel's works at the Louvre annex in Paris), later years saw her writing much more infrequently of the countryside's beauties.[38] Her arthritis and back problems continued to plague her and she spoke of few emotional commitments in New Zealand, apart from her old cat and her garden. While she appeared to have been well accepted into the artistic community in New Zealand, crossing swords with the Suter Art Gallery in her final year cannot have left her with many fond feelings for gallery administrators in that country. Increasingly, her thoughts turned to family matters; from her point of view it was up to the experts to formulate their own theories of why and how her compositions worked. In the 1981 New Zealand catalogue that commemorated the anniversary of her birth, Campbell Ewing commented that such works as *Pinus insignis*, *The glen* and *The lake* were notable for their classical restraint. In these works it seemed that Mabel's mind had found an appropriate medium. In her art she was able to reconcile 'what one felt, saw and heard' with the 'landscape's seeming order'. In these pictures she maintained a very strong and stable image, even though the landscape changed dramatically. The rhythmical patterning of Mabel's prints had an influence on their foreground, middle ground and background. In her final days of printmaking she appeared settled in herself, with perceptions of the landscape that brought a new kind of order to her work.[39]

Some would say that criticism from the New Zealand galleries was all she gained from her years in that country. It is likely, however, that living in a 'rakish red house on stilts (about to walk away) with an iron pipe for a chimney' deepened her love for her own baronial castle and its gardens.[40]

[1] John Hewitt, 'Foreword: the Lady Mabel Annesley's gift', *Belfast Museum and Art Gallery: quarterly notes*, lxi (June 1939), p. 1.

[2] *Atsib*, p. 114.

[3] Ibid., p. 102.

[4] A. Wall, 'From the Suter', *The Nelson Evening Mail*, 25 February 1984.

[5] *Atsib*, p. 106.

[6] Ibid., p. 107.

[7] Wall, 'From the Suter'.

[8] Noel Rooke to Margaret Pilkington, 1 December 1916 (Margaret Pilkington Archive, John Rylands University Library, Manchester).

[9] Mabel Annesley to Margaret Pilkington, 26 October (no year given) (Whitworth Art Gallery, Manchester).

[10] *Atsib*, pp. 110, 116.

[11] Suter Art Gallery, *Collected works of the Lady Mabel Annesley 1881–1959: an exhibition commemorating the centenary of her birth* (Nelson, New Zealand, 1981).

[12] Ibid., p. 5.

[13] Ogilvie to Black, 5 February 1980.

[14] *Atsib*, p. 116.

[15] Ibid., p. 118.

[16] Ibid., p. 119.

[17] Ibid.

[18] Ibid.

[19] Ibid., p. 120.

[20] Mabel Annesley to Margaret Pilkington, n.d. (Whitworth Art Gallery, Manchester).

[21] Patinir, Joachim (d. *c.* 1524) is documented in the Antwerp Guild in 1515. Durer, who owned a picture by him, mentions him as a landscape painter, attended the festivities at his second marriage in 1521, and drew his portrait. His small landscapes have something in common with Antwerp Mannerism in that they are cool in colour and very blue in the distance [...] they offer a wonderful mixture of fantasy and naturalistic detail that presage the more naturalistic landscapes of Brueghel. (Peter and Linda Murray, *A dictionary of art and artists* (Harmondsworth, 1959)).

[22] Mabel Annesley to Margaret Pilkington, 4 January (no year given) (Whitworth Art Gallery, Manchester).

[23] Constance Malleson to Mabel Annesley, n.d. (BRAMU, Colette collection).

[24] 'Double anniversary', *The Nelson Evening Mail*, 22 July 1981.

[25] Patrick Bowe and Edward Malins, *Irish gardens and demesnes from 1830* (London, 1980), p. 69.

[26] Mabel Annesley to Margaret Ogilvie, 4 December (no year given) (BRAMU, Colette collection).

[27] Mabel Annesley to Margaret Ogilvie, n.d. (BRAMU, Colette collection).

[28] Ibid.

[29] Mabel Annesley to Margaret Pilkington, 29 July (no year given) (Whitworth Gallery, Manchester).

[30] Mabel Annesley to Margaret Ogilvie, 4 March (no year given) (BRAMU, Colette collection).

[31] Mabel Annesley to Margaret Ogilvie, 3 June (no year given) (BRAMU, Colette collection).
[32] Stewart MacLennan, 'The exhibition introduced' in Victoria University College, Regional Council of Adult Education, Community Arts Service, *The Lady Mabel Annesley: wood engravings, linocuts, silverpoints* (Wellington, New Zealand, 1951).
[33] Mabel Annesley to Constance Malleson, n.d. (BRAMU, Colette collection).
[34] Ibid.
[35] Mabel Annesley to Margaret Ogilvie, n.d. (BRAMU, Colette collection).
[36] Mabel Annesley to Margaret Ogilvie, 14 September 1952 (BRAMU, Colette collection).
[37] Susan M. Butterworth, *The Suter: one hundred years in Nelson* (Nelson, New Zealand, 1999), p. 73.
[38] 'Irish artist hasn't forgiven Churchill', 16 January 1950 (Museum of New Zealand Te Papa Tongarewa, Wellington, vertical file).
[39] Suter Art Gallery, *Collected works*, p. 5.
[40] Mabel Annesley to Margaret Pilkington, 29 July 1949 (Whitworth Art Gallery, Manchester).

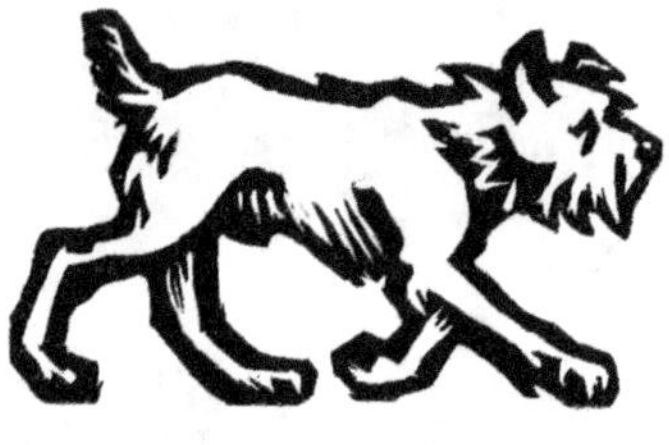

Dog, 25 × 45, *As the sight is bent*, p. 42.

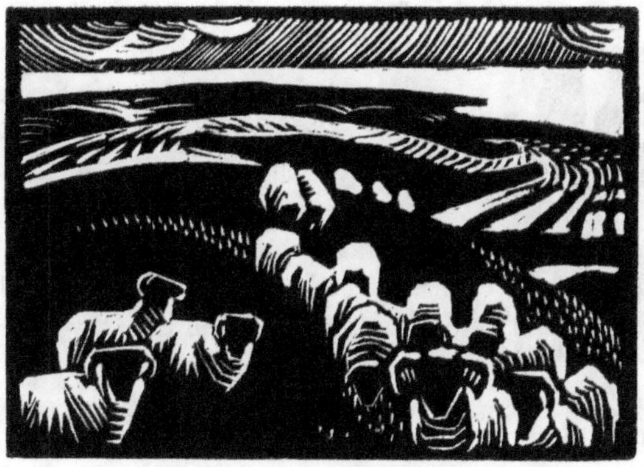

The truant, 49 × 71, *County Down songs*, p. 20.

6
Conclusion

Two years before her death in 1959, Mabel Annesley published a short, concise essay that furnished the background to the work of Irish artists Mainie Jellett and Evie Hone. It was to be her swansong as an artistic theorist. The essay was a defence of modern abstract art and said as much about Mabel's own early years as it did about those of her two contemporaries. Mabel began by referring to an exhibition of modern French pictures that took place in London in 1910. Rejecting the representation of natural shapes, the pictures sought to 'translate inward meaning into visible form'.[1] Mabel gathered around her subjects the atmosphere of the age in which they lived: it was an age of ground-breaking innovations in the arts, valuable for anyone wishing to trace the artistic influences of those characters who helped Mabel develop her own sensibilities. The Dublin Painters of the 1920s were at the centre of an enterprising group of artists. Kindred spirits were drawn to the Painters – artists like Harriet Kirkwood, Jack B. Yeats, Paul Henry and Grace Henry. In Mabel's opinion Paul Henry was a genius who held no 'high-faluting views'. Letitia Hamilton, Charles Lamb, Sarah Purser and Harry and Margaret Clarke were also part of this circle. Mabel was given an insight into the working of the Cuala Press when Elizabeth Yeats took her to that press just when they were printing the exquisite but all-too-short autobiography of John Butler Yeats. George Russell, with brown beard and broad-brimmed hat, was also a visitor to the Dublin Painters. It was in the 1920s that Mainie Jellett and Evie Hone, straight from Paris, introduced the idea of completely non-representational abstract design. 'This was their world, one in which they went their different ways and created their visual imagery.'[2]

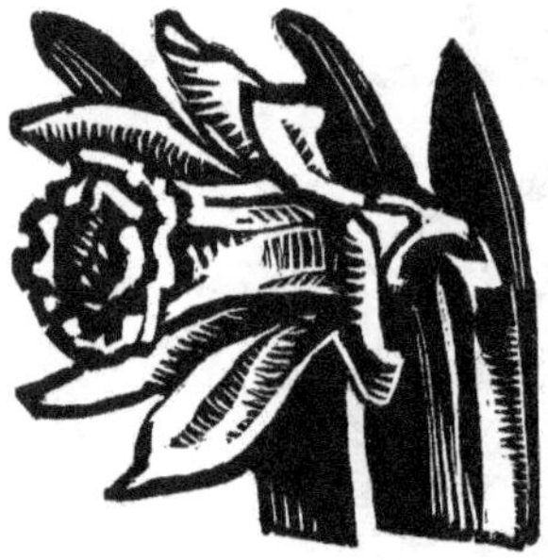

Daffodil, 40 × 40,
As the sight is bent, p. 148.

This, too, was Mabel Annesley's world – the world of Yeats and Henry, Purser and Hone, and George Russell – and it was the world from which she had been exiled during her time in New Zealand. Alas, that world had vanished by the time Mabel returned to Britain in 1953 and her own spirit had been quenched by sadness and irritability, ill health and flagging strength. It was only the knowledge of what she and her family had done and been that gave her the courage to stand side by side with her artistic contemporaries.

Mabel Annesley's last years were to be spent in a small Suffolk village not far from Lavenham, where her sister Constance lived. Her cottage in the little town of Long Melford, at the end of a row of houses, was aptly named End Cottage. To make the little house into a home required 'courage and patience and endurance. But she had all those – and a chunk of common sense as well.'[3] It was that common sense that brought her back from New Zealand to spend her final days relatively close to her son in Ireland. In a letter from 6 April 1956 she described her new cottage to her granddaughter, Margaret Ogilvie. Six miles from Lavenham, it was very small with a good sitting room, out of which a stair led to a lobby. There was one good bathroom with a bath and outside was a beautiful village street. The garden was tiny and the cottage had many drawbacks, including being very old. It was, however, very cheap.[4]

From Long Melford Mabel believed she could watch over Castlewellan, about whose future she harboured great uncertainty. She also felt it was important to watch over the two boys of Gerald's second marriage. A great part of her day was taken up with reading, as her granddaughter wrote in 1980 to Eileen Black. Mabel was very well read, having access as a child to the fine library at Castlewellan. She read seriously and her thoughts were very deep. Parcels of books used to arrive from the London library and Margaret remembered taking them into her grandmother's sitting room, which overlooked a spring garden and the lake and mountains beyond. Mabel, with her crippling arthritis, would often be lying on a sofa wrapped in a vast north African sheepskin. Books were very precious to her and she had a fine collection of modern limited first editions. 'The money she earned from the engravings,' Mabel said, 'was usually put to acquiring books.'[5]

Her arthritic hands in particular were in a sad state, needing 'somehow to be kept from the cold'.[6] Mabel was also troubled by the state of her family's affairs, writing that a gulf had opened in which Margaret and her father appeared to have turned against family loyalties, so that Mabel feared for the future. 'Opinions,' she said, 'are one thing[;] bullets are the outcome.'[7] Presumably Mabel was referring to Gerald's political leanings, as an Irish nationalist, and to her own defiantly steadfast status as a unionist. Soon, however, she recovered her affection for her son and granddaughter. A few months later, she wrote of her great love for Margaret and her longing to see her.

Mabel seemed to have had regular visitors to End Cottage, including the family of her granddaughter, Patricia, and the sister of her beloved friend Fish – 'a large Cockney typist'.[8]

Twice a week she visited a hospital in Sudbury for electric treatment for her arthritis. In spite of this pain and discomfort she revelled at the news of Margaret's marriage to Farquhar Ogilvie, a spirited Scot whom Margaret had met while living and working in Edinburgh. As a worthy daughter to Hugh Annesley, Mabel continued to take an interest in her small 'pocket hankie of a garden'.[9] Mabel was a multi-talented artist; although the piece is undated, she appears to have tried her hand at woodcarving, leaving a carved wooden box, which is now in the collection of the Down County Museum.

To Mabel's old-fashioned mind, Gerald's third marriage – to his housekeeper, Lil – was quite unacceptable. She was frank and open about her feelings for Lil and wrote to Margaret that it would be a shame if Gerald's third marriage divided the family. She was sorry but it was unthinkable that she meet Lil. If Lil were to go to Margaret's wedding, Mabel would not.[10] In the end, Mabel did go to the wedding and had a splendid time, meeting Margaret's husband and reconciling with Margaret's other grandmother, Lady Roden, after a long period of separation.

From Long Melford, close to the end of 1957, she wrote that she had been 'chopping a wood block again', and that this had lifted her spirits so much she could seriously consider the matter of never going to Castlewellan again. She asked that her books be sent from Ireland to Scotland, where Margaret was living. She hoped that her watercolours and watercolour paper would be sent directly to Long Melford, along with an envelope with all of her designs for toys, perfected during her stay with Fish in Connemara.

During the two years before her death, Mabel suffered from 'queer dizzy heads'. She had days when she forgot everything and the doctor told her to keep quiet because of her blood pressure.[11] She longed constantly for her books and asked for the return of her small woodblocks as well. Margaret's gift of a Paul Klee book 'simply enchanted her', providing a tremendous emotional support when she found herself in hospital with a 'very up-to-date flu'.[12] Once out of hospital her spirits returned and she found herself fantasising about

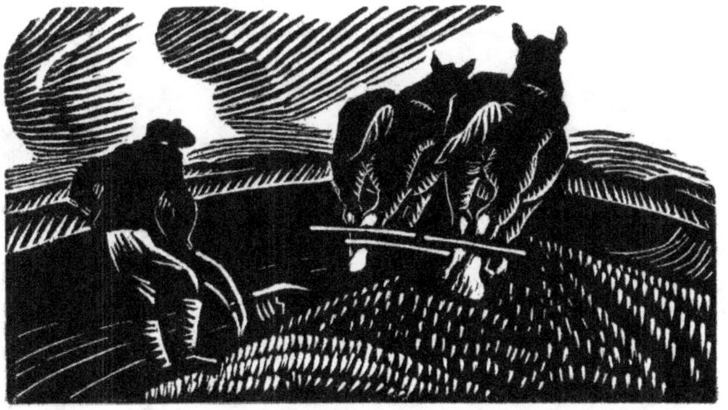

The ploughman,
46 × 83, *Songs from Robert Burns*, p. 10.

Castlewellan and her great hope that Rory (Gerald's oldest son) would return the estate to its former stability.[13]

Sadly, however, Mabel's life seemed only to fall more deeply into a shadow of worry. Though she rejoiced at the birth of Margaret's first child – 'too entrancing for words' – she was concerned that housekeeping, baby-minding and cooking would be too much for her beloved granddaughter, suggesting that Margaret and Farquhar 'go and dance again'.[14] Still perfectly lucid, with sloping but easily legible handwriting, she took joy where she could, though every day seemed to bring an increased deafness – perhaps inherited, since both of her sisters and her father had suffered from the problem in their later years.

Mabel's fondness for cats seemed to deepen with old age, and she succumbed to the charms of her neighbour's black kitten, who was caught by an Alsatian inside his front door. Though nearly shaken to death, his tiny sharp claws caused the dog to drop him. He was so frightened, however, that he settled into Mabel's house and would not go home.[15] With her cat and her frequent letters and gifts from Margaret, Mabel seemed happy enough in her very warm 'comfy little cottage'.[16]

One early 1959 letter finds her worrying as ever about Gerald's health, with only a postscript to say, 'I fell down my corkscrewy stairs and knocked out a front tooth.'[17] This simple admission was followed by a letter saying, just as simply, that her ever-problematic back had worsened and, though she did not feel ill, she just could not walk more than a few steps nor sit up on a straight-backed chair for more than a moment.[18] Her last letter to Margaret preceded her death by only a few months. It was written from the hospital in Bury St Edmunds. From there she lamented that being in a small hospital away from her garden full of tulips was more than she could bear, and wrote, 'They say they can cure me in 2 or 3 weeks.'[19] In fact, there was no cure, and Mabel Annesley died on 19 June 1959. The cause of death was cited as myelomatosis, or inflammation of the spinal cord.

The Down Recorder noted the passing of Lady Mabel Annesley, saying that she was an artist 'of distinction'. Her wood engravings and watercolours had allowed her to achieve 'a high place in the world of art'. Gracious and enthusiastic, she would be remembered in Newcastle as a pioneer of the Women's Institute. Her funeral took place quietly at Long Melford, Suffolk.[20]

The Times of London also recorded her death with this eulogy:

> Lady Mabel's death severed a link with Victorian times. Possessing an incorruptible sense of duty and tradition, she also possessed an understanding which was most vital in the world of modern art. Though she shied away from publicity, her engravings had been internationally valued and A.E. (George Russell) compared them with William Blake's black and white engravings. Her work was in the British Museum; and she was elected an honorary member of the Society of Wood Engravers of which she had long been a member. Married to Gerald Sowerby, flag lieutenant to Admiral Prince Louis of Battenberg, she was a young widow when she succeeded to the family estate of Castlewellan. It was then that she took back her maiden name, and plunged into the task of maintaining the baronial castle and its gardens sheltered by the Mourne Mountains. An exemplary landowner, Lady Mabel showed the same bravery in a troubled Ireland as her father, the fifth Earl Annesley,

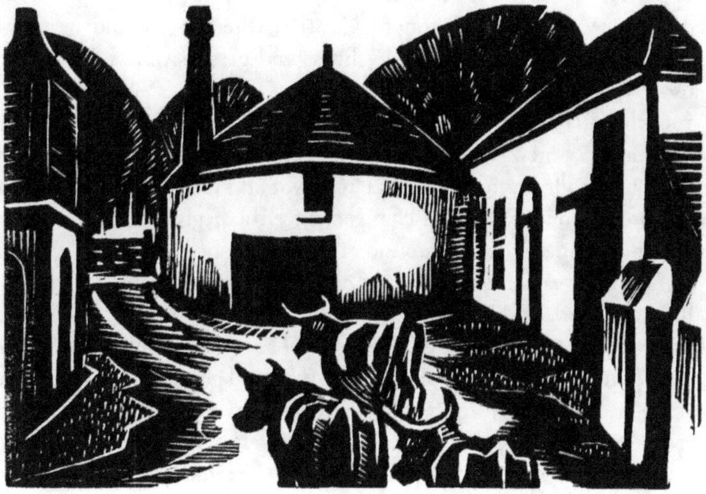

Round house, 65 × 95, *As the sight is bent*, p. 17.

> had shown in the Crimean War. Fundamentally, however, it was 'an intense and profound feeling for beauty in nature and in art' that was the inspiration of her inner life.[21]

In May 1960, less than a year after her death, an exhibition opened at the Whitworth Gallery in Manchester devoted to the work of three wood engravers: Mabel Annesley, Robert Gibbings and Gwen Raverat. Mabel's sister Constance wrote a review of the exhibition, in which she commented that Mabel's depiction of Northern Ireland greatly resembled the western Scotland she had depicted in the Golden Cockerel book *Songs from Robert Burns*. In the Burns country, Constance wrote, only the Mournes of Ulster were lacking. The Whitworth show also exhibited Mabel's work for Duckworth, *County Down songs* and *Apollo in Mourne* (both written by Richard Rowley). Rowley's poetry in *County Down songs* was quite full of Northern Ireland's unmistakable humour. It was, indeed, the frontispiece to *County Down songs* which, exhibited at the International Art Exhibition in Stockholm (1927), so captured the taste of the then crown prince (and later king of Sweden) that he promptly acquired it for his private collection.[22]

Some years after the Whitworth exhibition, two events occurred which would have greatly affected Mabel. The first was the publication of her finely crafted autobiography, *As the sight is bent*, in 1964. Constance, Mabel's writer sister, edited the prose work with its illustration, bringing it to the attention of a public who might otherwise never have seen Mabel's engravings. Although the first publisher Constance approached, Faber and Faber, rejected the autobiography because Mabel was very reticent about anything personal, the Museum Press in London went on to release the book to a warmly receptive audience.[23] Katherine Chorley wrote to Constance concerning the publication of *As the sight is bent*, saying that it contained the perfect marriage between illustration and script, one which was rarely found in illustrated books. Visual artists, thought Chorley, when they could write at all, often conveyed their personal vision with great liveliness and persuasiveness. In Mabel's case the reader was also given many interesting reflections on visual art.[24] The reviewer from *The Guardian* wrote that the Lady Mabel was an artist 'who sought passionately the essential things of life evocative'.[25] Stewart MacLennan, director of the National Art Gallery of New Zealand, wrote that her illustrations sparkled 'with wit and interest'. The book itself offered a fascinating record of how society had changed since the beginning of the century. It also portrayed with some intimacy the background of 'a distinguished and keenly observant visitor' who had lived for some years in New Zealand.[26]

The second notable event that followed the death of Mabel Annesley was the sale of the Annesleys' Castlewellan estate to the Department of Forestry in 1965, in order to preserve the gardens as public grounds managed by the Northern Ireland government. The castle itself was eventually turned into a Christian conference centre, preserving much of the entrance, library and ballroom in their original condition, while turning the upper floor into bedrooms for visiting Irish youths. The sale of the estate as forest park and arboretum kept the Ulster grounds available for all Northern Irish people (and visitors) to traverse – something that would have been impossible if the estate had been sold as a hotel, a course of action Gerald Annesley had considered early on. Upon the opening of Castlewellan Forest Park, *The Belfast Telegraph* wrote that by keeping some of the vestiges of the garden and castle the lives of all of the family, including the gifted Lady Mabel, could be felt in the atmosphere of Castlewellan. The intruder (for that was how the reviewer considered himself) was rewarded for his visit by a strong sense of the people who had lived there and impregnated the walls and windows with something of themselves.[27]

One final word can be given to Mabel Annesley herself, for she is properly remembered as an exquisite prose writer as well as a visual artist. In her essay on her friends Mainie Jellett and Evie Hone she evolved a theory of art that might well be applied to her own works. It was Sylvia Cooke-Collis – an artist who had, Mabel thought, a lovely language of her own – who took her to Mainie Jellett's studio. On that visit Mabel saw not only countless studies for abstract designs, but also studies of people, fields and seas. The geometrical studies went far beyond symmetrical patterns and the drawings of fields and people were made simple and thoroughly accessible. Objects related to each other through pattern and design. They became, finally, personal statements that were converted by their inward meaning into visible form. They had, themselves, become symbols of a greater meaning.[28]

A fitting symbol of Mabel Annesley's life might be found by anyone willing to visit the churchyard in Long Melford where she lies. In the overgrown cemetery, amidst ancient and modern tombstones, is the final resting place of this County Down woman. Marked by a simple monolith of the same granite as that from which her beloved Castlewellan Castle had been built, the place embodies the very qualities that Mabel Annesley's life represents. Plain, resolute, enduring, the flat granite stone which Gerald Annesley sent to mark his mother's grave recalls most poignantly the life of an artist who was as steadfast, determined and true as the Ulster bedrock upon which her very nature was founded.

[1] Mabel Annesley, 'A background', in Stella Frost (ed.), *A tribute to Evie Hone and Mainie Jellett* (Dublin, 1957), p. 3.
[2] Ibid.
[3] Malleson, *After ten years*, p. 187.
[4] Mabel Annesley to Margaret Ogilvie, 1956 (BRAMU, Colette collection).
[5] Ogilvie to Black, 5 February 1980.
[6] Mabel Annesley to Margaret Ogilvie, n.d. (BRAMU, Colette collection).
[7] Ibid.
[8] Ibid.
[9] Ibid.
[10] Ibid., 9 July [1957].
[11] Ibid., 27 November [1957].
[12] Ibid. [1958].
[13] Ibid., 14 March [1958].
[14] Ibid., 29 August [1958].
[15] Ibid.
[16] Ibid.
[17] Ibid., 26 March 1959.
[18] Ibid.
[19] Ibid.
[20] *The Down Recorder*, 27 June 1959.
[21] *The Times*, 27 June 1959.
[22] Colette O'Niel, 'The three wood engravers exhibition' (BRAMU, Colette collection).
[23] Faber and Faber to Constance Malleson, 9 January 1962 (BRAMU, Colette collection).
[24] Katharine Chorley to Constance Malleson, 25 June 1964 (BRAMU, Colette collection).
[25] *The Guardian*, 5 June 1964.
[26] *Wellington Evening Post*, November 1964.
[27] *Belfast Telegraph*, n.d.
[28] Annesley, 'A background', p. 3.

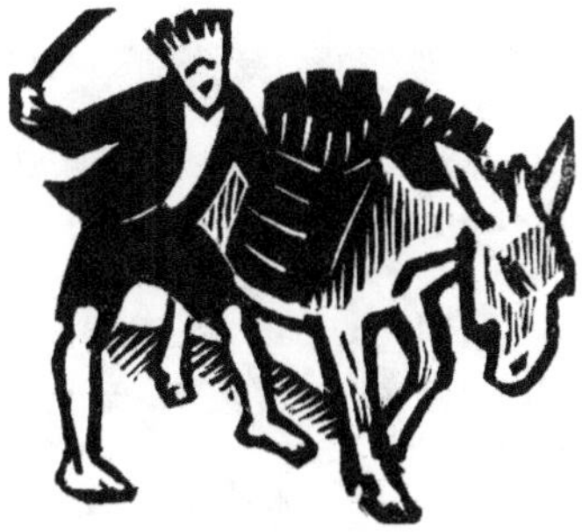

Boy with donkey,
37.5 × 45, *As the sight is bent*, p. 50.

SELECTED BIBLIOGRAPHY

Illustrated and/or written by Mabel Annesley

Annesley, Mabel, *As the sight is bent: an unfinished autobiography* (London, 1964).

Burns, Robert, *Songs from Robert Burns, selected by A.E. Coppard, with wood engravings by Mabel M. Annesley* (Waltham, 1925).

Rowley, Richard, *Apollo in Mourne: a play in one act, with woodcuts by Lady Mabel Annesley* (London, 1926).

—, *County Down songs* (London, 1924).

Books

Andrews, Martin J., *The life and work of Robert Gibbings* (Bicester, 2003).

Anglesea, Martyn, *William Conor: the people's painter* (Belfast, 1999).

—, *The Royal Ulster Academy of Arts* (Belfast, 1981).

Arnold, Bruce, *Irish art: a concise history* (rev. ed., London and New York, 1977).

Ballard, Linda May, *Forgetting frolic: marriage traditions in Ireland* (Belfast, 1998).

Bell, Sam Hanna, Nesca A. Robb and John Hewitt (eds), *The arts in Ulster: a symposium* (London, 1951).

Blamires, David, Patricia Jaffé *et al.*, *Margaret Pilkington, 1891–1974* (Buxton, 1995).

Bowe, Nicola Gordon, *The life and work of Harry Clarke* (Dublin and Portland, Oregon, 1994).

Bowe, Patrick and Edward Malins, *Irish gardens and demesnes from 1830* (London, 1980).

Bowen, Elizabeth, *Bowen's Court* (New York, 1942).

Brady, Ciaran, Mary O'Dowd and Brian Walker (eds), *Ulster: an illustrated history* (London, 1989).

Brown, Terence, *Ireland: a social and cultural history 1922–1985* (London, 1981).

Burke, Bernard, *Burke's genealogical and heraldic history of the landed gentry* (London, 1970).

—, *Burke's genealogical and heraldic history of the peerage, baronetage and knightage* (London, 1928).

Butterworth, Susan M., *The Suter: one hundred years in Nelson* (Nelson, New Zealand, 1999).

Crozier, Maurna (ed.), *Cultural traditions in Northern Ireland* (Belfast, 1989).

Davis-Goff, Annabel, *Walled gardens: scenes from an Anglo-Irish childhood* (New York, 1989).

De Burgh, Lydia, *Another way of life* (Downpatrick, 1999).

Delany, Mary, *Letters from Georgian Ireland: the correspondence of Mary Delany, 1731–68* (Angélique Day, ed., Belfast, 1991).

Dodgson, Campbell, *Contemporary English woodcuts* (London, 1922).

Evans, E. Estyn, *Ireland and the Atlantic heritage: selected writings* (Dublin, 1996).

—, *The personality of Ireland: habitat, heritage and history* (Cambridge, 1973).

Falls, Cyril, *The birth of Ulster* (London, 1936).

Foster, R.F., *Modern Ireland 1600–1972* (Harmondsworth, 1989).
Frost, Stella (ed.), *A tribute to Evie Hone and Mainie Jellett* (Dublin, 1957).
Garrett, Albert, *A history of British wood engraving* (Tunbridge Wells, 1978).
Genet, Jacqueline (ed.), *The Big House in Ireland: reality and representation* (Dingle, County Kerry and Savage, Maryland, 1991).
Gibbings, Robert, *The wood engravings of Robert Gibbings: with some recollections by the artist* (Patience Empson, ed., London, 1959).
Glassie, Henry, *Passing the time in Ballymenone: culture and history of an Ulster community* (Bloomington, Indiana, 1982).
Glenavy, Lady Beatrice, *Today we will only gossip* (London, 1964).
Glendinning, Victoria, *Jonathan Swift* (London, 1998).
Green, Henry, *Loving* (London, 1948).
Hamilton, J., *Wood engraving and the woodcut in Britain,* c. *1890–1990* (London, 1994).
Hewitt, John and Mike Catto, *Art in Ulster* (Belfast, 1977).
Hill, Myrtle and Sarah Barber (eds), *Aspects of Irish studies* (Belfast, 1990).
Holmes, Janice and Diane Urquhart (eds), *Coming into the light: the work, politics and religion of women in Ulster 1840–1940* (Belfast, 1994).
Horne, Alan, *A dictionary of 20th century British book illustrators* (Woodbridge, 1994).
Jaffé, Patricia, *Women engravers* (London, 1988).
Jolliffe, John, *Woolf at the door: Duckworth, 100 years of Bloomsbury behaviour* (London, 1998).
Kennedy-Pipe, Caroline, *The origins of the present Troubles in Northern Ireland* (London and New York, 1997).
Kennedy, S.B., *Irish art and modernism 1880–1950* (Belfast, 1991).
Killen, John, *John Bull's famous circus: Ulster history through the postcard, 1905–1985* (Dublin, 1985).
Kirkus, A. Mary, *Robert Gibbings: a bibliography* (London, 1962).
Londonderry, Edith, Marchioness of, *Retrospect* (London, 1938).
Lyons, F.S.L., *Culture and anarchy in Ireland 1890–1930* (Oxford, 1979).
—, *Ireland since the Famine* (London, 1971).
MacCarthy, Fiona, *Eric Gill* (London, 1989).
Malleson, Constance, *After ten years* (London, 1931).
—, *The coming back* (London, 1933).
—, *Fear in the heart: a novel* (London, 1936).
Mansergh, Nicholas, *The Irish question 1840–1921: a commentary on Anglo-Irish relations and on social and political forces in Ireland in the age of reform and revolution* (3rd ed., Toronto and Buffalo, New York, 1975).
Monk, Ray, *Bertrand Russell: the spirit of solitude* (London, 1996).
—, *Bertrand Russell: the ghost of madness, 1921–70* (London, 2000).
Murray, Peter and Linda Murray, *A dictionary of art and artists* (Harmondsworth, 1959).
O'Brien, Conor Cruise, *States of Ireland* (London, 1972).
O'Dowd, Liam (ed.), *On intellectuals and intellectual life in Ireland: international, comparative, and historical contexts* (Belfast, 1996).

O'Dowd, Mary and Sabine Wichert (eds), *Chattel, servant or citizen: women's status in church, state and society* (Belfast, 1995).
O'Grady, John, *The life and work of Sarah Purser* (Dublin, 1996).
O'Sullivan, Seumas, *Essays and recollections* (Dublin and Cork, 1944).
Peppin, Brigid and Lucy Micklethwait, *Book illustrators of the twentieth century* (New York, 1984).
Petteys, Chris, *Dictionary of women artists: an international dictionary of women artists born before 1900* (Boston, 1985).
Proudfoot, Lindsay and W. Nolan (eds), *Down: history and society: interdisciplinary essays on the history of an Irish county* (Dublin, 1997).
Pyle, Hilary, *Jack B. Yeats: a biography* (London, 1970).
Raverat, Gwen, *Period piece: a Cambridge childhood* (London, 1952).
Robinson, Lennox, *Curtain up: an autobiography* (London, 1942).
Rowley, Richard, *Apollo in Mourne: poems, plays and stories* (Victor Price, ed., Belfast, 1978).
Russell, Bertrand, *The autobiography of Bertrand Russell: volume 2, 1914–1944* (London, 1968).
Selborne, Joanna, *British wood-engraved book illustration 1904–1940: a break with tradition* (Oxford, 1998).
Snoddy, Theo, *Dictionary of Irish artists: 20th century* (Dublin, 1996).
Stewart, A.T.Q., *The narrow ground: aspects of Ulster, 1609–1969* (London, 1977).
—, *The Ulster crisis: resistance to Home Rule, 1912–1914* (London, 1967).
Stewart, Ann M., *Irish art societies and sketching clubs: index of exhibitors 1870–1980* (2 vols, Dublin, 1997).
Unknown, *British printmakers 1855–1955: a century of printmaking from the etching revival to St Ives* (London, 1992).
Unknown, 'Sir Francis Grant' in L. Stephen and S. Lee (eds), *Dictionary of national biography* ('G' vol., London, 1885–1901).
Walker, George A., *The inverted line* (Erin, Ontario, 2000).
Walker, J. Crampton, *Irish life and landscape* (Dublin, 1927).
Wallace, R.T., *Castlewellan Castle: a short history* (n.p., 1986).
White, Terence de Vere, *The Anglo-Irish* (London, 1972).
—, *A fretful midge* (London, 1957).
Wilson, Judith, *Conor 1881–1968: the life and work of an Ulster artist* (Belfast, 1981).

Catalogues

Batsford Gallery, *Exhibition of silverpoints, watercolours and wood engravings by Mabel Annesley: exhibition catalogue* (London, 1933).
Musée d'Art Ancien (Musées Royaux des Beaux-Arts de Belgique), *Exposition d'art irlandais* (Brussels, 10 May–8 June 1930).
Portsmouth City Museum and Art Gallery, *British wood engraving of the 20s and 30s* (Portsmouth, 7 October–27 November 1983).

Society of Wood Engravers, *Engraving then and now: the retrospective 50th exhibition of the Society of Wood Engravers* (Richmond, Surrey, 1970).

Studio One Gallery, Museum of Oxford, '*Shall* we *join the ladies?*': *wood engravings* (Oxford, 1979).

Suter Art Gallery, *Collected works of the Lady Mabel Annesley 1881–1959: an exhibition commemorating the centenary of her birth* (Nelson, New Zealand, 1981).

Ulster Museum, *Concise catalogue of the drawings, paintings and sculptures in the Ulster Museum* (Belfast, 1986).

Ulster Unit, *Ulster Unit: exhibition of contemporary art* (Belfast, 18–29 December 1934).

Victoria University College, Regional Council of Adult Education, Community Arts Service, *The Lady Mabel Annesley: wood engravings, linocuts, silverpoints* (Wellington, New Zealand, 1951).

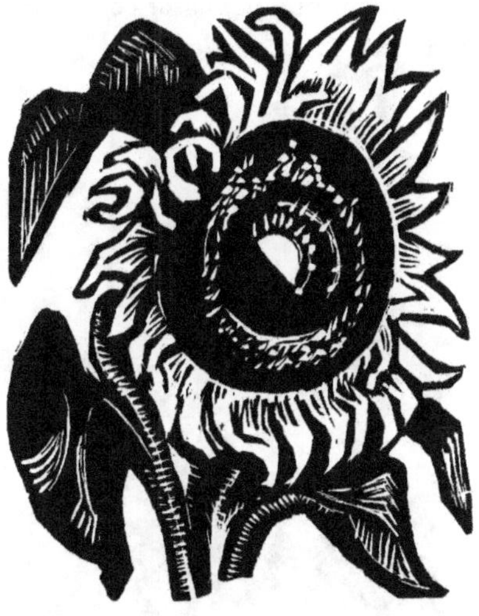

Sun flower, 65 × 55, *As the sight is bent*, p. 136.

MABEL ANNESLEY: THE RELIEF PRINTS

Notes

The prints reproduced in this book are taken from the four books illustrated by Mabel Annesley (see selected bibliography), collections of the Ulster Museum, the British Museum, the Whitworth Gallery, the Suter Art Gallery, Central St Martins College of Art and Design, the National Art Gallery of New Zealand, the Museum of New Zealand Te Papa Tongarewa, the Suter Art Gallery and private collections. Photographs are reproduced with the kind permission of Margaret Ogilvie.

Sizes are given in millimetres, height by width.

All titles are those given by the artist or gallery. Illustrations in books are identified by the title of the book and the page number where no title is given.

Since the majority of Mabel Annesley's prints were not dated, only those illustrations appearing in books can be accurately dated; many remaining prints remain undated.

Some of the prints have the edition sizes; like other female contemporaries, Annesley issued plates informally, often without numbering or editioning them. Some of her book illustrations were also editioned as single sheet prints.

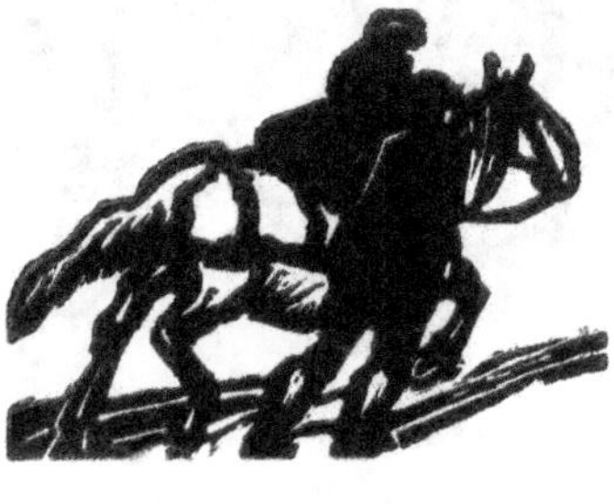

Tibbie Dunbar,
32 × 45, *Songs from Robert Burns*, p. 1.

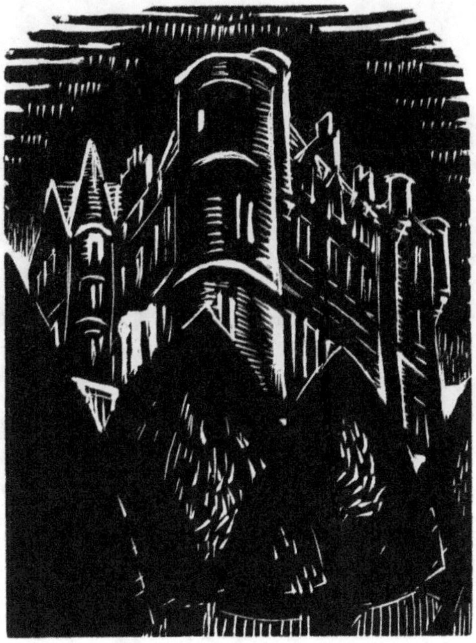

Castle, 85 × 65, *As the sight is bent*, p. 11.

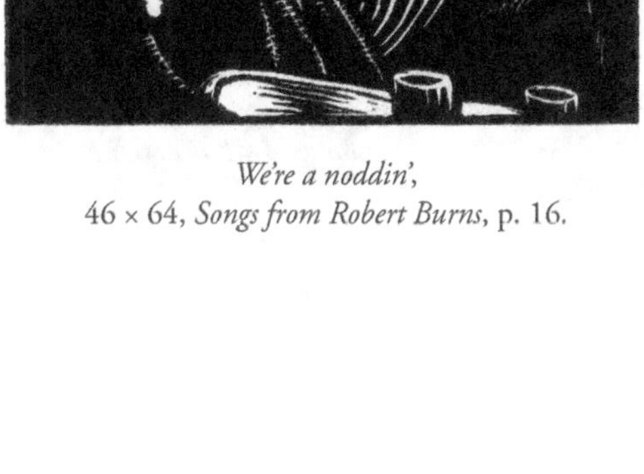

We're a noddin',
46 × 64, *Songs from Robert Burns*, p. 16.

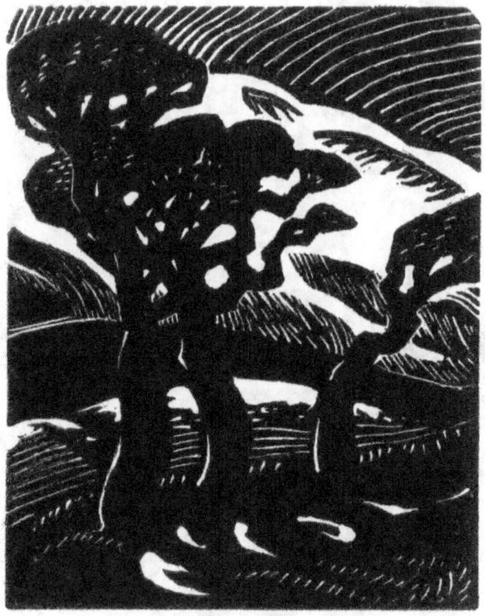

Up in the morning early,
70 × 58, *Songs from Robert Burns*, p. 4.

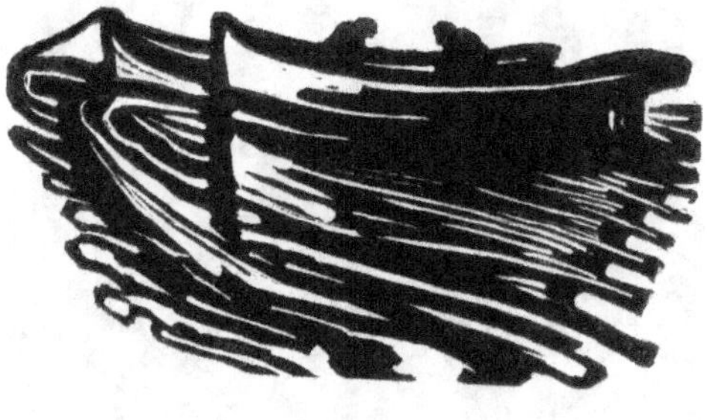

Go fetch me a pint of wine,
33 × 69, *Songs from Robert Burns*, p. 37.

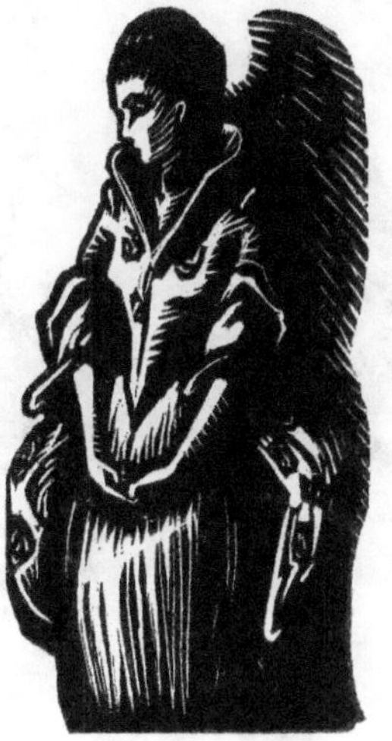

My lady's gown,
64 × 33, *Songs from Robert Burns*, p. 94.

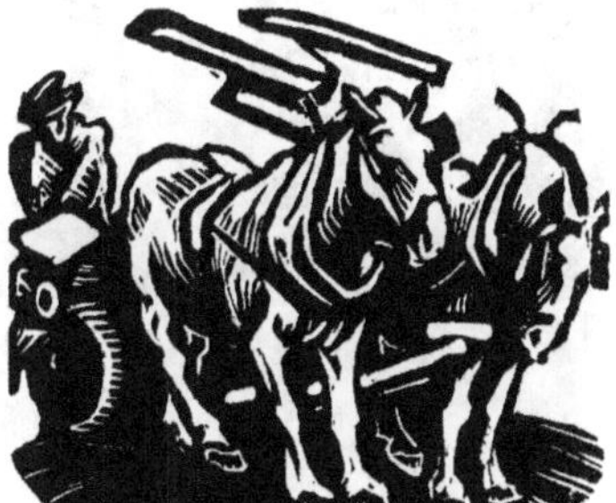

Tub cart, 40 × 45, *As the sight is bent*, p. 25.

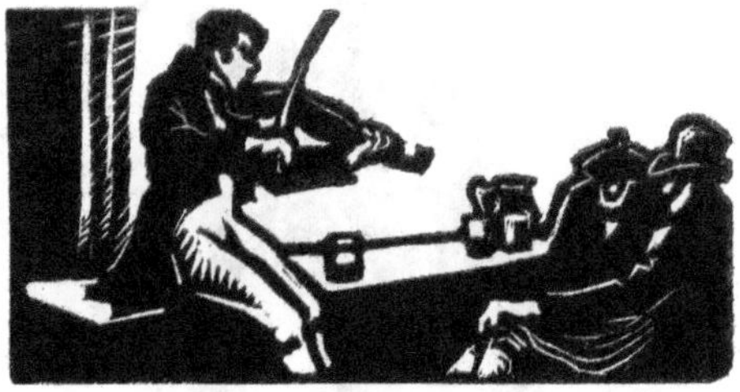

Rattlin' roarin' Willie,
30 × 61, *Songs from Robert Burns*, p. 30.

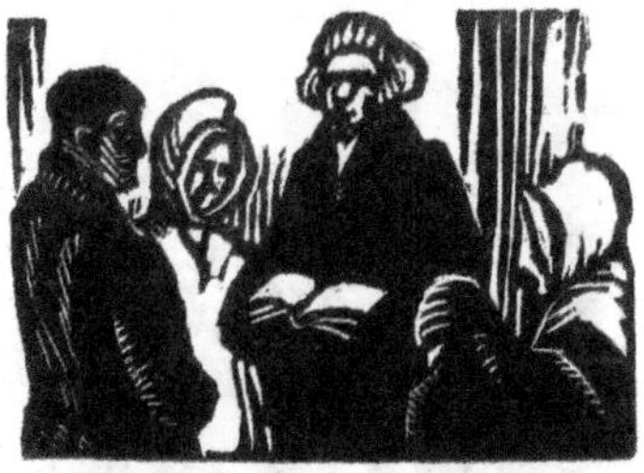

Sweet lass may I do that,
32 × 46, *Songs from Robert Burns*, p. 65.

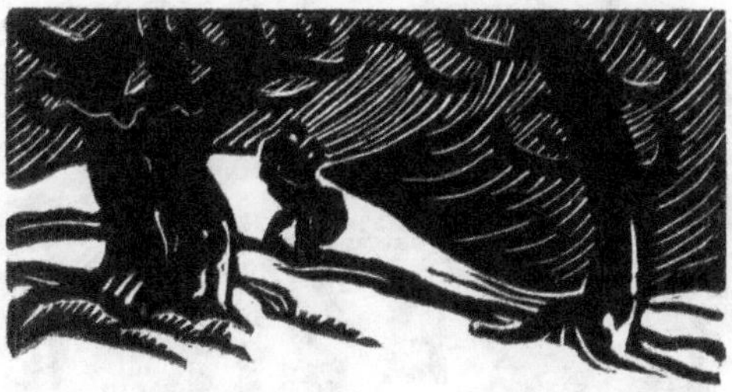

Oh, wert thou in the cauld blast, 32 × 64,
Songs from Robert Burns, p. 23.

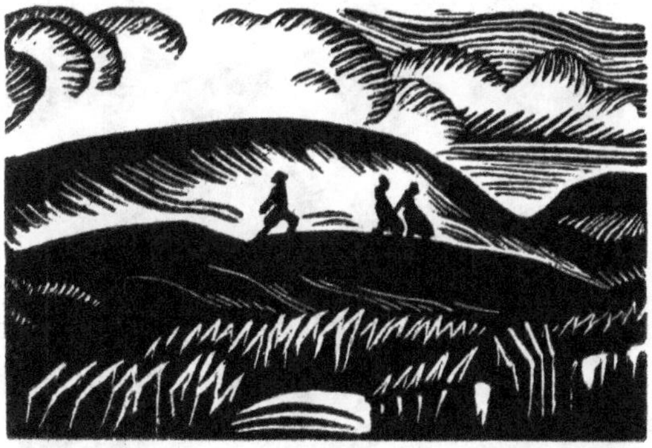

Untitled,
45 × 70, *Songs from Robert Burns*, p. 73.

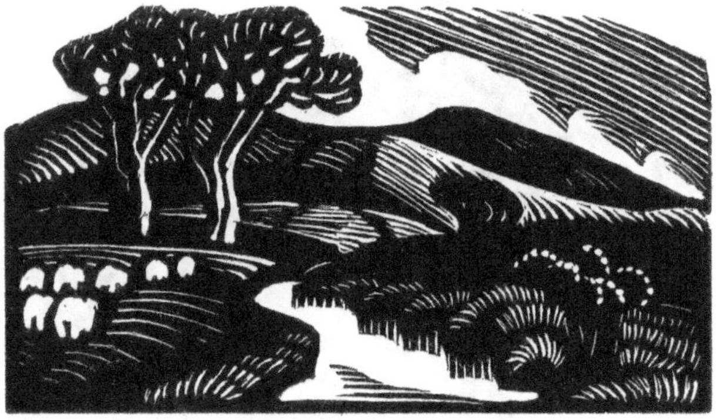

Ca' the yowes to the knowes,
45 × 83, *Songs from Robert Burns*, p. 100.

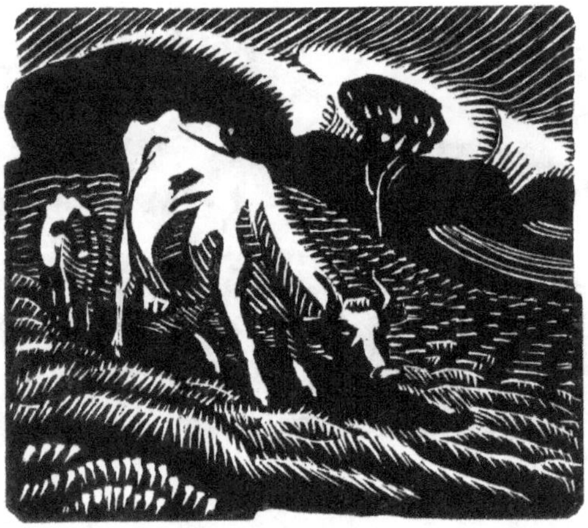

Jumpin' John, 57 × 67,
Songs from Robert Burns, p. 44.

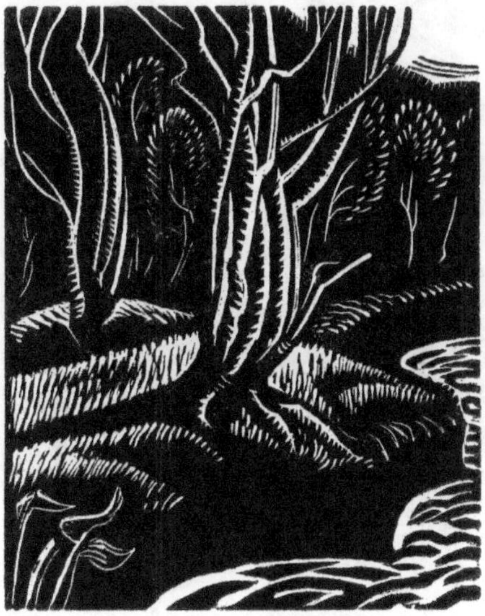

Highland Mary,
71 × 58, *Songs from Robert Burns*, p. 84.

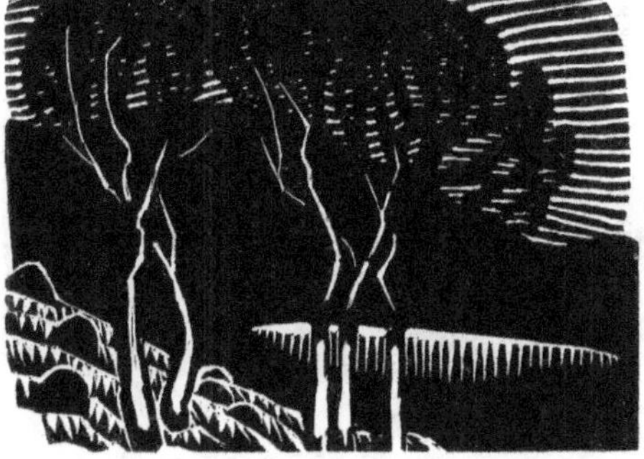

Cauld is the e'enin' blast,
44 × 61, *Songs from Robert Burns*, p. 80.

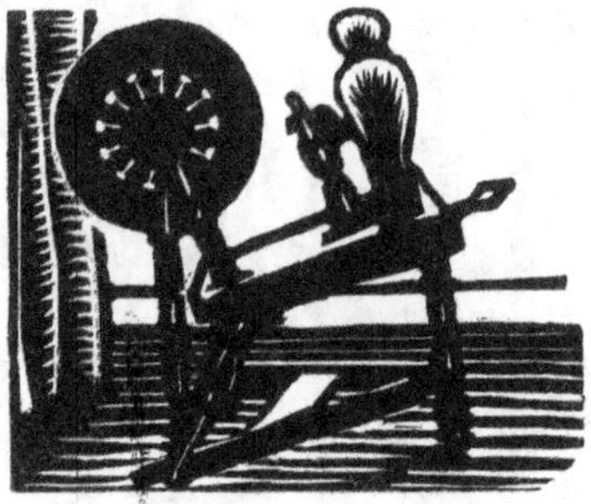

Duncan Davison, 38 × 46,
Songs from Robert Burns, p. 58.

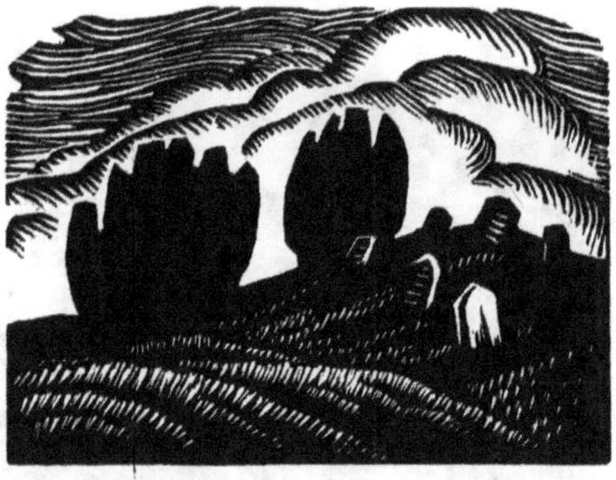

Lines to John Rankine, 44 × 60,
Songs from Robert Burns, p. 107.

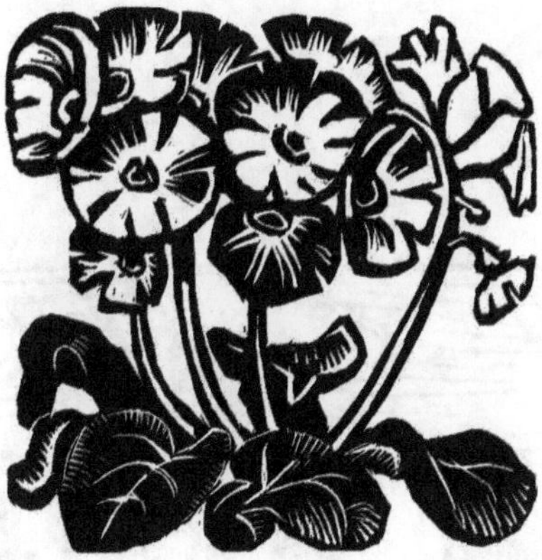

Blossoms,
52.5 × 52.5, *As the sight is bent*, p. 150.

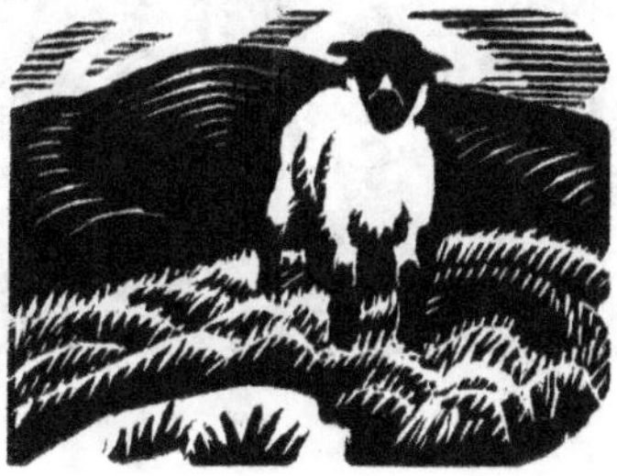

My hoggie, 33 × 45,
Songs from Robert Burns, p. 89.

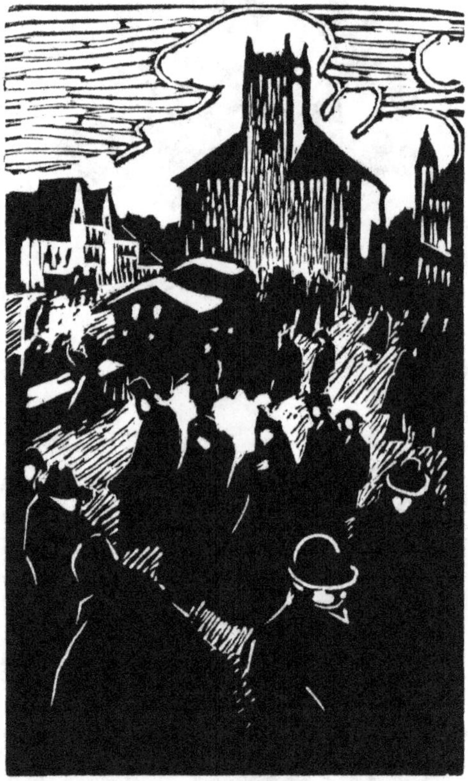

On Slieve-na-man, 101 × 63, *County Down songs*, p. 12.

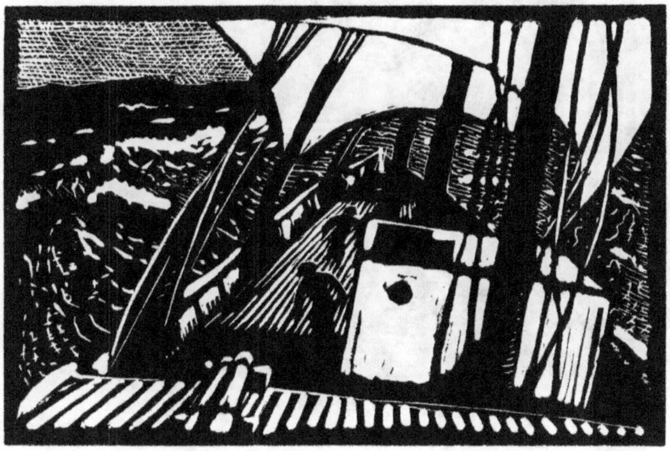

Untitled, 58 × 90, *County Down songs*, p. 19.

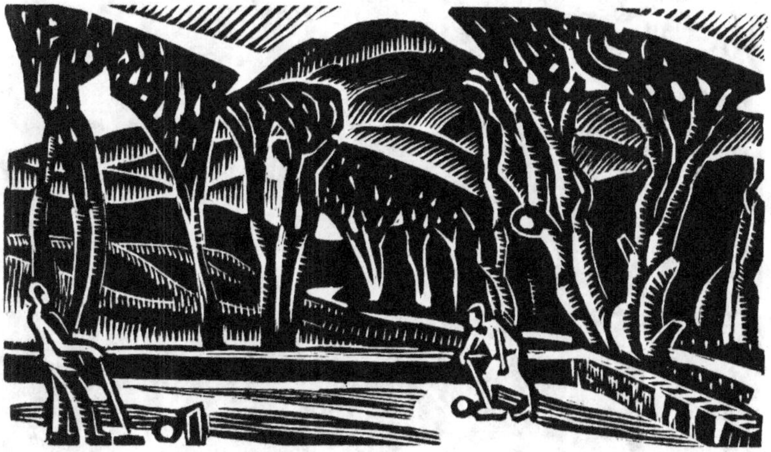

Winter croquet, 60 × 105, *As the sight is bent*, p. 55.

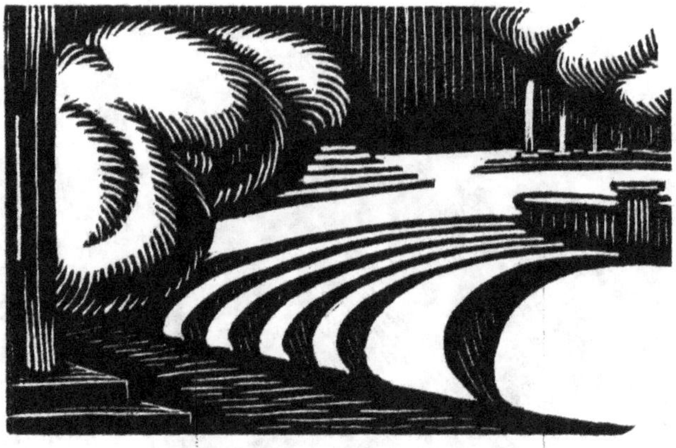

Untitled, 52 × 84, *Apollo in Mourne.*

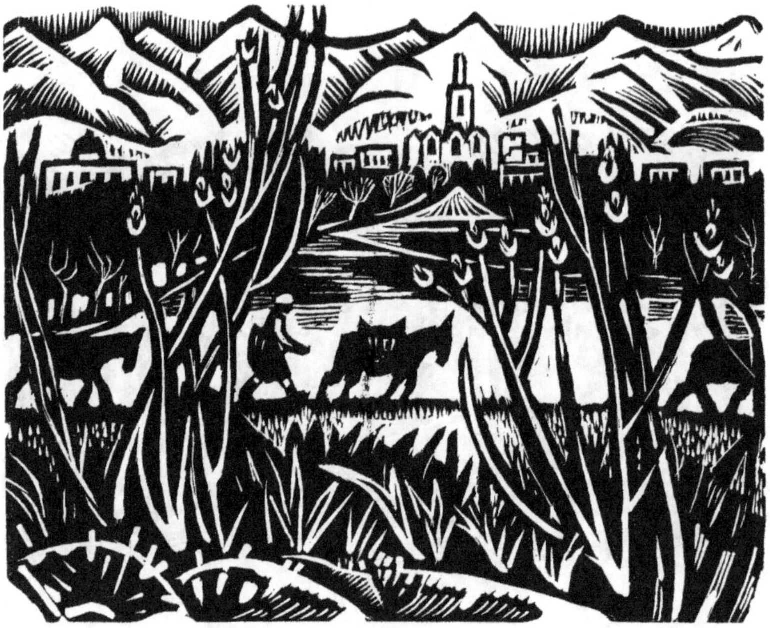

Paphos, 85 × 105, *As the sight is bent*, p. 99.

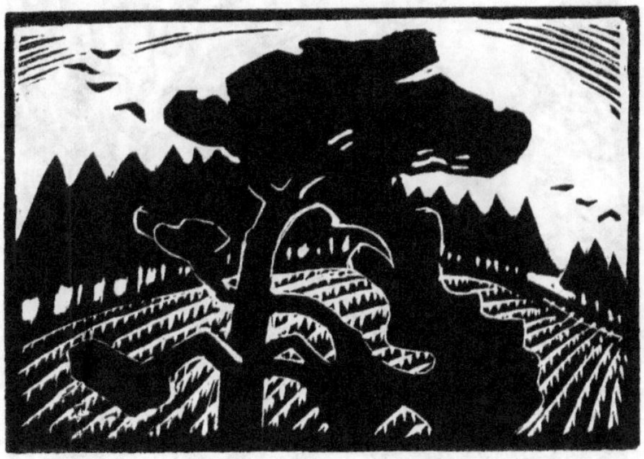

The wood-pigeon, 52 × 77, *County Down songs*, p. 28.

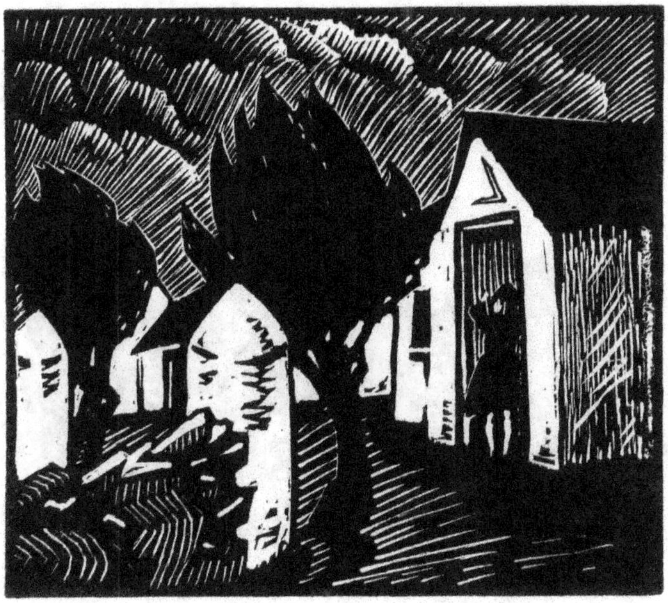

The door, 78 × 90, *County Down songs*, p. 23.

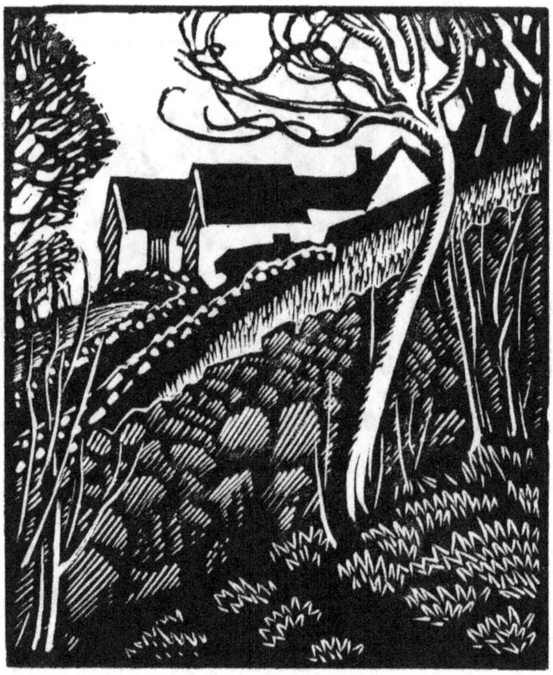

Clanawhillan, 88 × 75, *County Down songs*, p. 26.

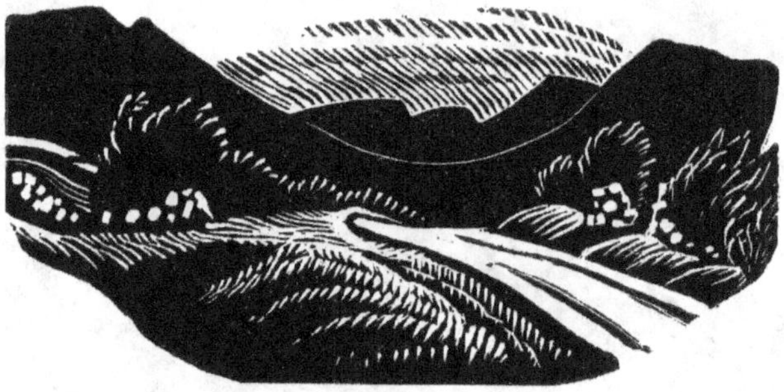

Untitled, wood engraving, 38 × 83.

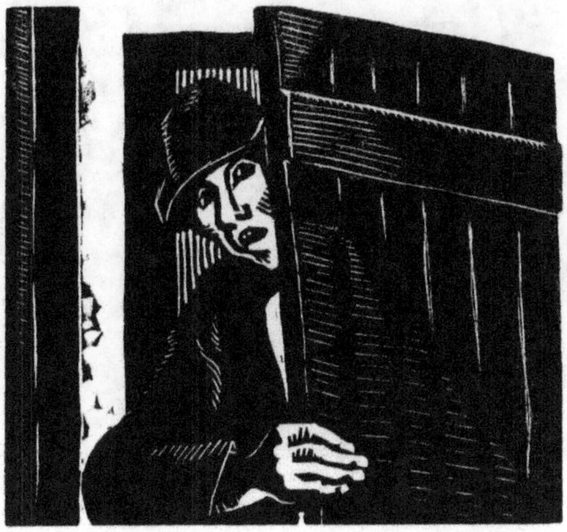

Untitled, 58 × 65, *Apollo in Mourne*, p. 28.

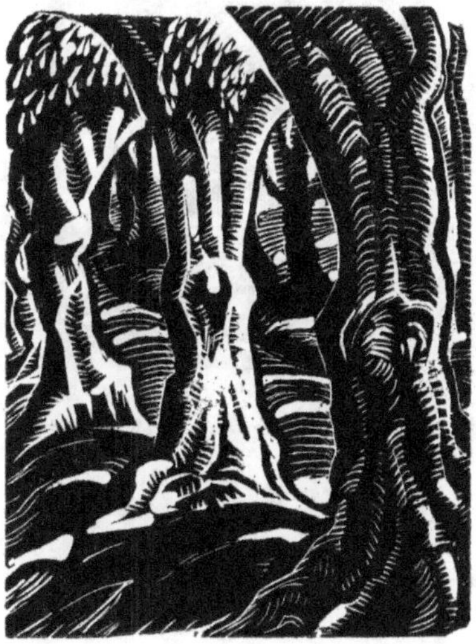

Untitled, wood engraving, 65 × 50.

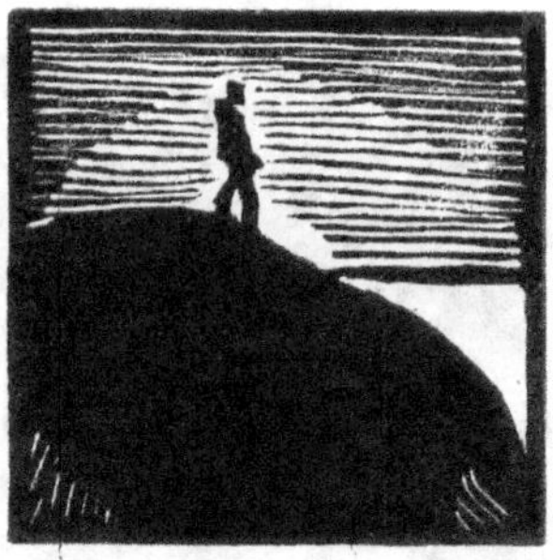

Day is prison, 38 × 39, *County Down songs*, p. 30.

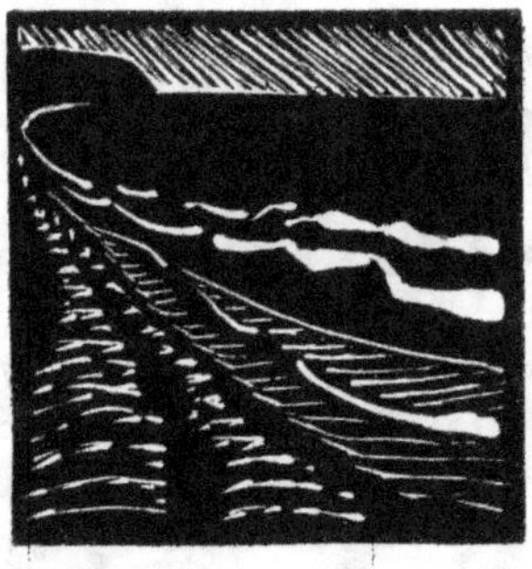

The door, 39 × 39, *County Down songs*, p. 22.

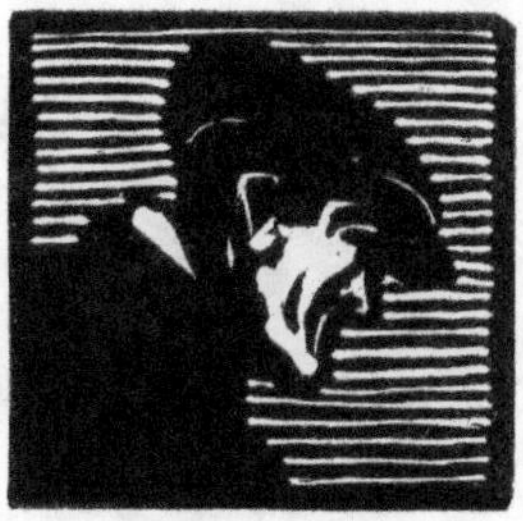

Poachin' Tom, 33 × 34, *County Down songs*, p. 35.

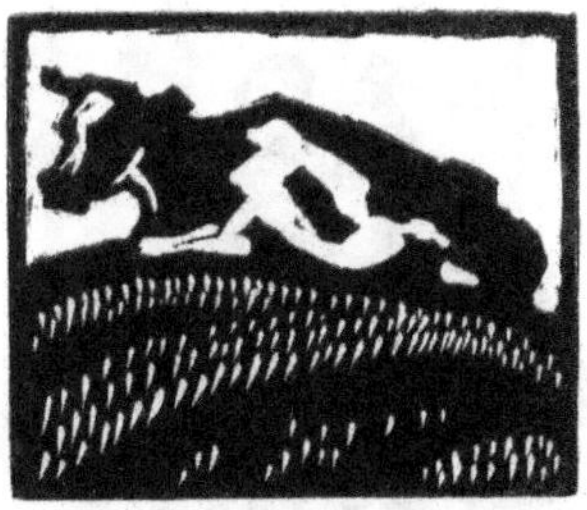

Clanawhillan, 32 × 39, *County Down songs*, p. 27.

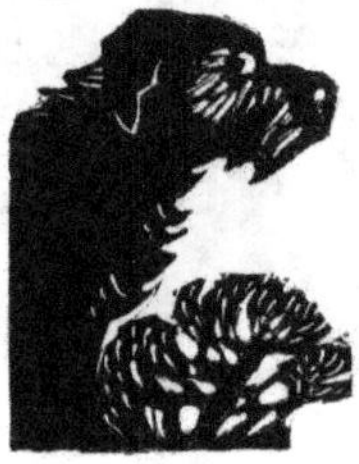

Poachin' Tom, 30 × 24, *County Down songs*, p. 35.

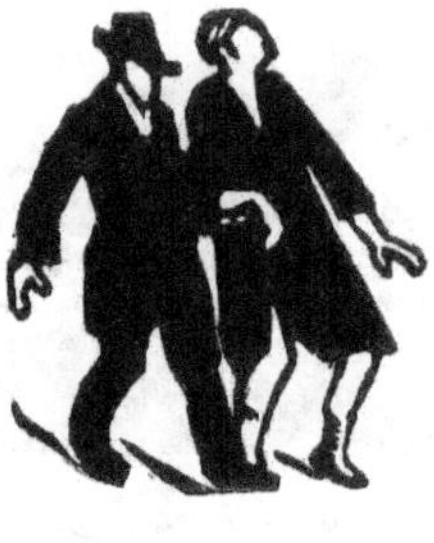

Untitled, wood engraving, 32 × 29.

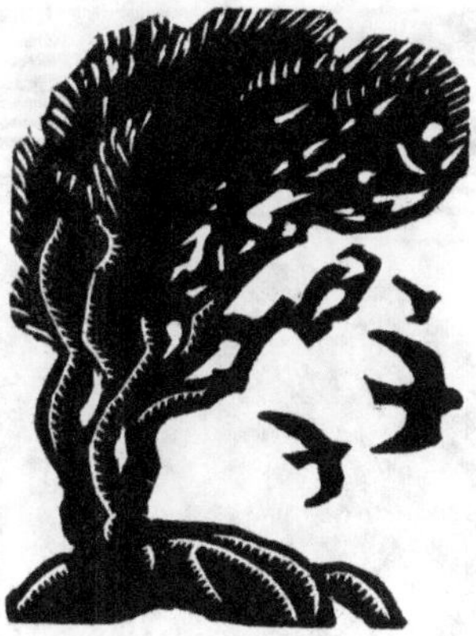

Untitled, wood engraving, 52 × 40.

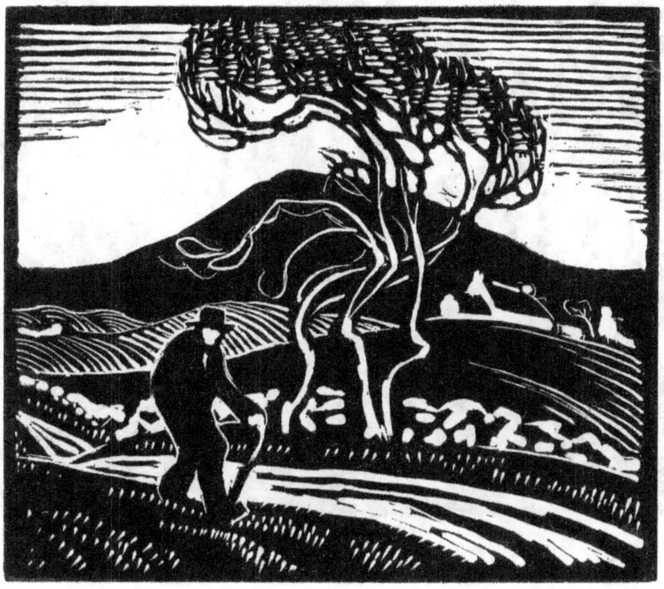

The beggar-man, 76 × 90, *County Down songs*, p. 33.

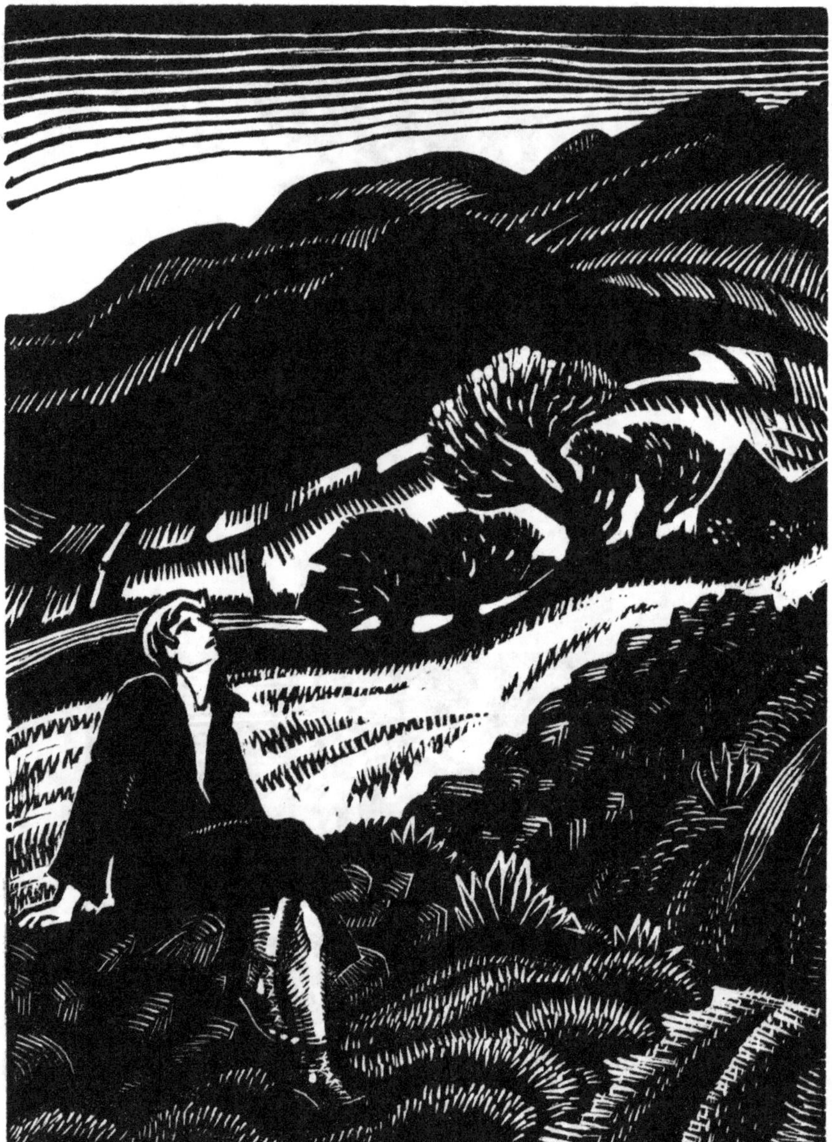

Untitled, wood engraving, 153 × 113.

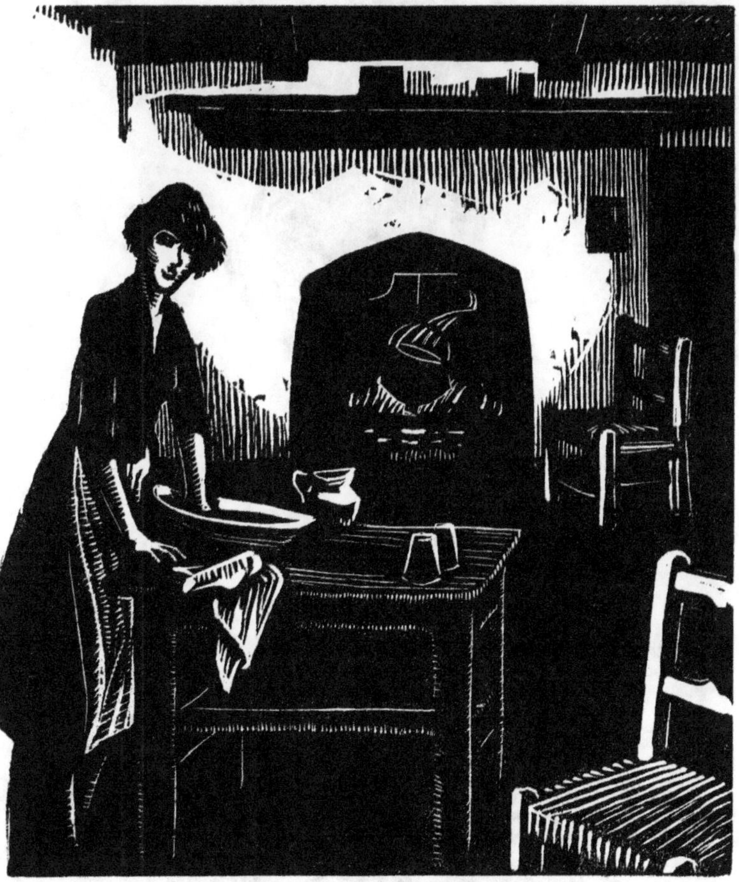

Untitled, 115 × 103, *Apollo in Mourne*, p. 20.

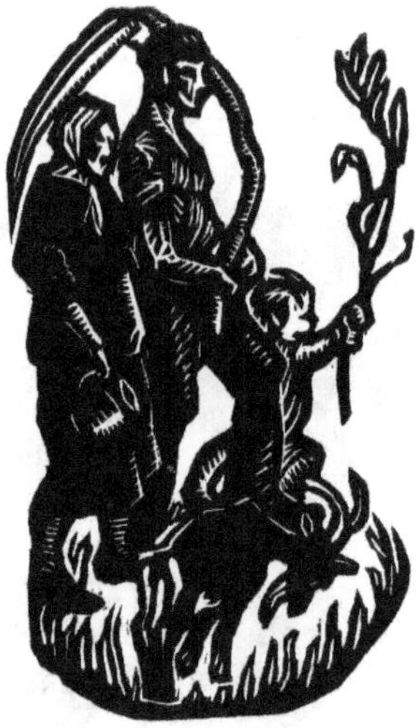

Untitled, wood engraving, 65 × 48.

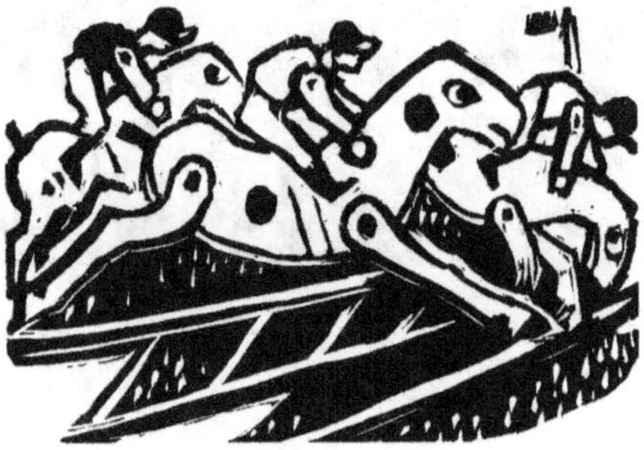

Toy horses, 40 × 57.5, *As the sight is bent*, p. 35.

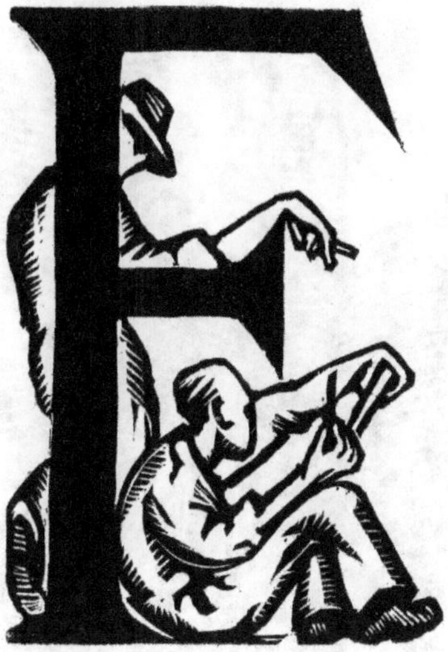

Untitled, wood engraving, 67 × 48.

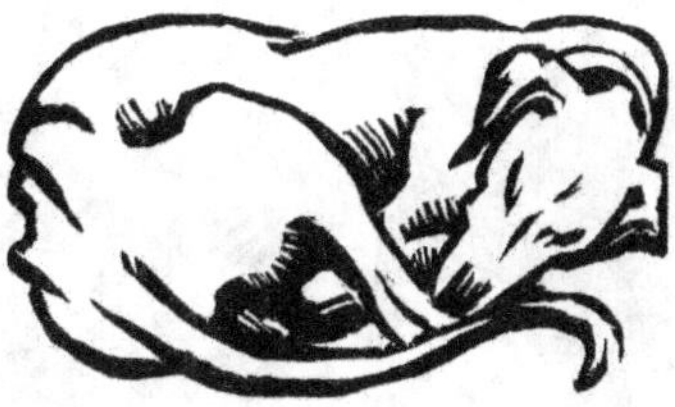

Hunting dog, 25 × 45, *As the sight is bent*, p. 98.

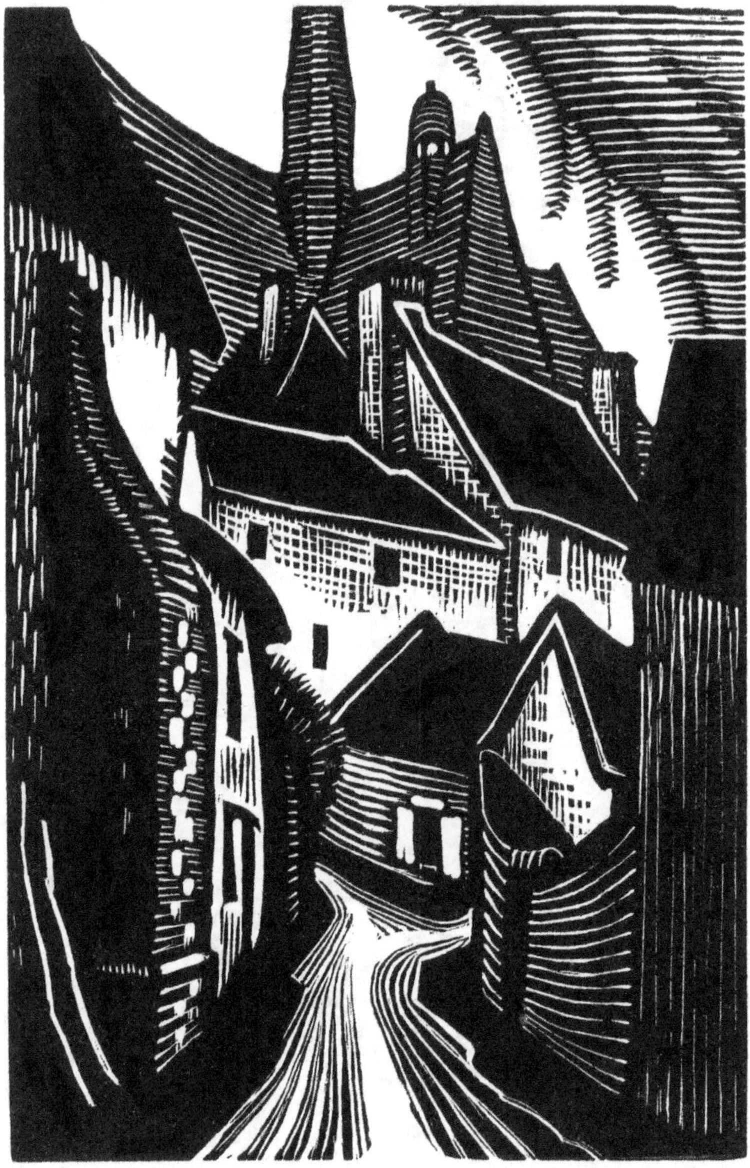

Montresor, wood engraving
(Museum of New Zealand Te Papa Tongarewa), 53 × 103 (no. 5 of 30).

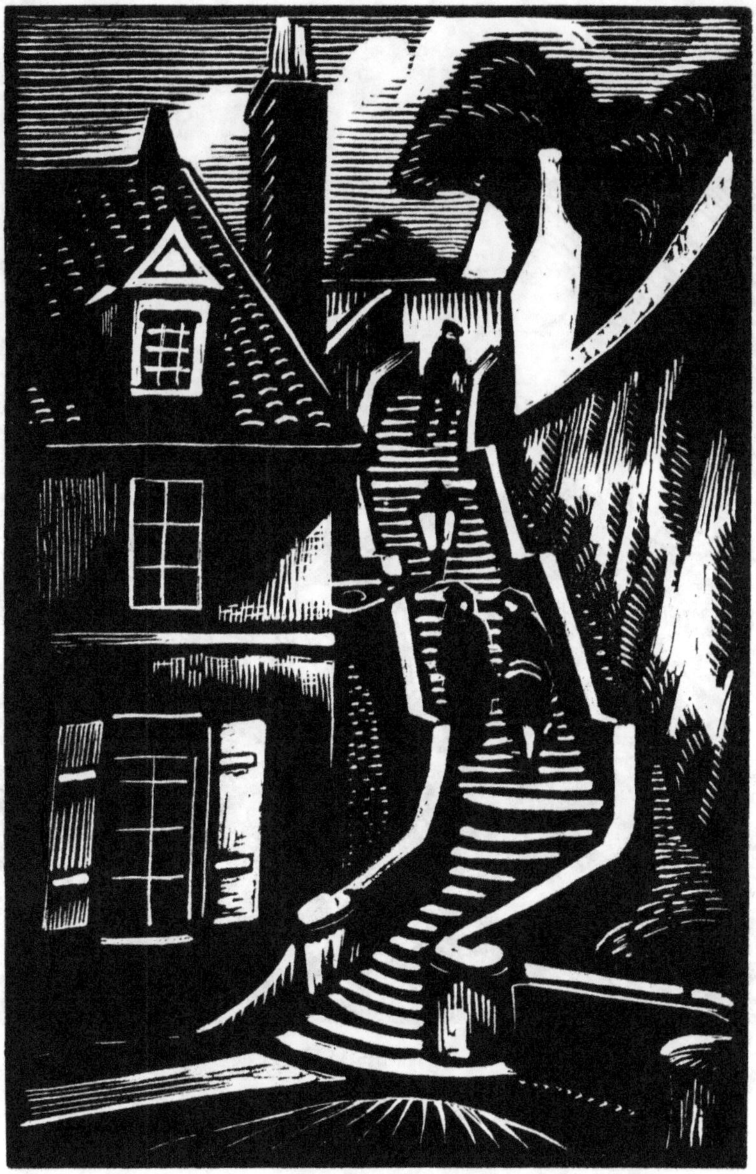

L'escalade, wood engraving (Museum of New Zealand Te Papa Tongarewa), 154 × 104 (no. 14 of 25).

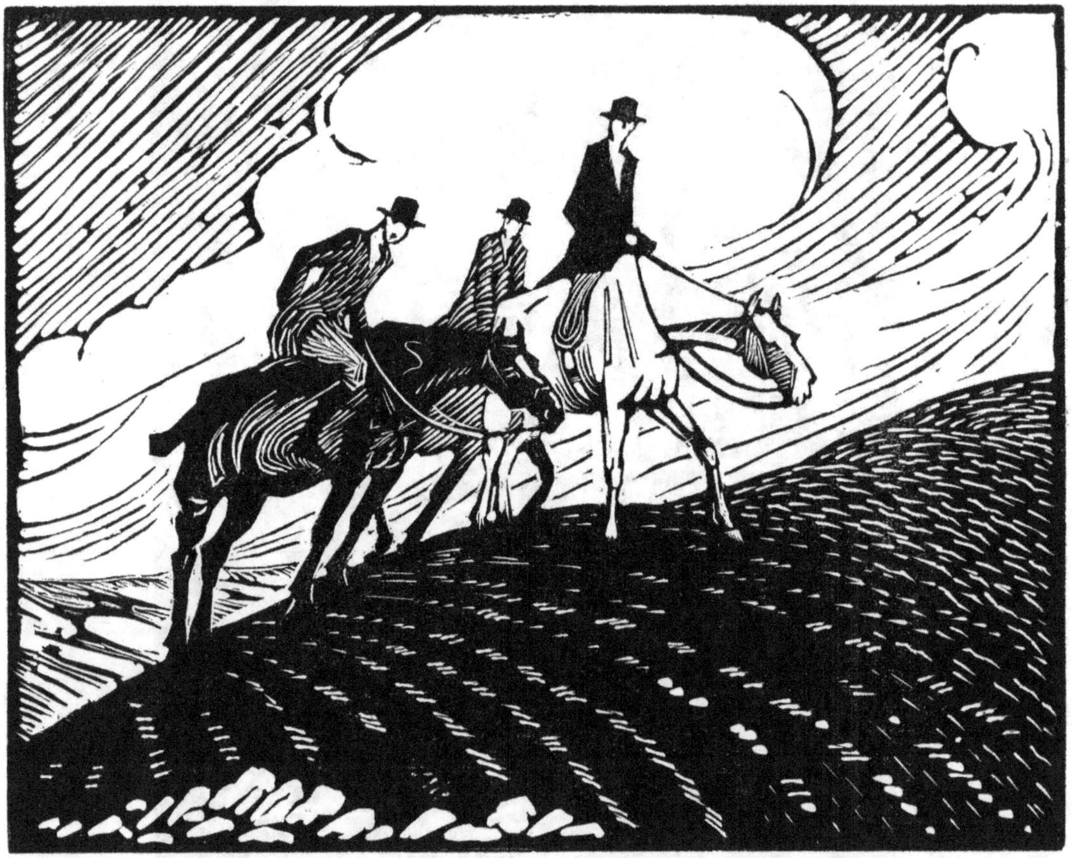

A hunting scene, wood engraving (British Museum), 112 × 145 (no. 12 of 50).

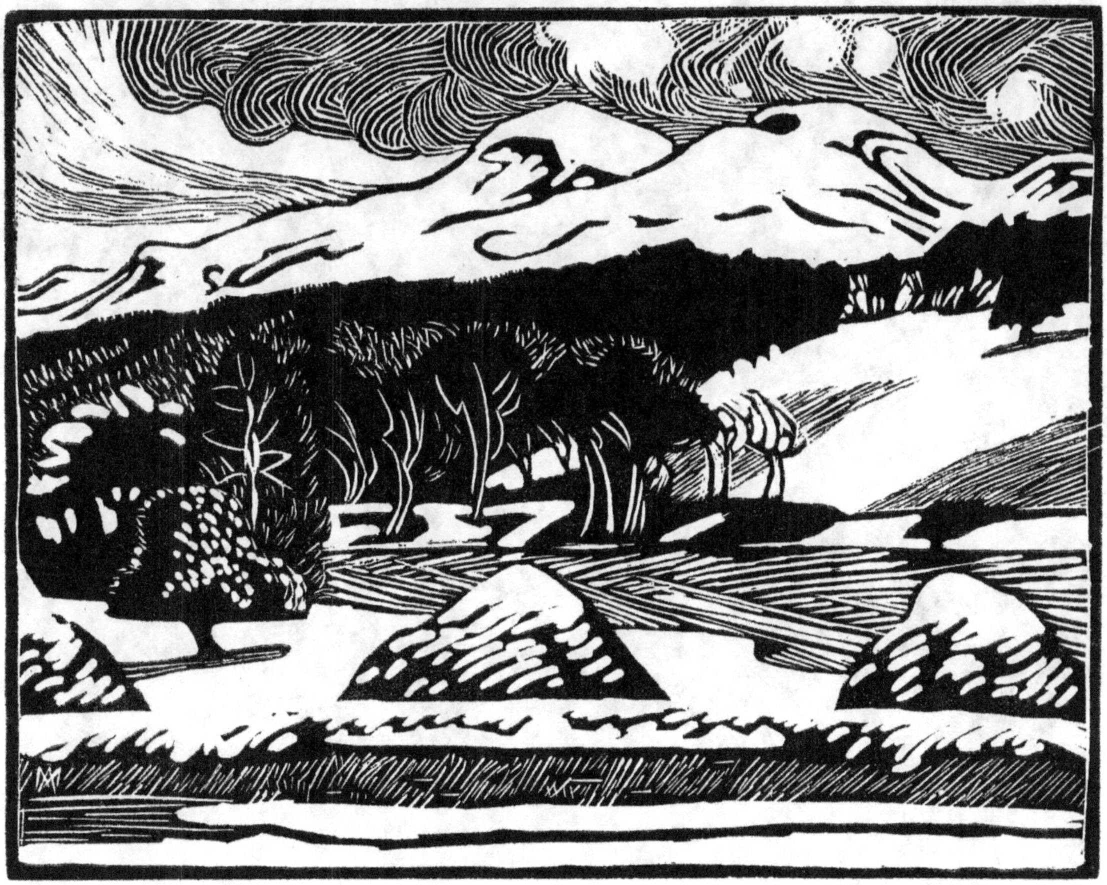

Snow, wood engraving (Central St Martins College of Art and Design), 115 × 153.

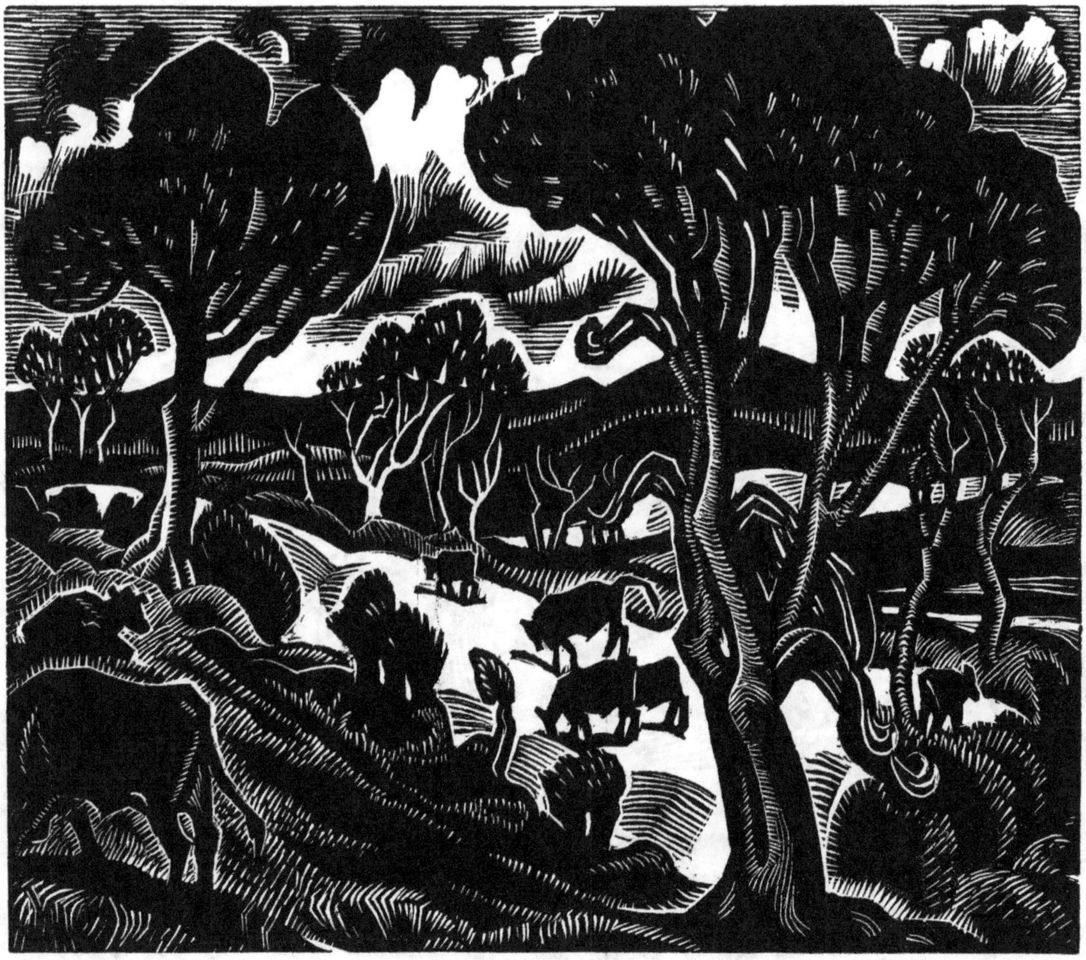

Pastureland, wood engraving, *c.* 1939
(Ulster Museum), 125 × 149 (no. 4 of 25).

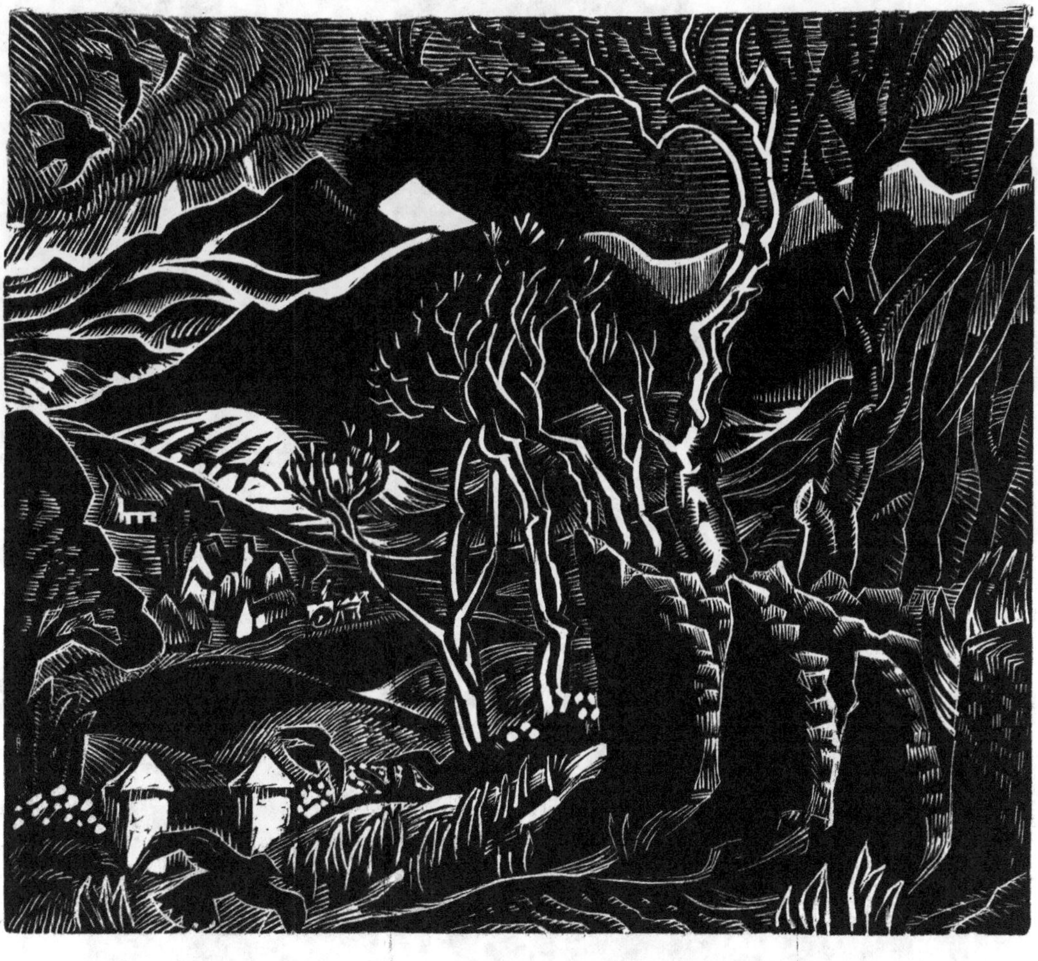

Winter, Carmeen, wood engraving,
122 × 143 (no. 3 of 20).

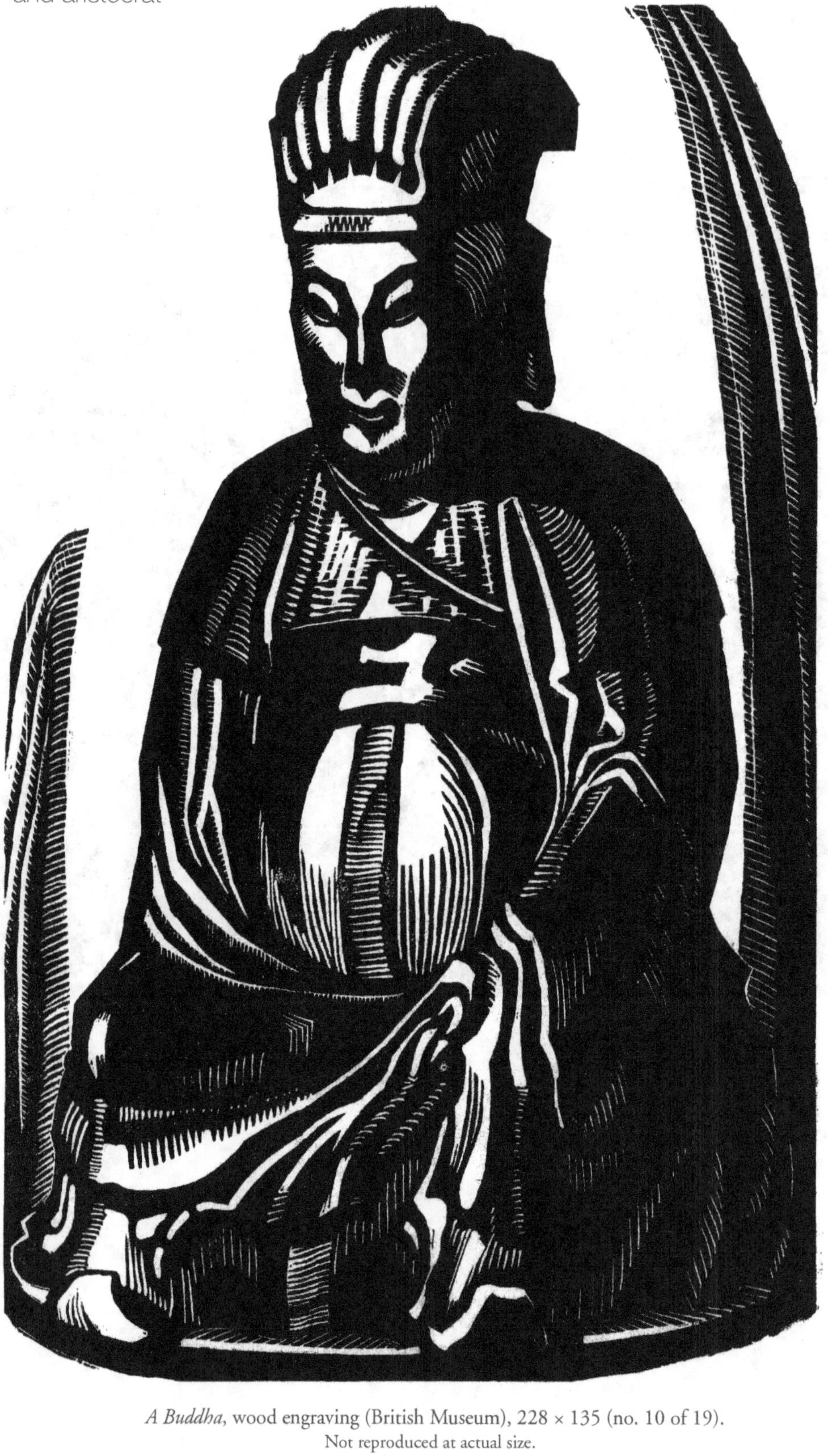

A Buddha, wood engraving (British Museum), 228 × 135 (no. 10 of 19).
Not reproduced at actual size.

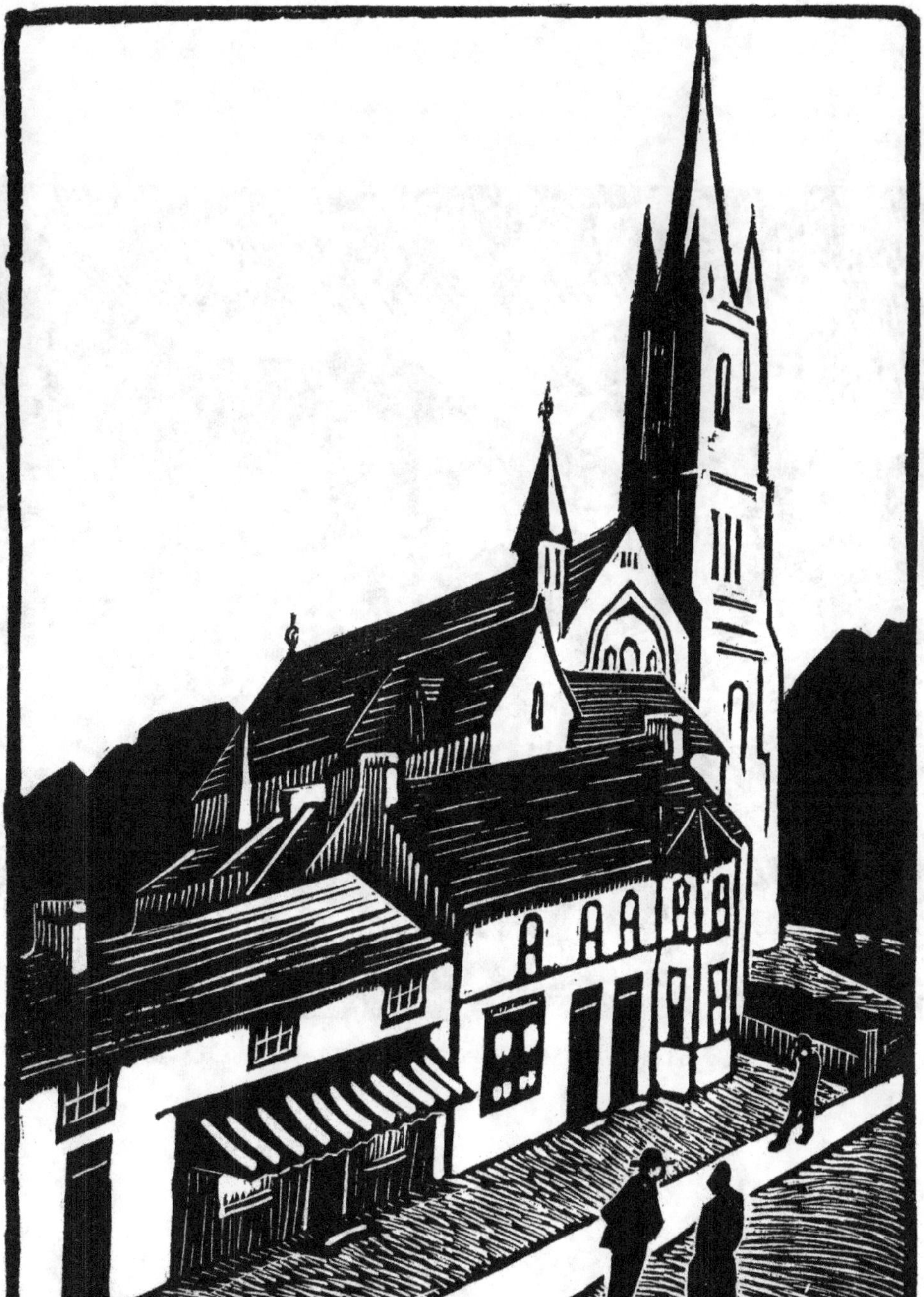

The chapel, wood engraving (National Art Gallery of New Zealand), 177 × 127 (no. 4 of 100).

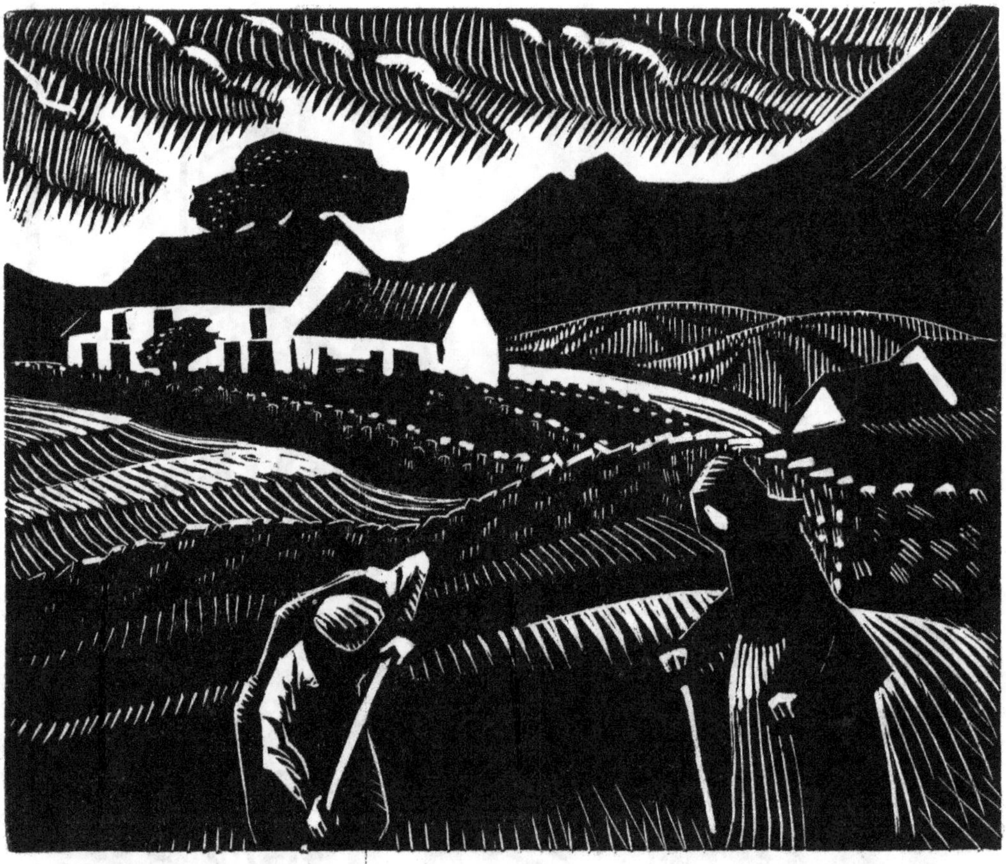

Foot of Bignian, wood engraving (Museum of New Zealand Te Papa Tongarewa), 111 × 138.

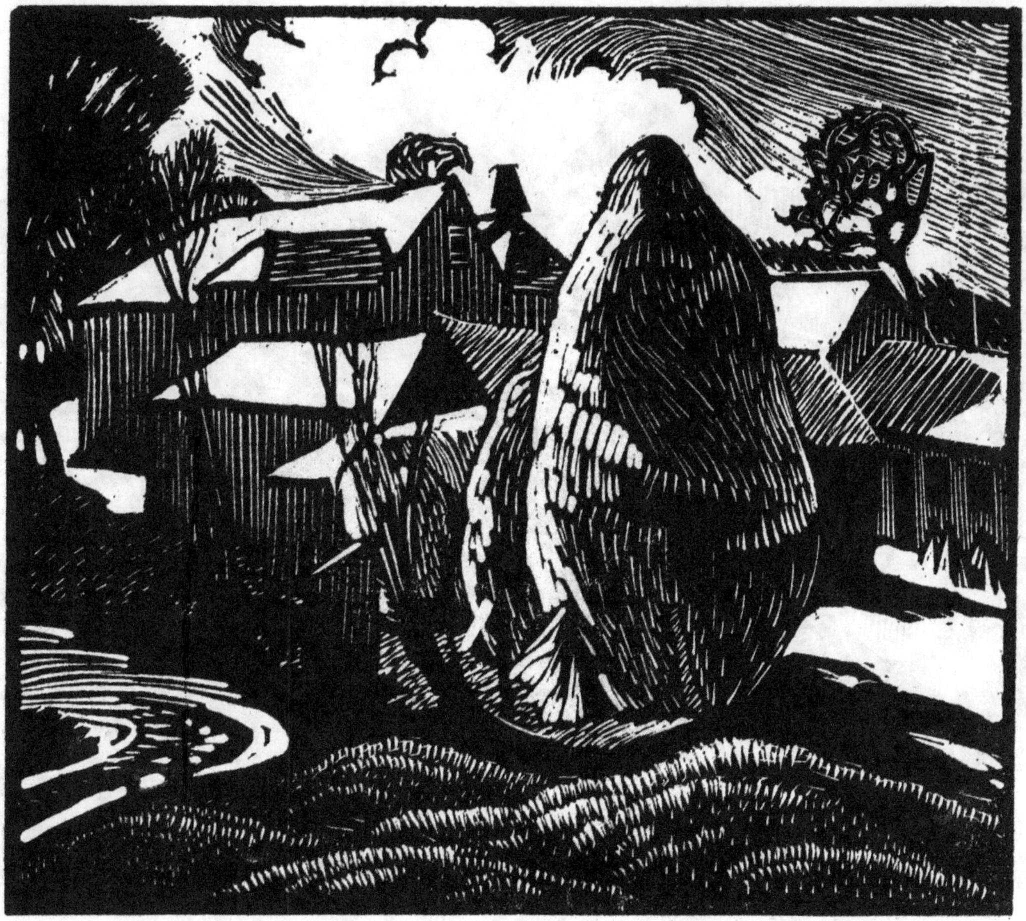

Tow stacks, wood engraving, *c.* 1939 (Ulster Museum) 120 × 140.

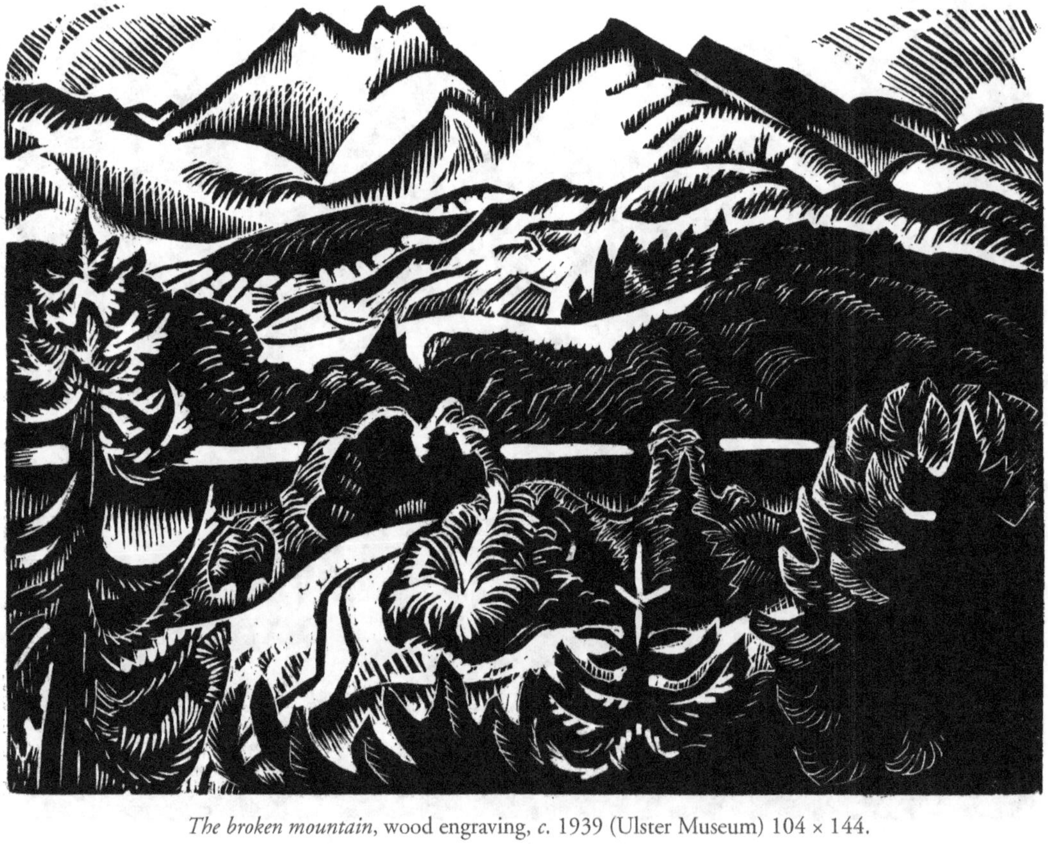

The broken mountain, wood engraving, *c.* 1939 (Ulster Museum) 104 × 144.

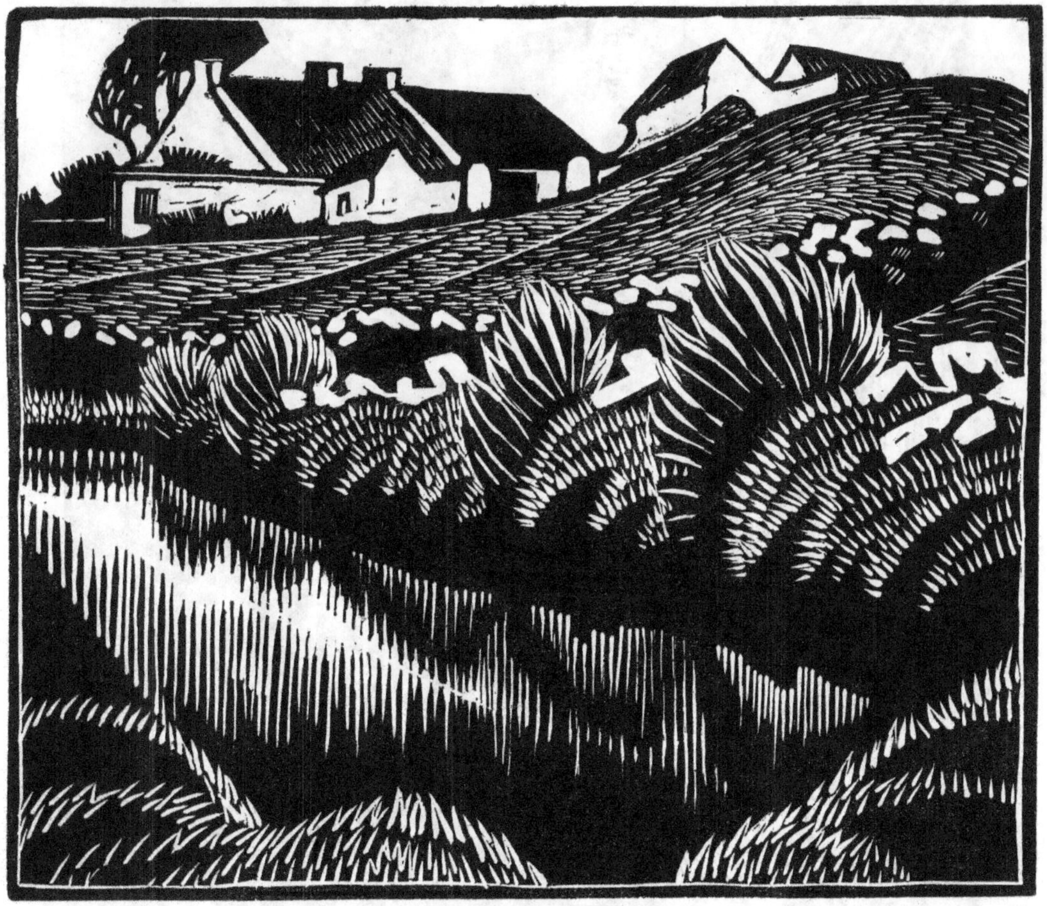

Flax dam, wood engraving, *c.* 1939 (Ulster Museum), 118 × 143 (no. 2 of 10).

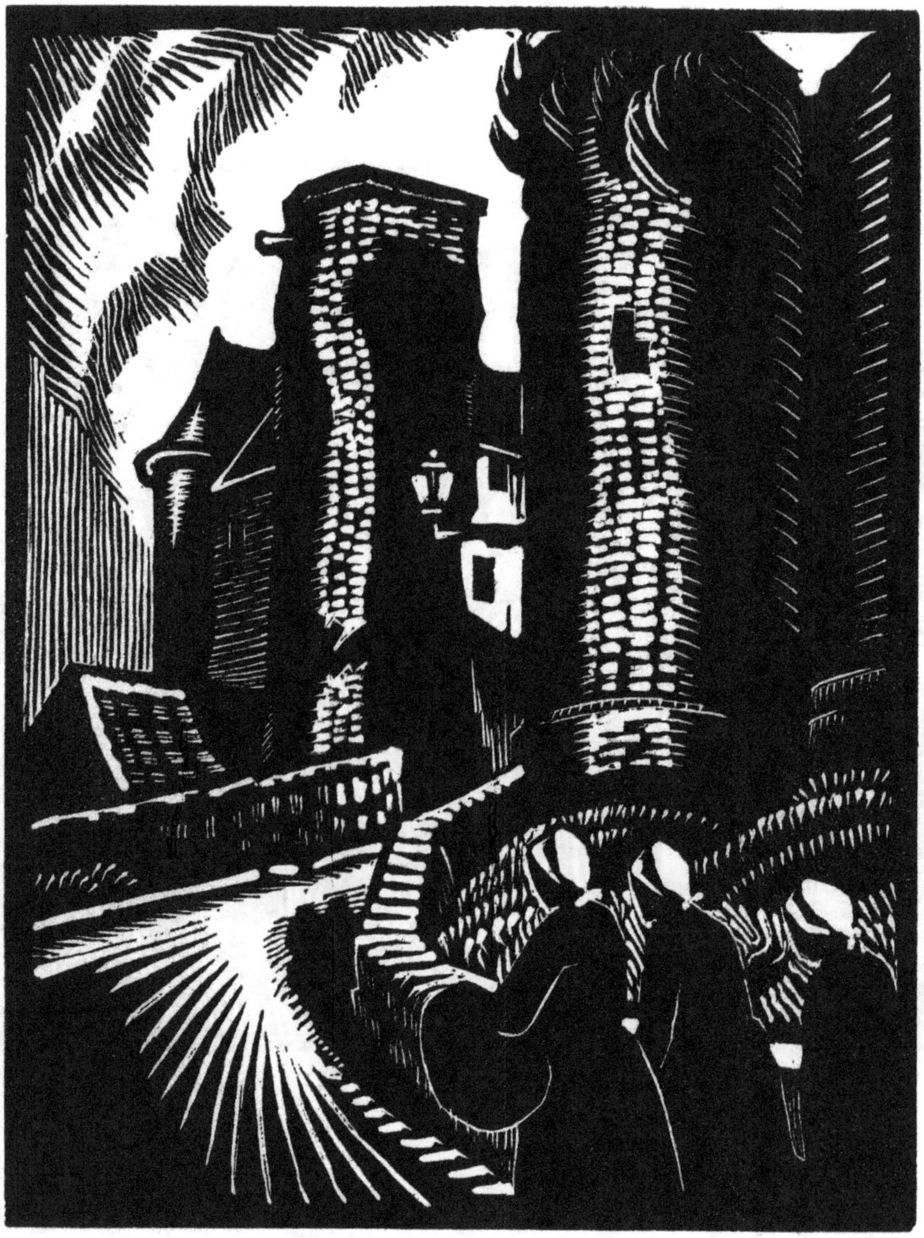

La porte, wood engraving, 162 × 126.

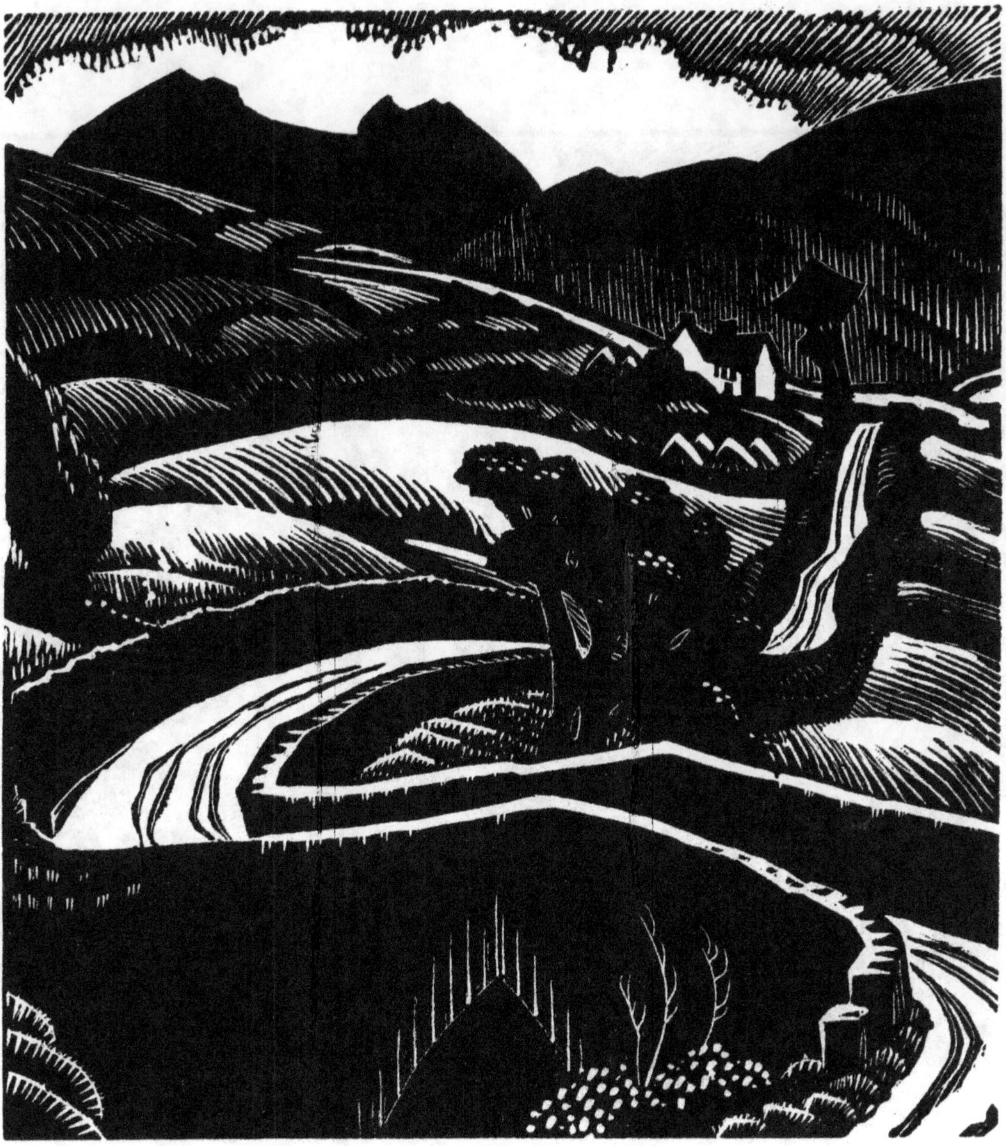

Clanawhillan Bridge, wood engraving
(Museum of New Zealand Te Papa Tongarewa), 155 × 138 (no. 13 of 25).

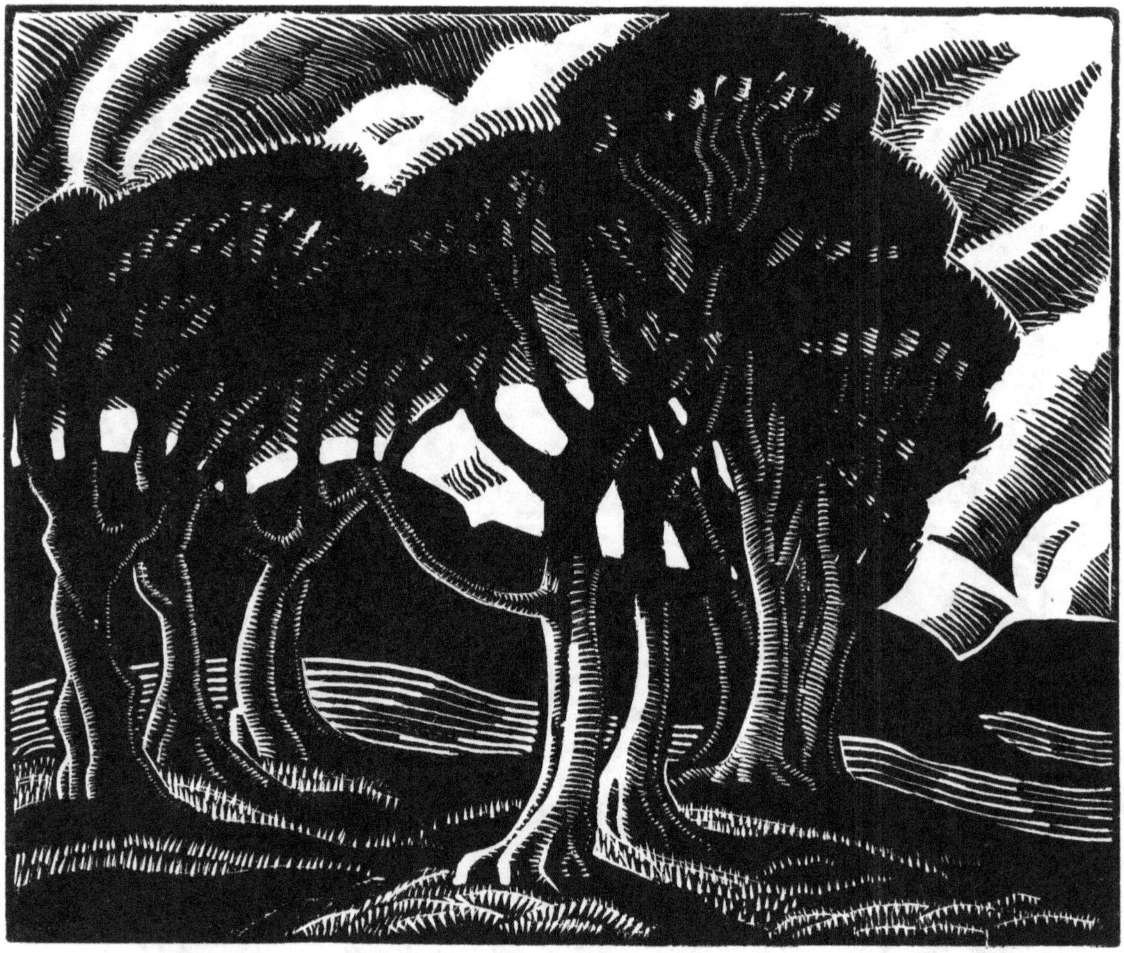

The park, wood engraving, *c.* 1939 (Ulster Museum), 124 × 153.

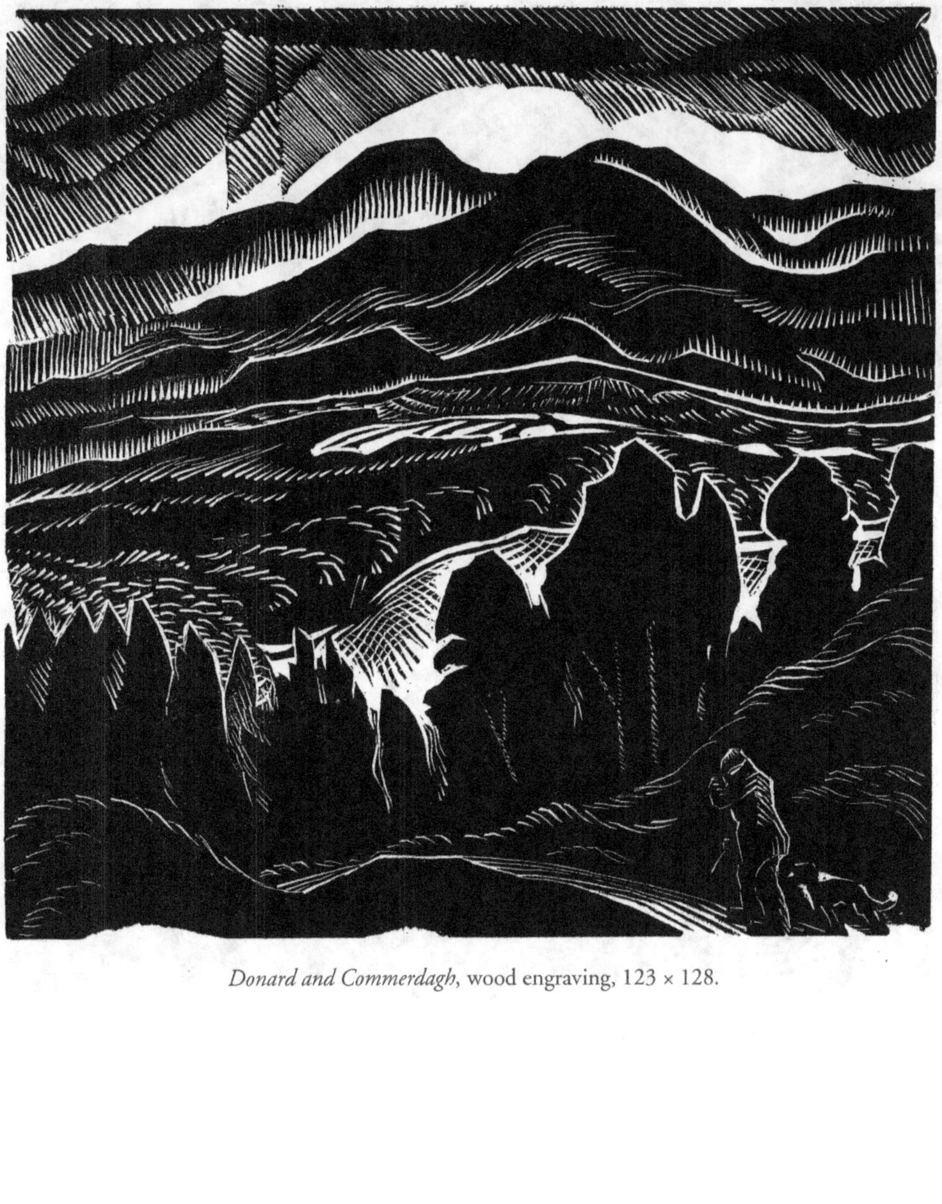

Donard and Commerdagh, wood engraving, 123 × 128.

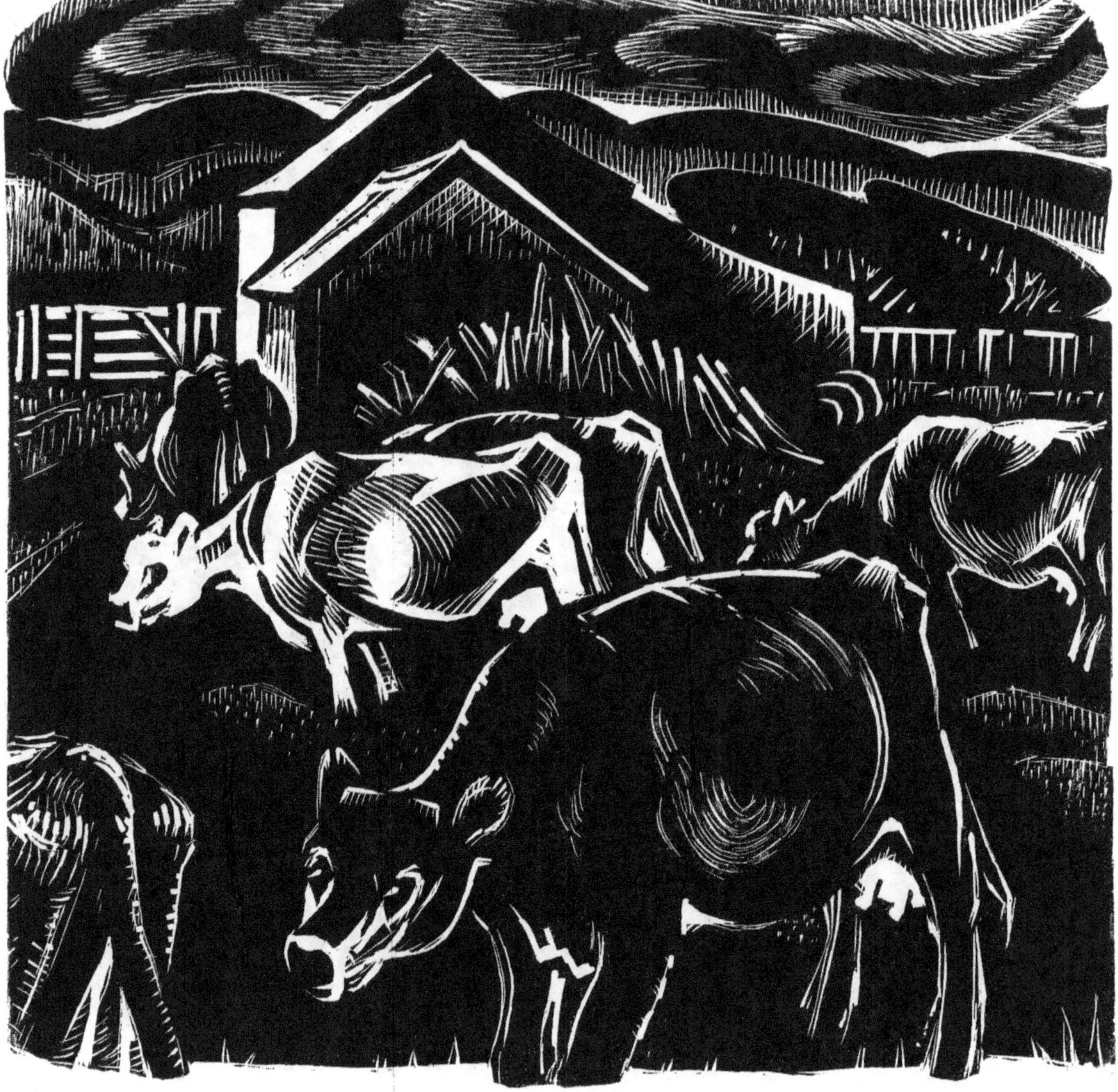

Cow farm, wood engraving, *c.* 1939 (Ulster Museum), 145 × 153 (no. 2 of 20).

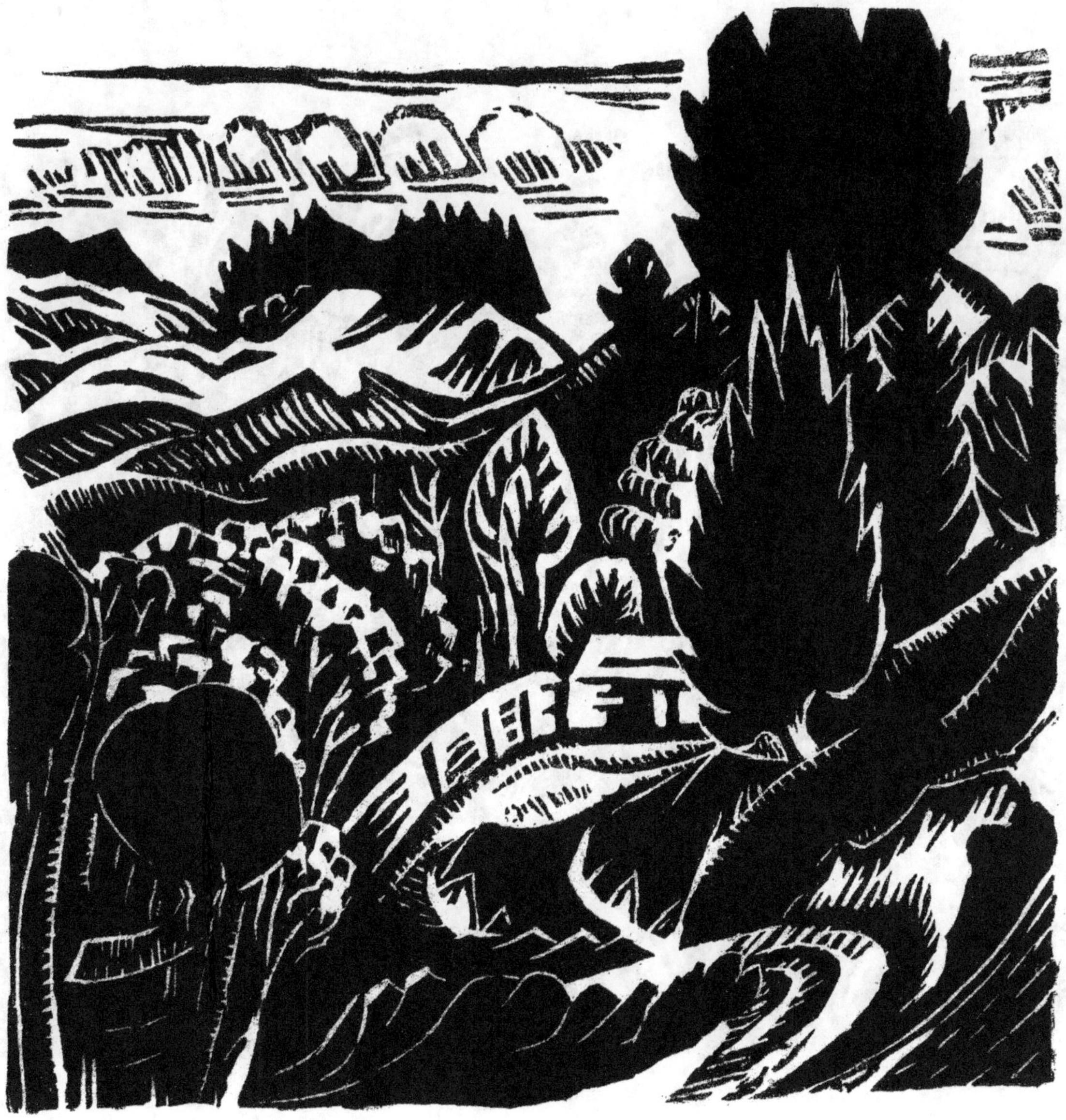

Little hills, linocut, *c.* 1940–45 (Suter Art Gallery), 150 × 152.

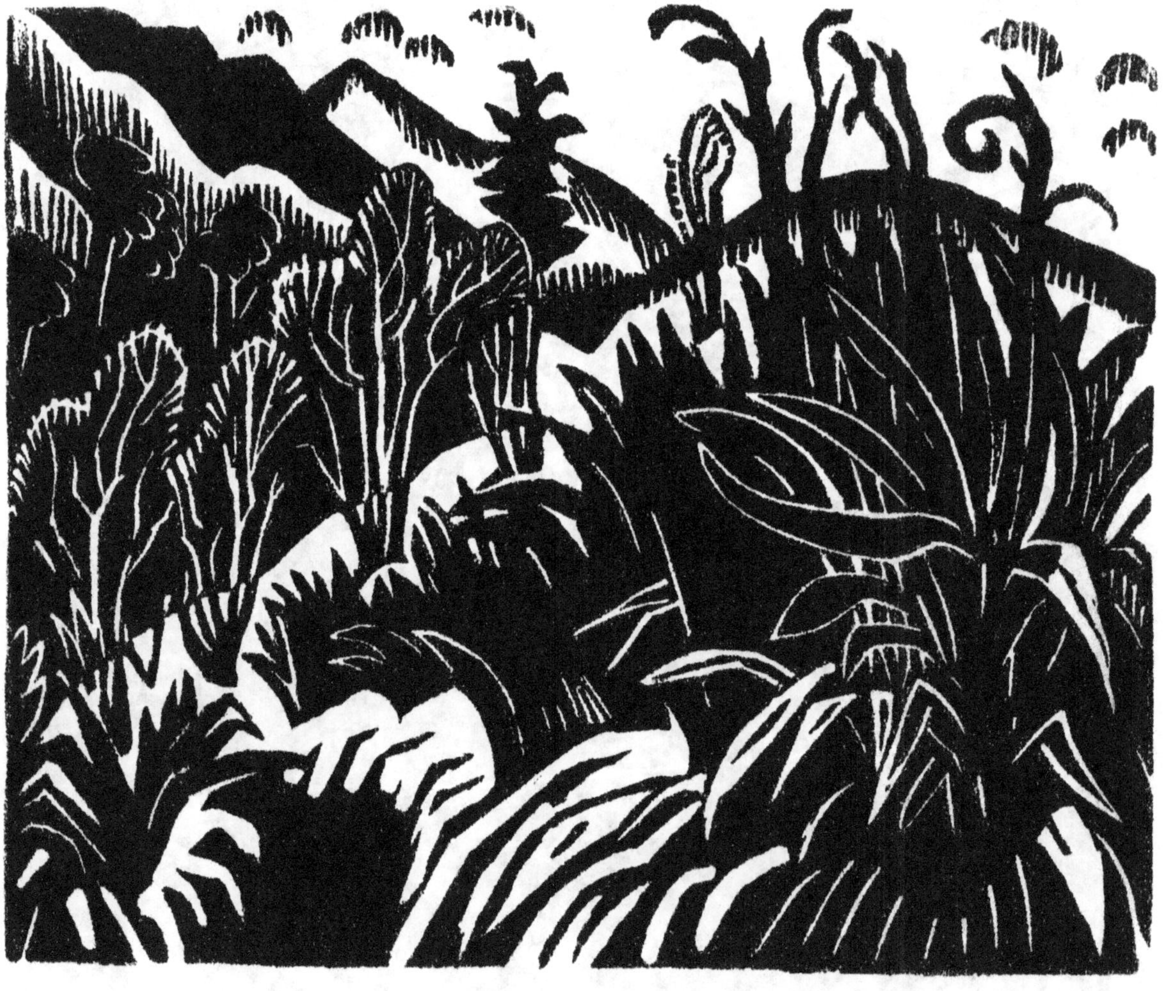

Pelorus Pass, linocut, *c.* 1940–45, 128 × 158.

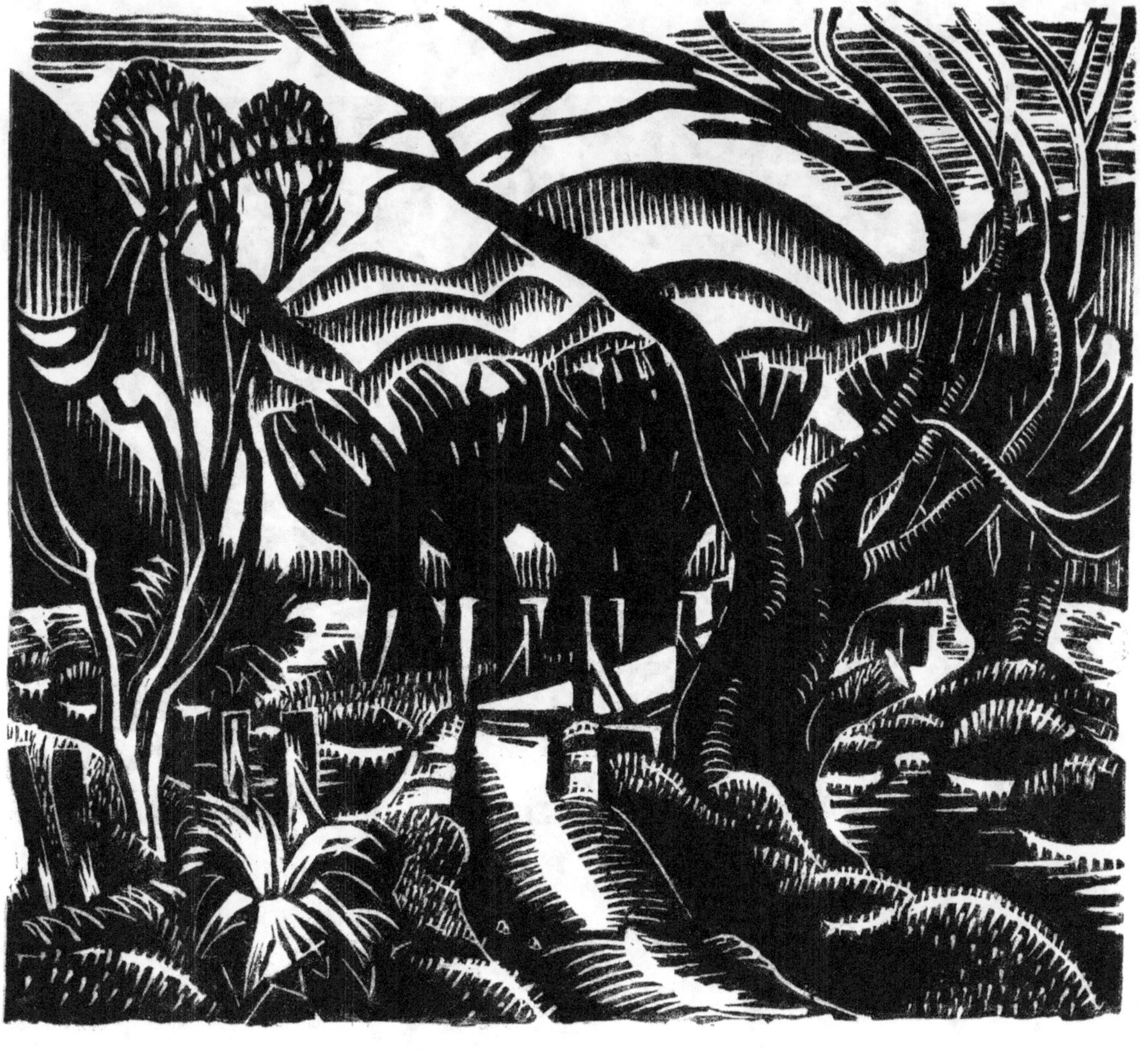

Willows, linocut, *c.* 1940–45 (Suter Art Gallery), 175 × 200.
Not reproduced at actual size.

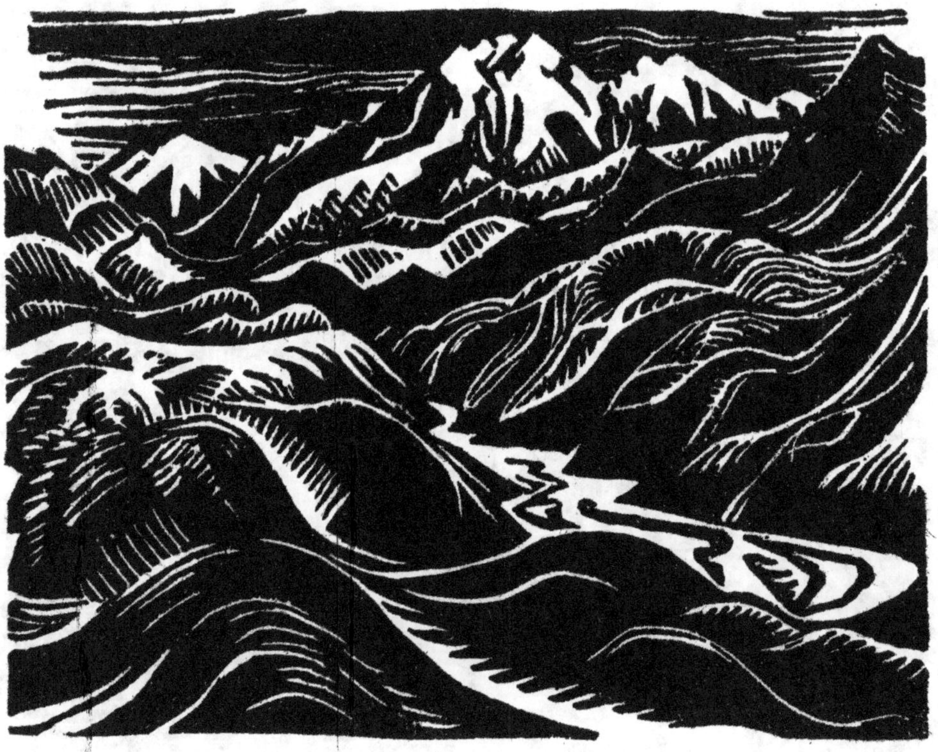

Rogerson River, linocut, *c.* 1940–45 (Suter Art Gallery), 97 × 115.

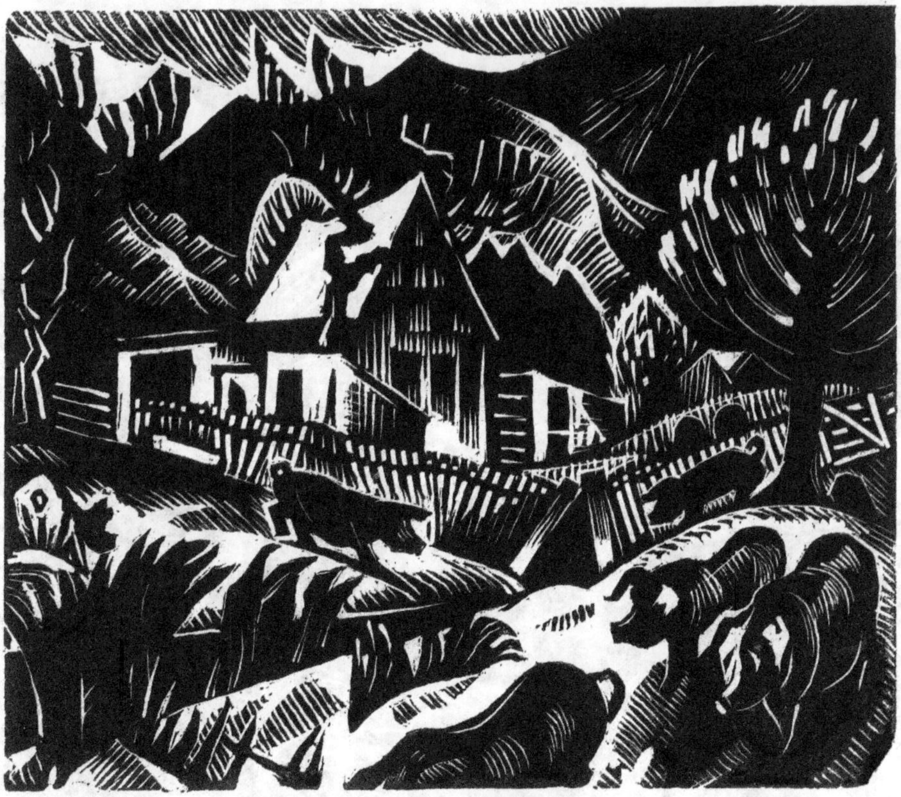

Pig farm, wood engraving, 103 × 122.

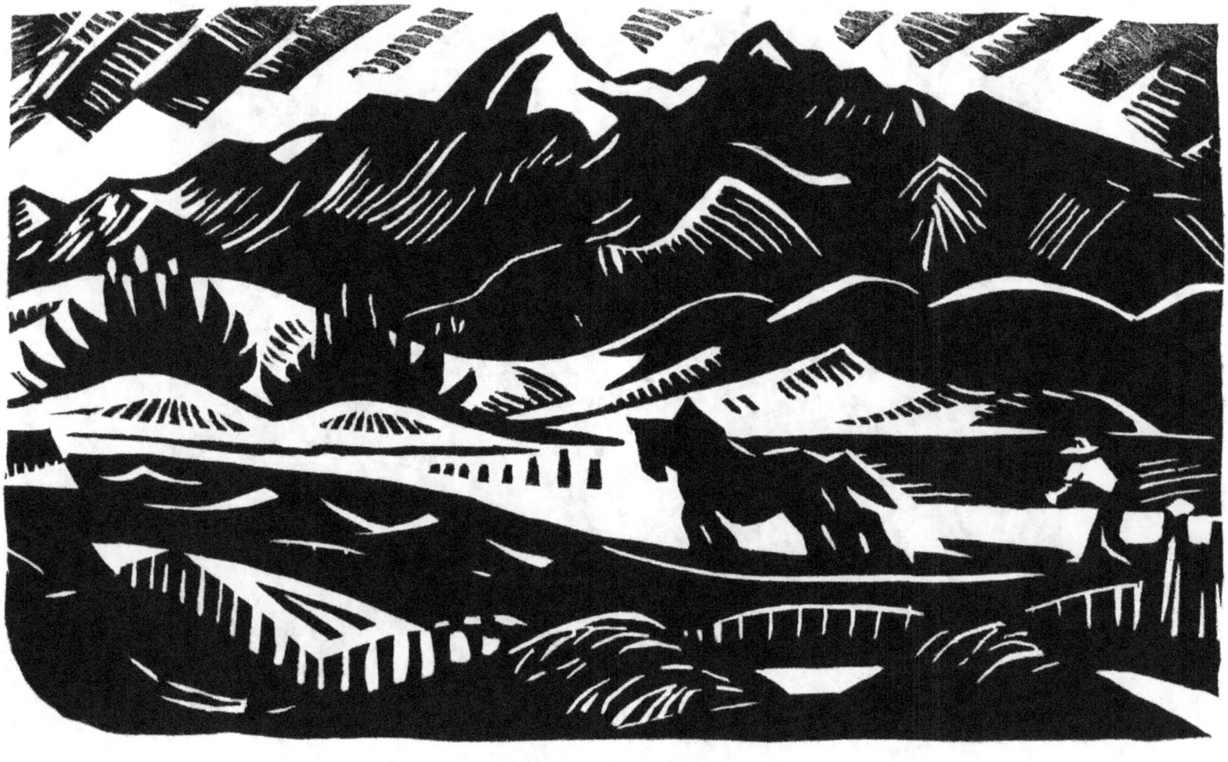

Anatoki, linocut, *c.* 1940–45 (Suter Art Gallery), 130 × 220.
Not reproduced at actual size.

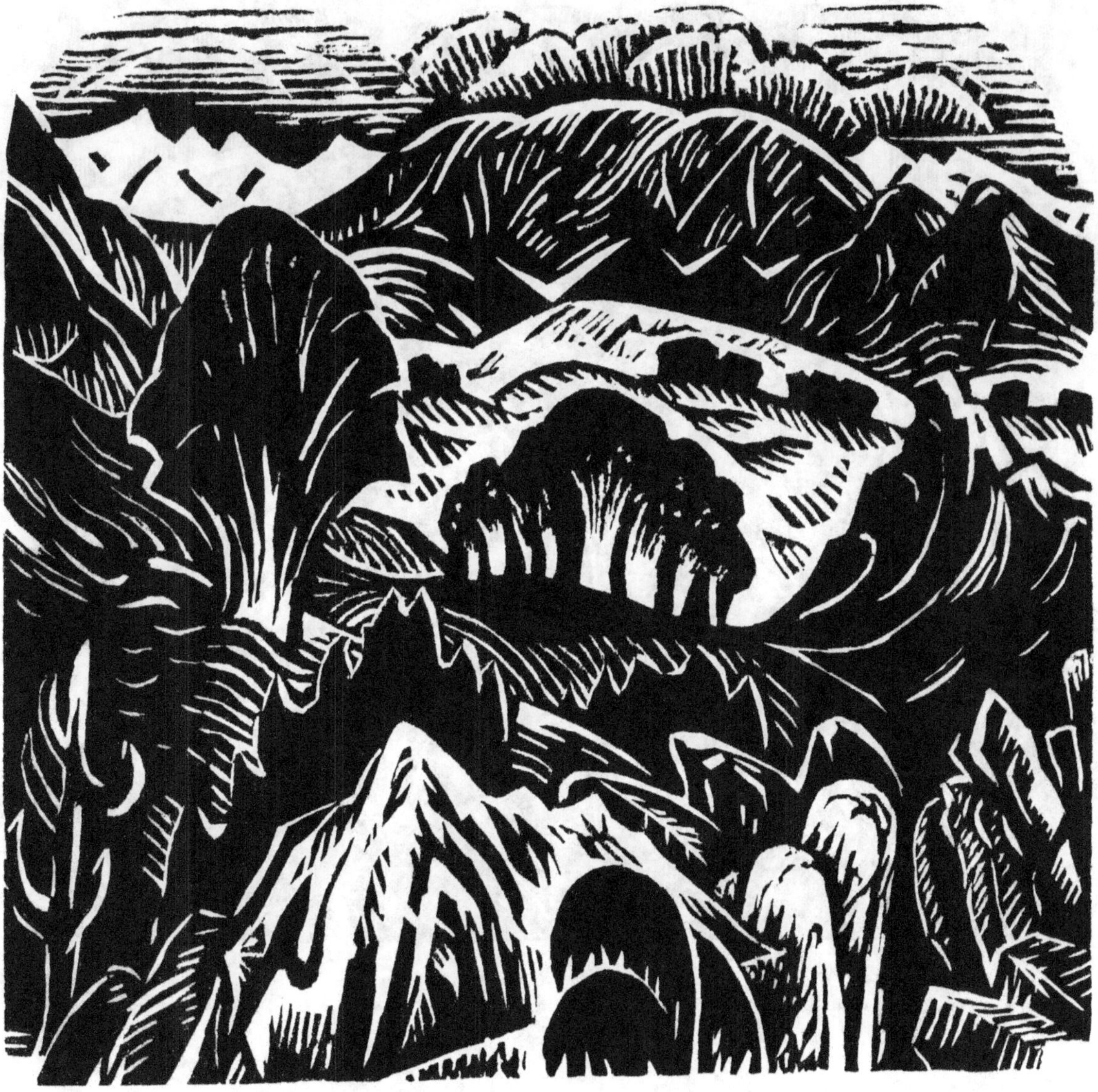

The glen, linocut, *c.* 1940–45 (Suter Art Gallery), 193 × 203.
Not reproduced at actual size.

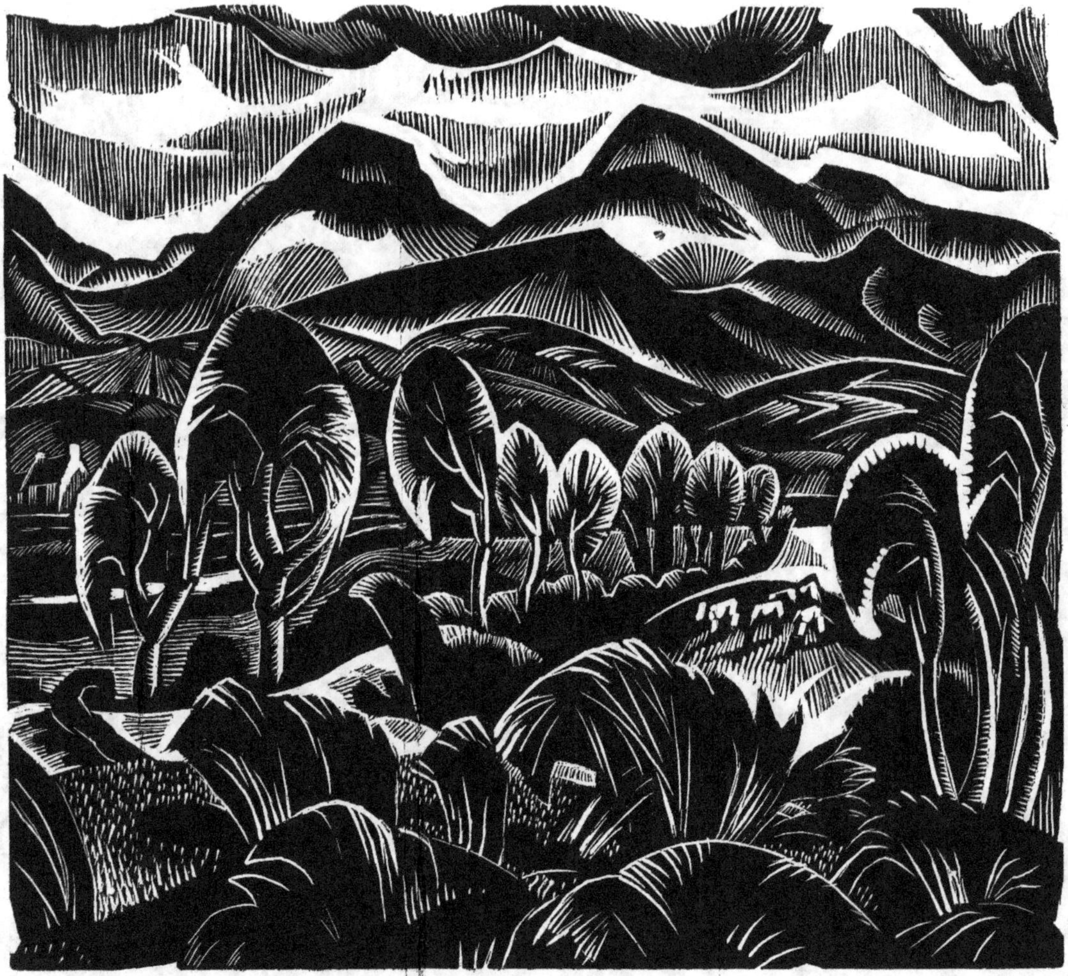

Mountains of Mourne, wood engraving
(Museum of New Zealand Te Papa Tongarewa), 128 × 147 (no. 11 of 18).

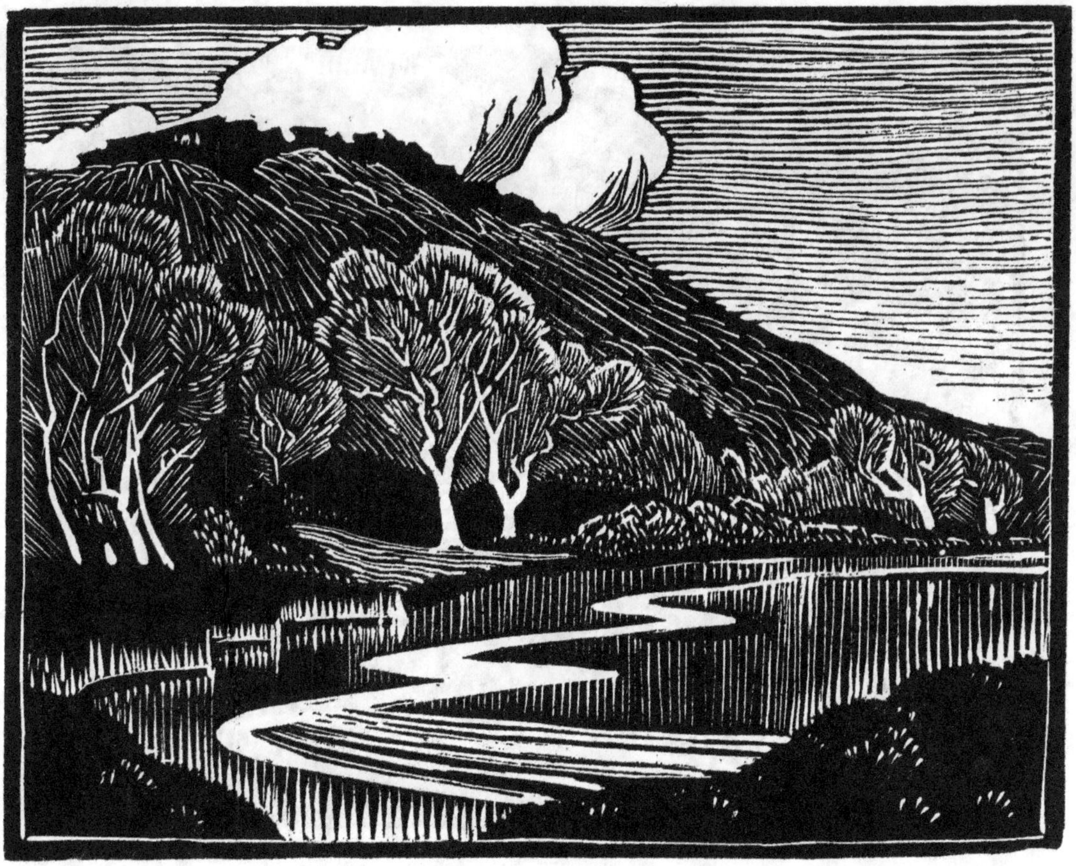

The lake, 113 × 143, frontispiece to *County Down songs*.

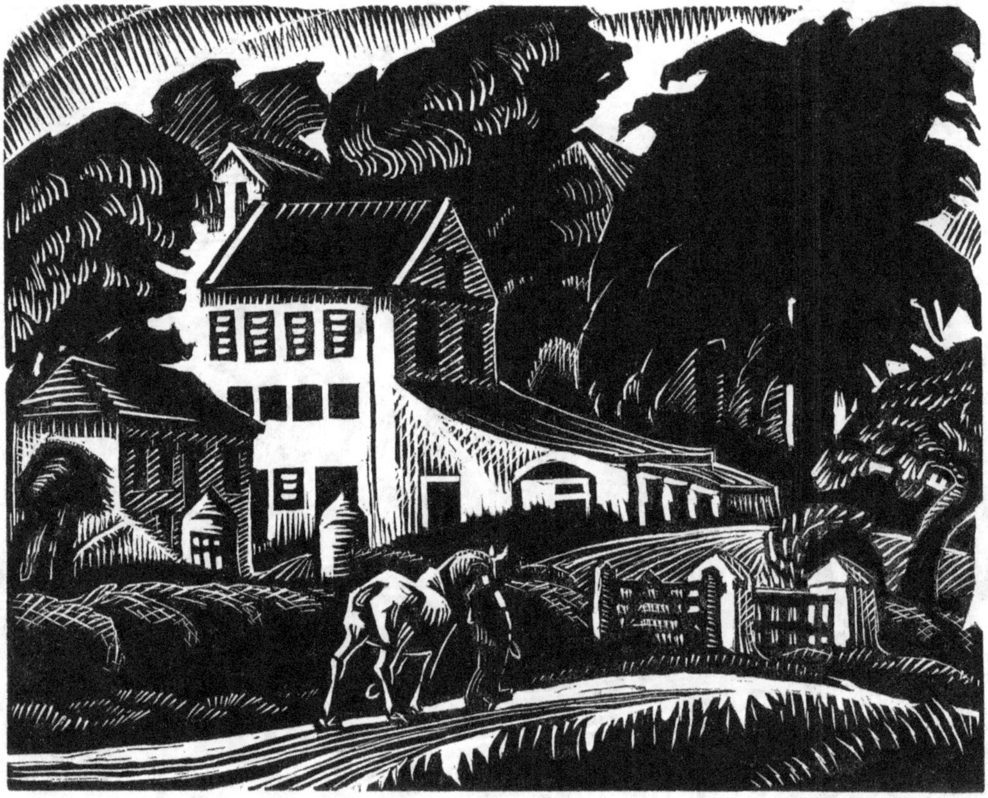

Untitled, wood engraving, 103 × 134 (no. 13 of 25).

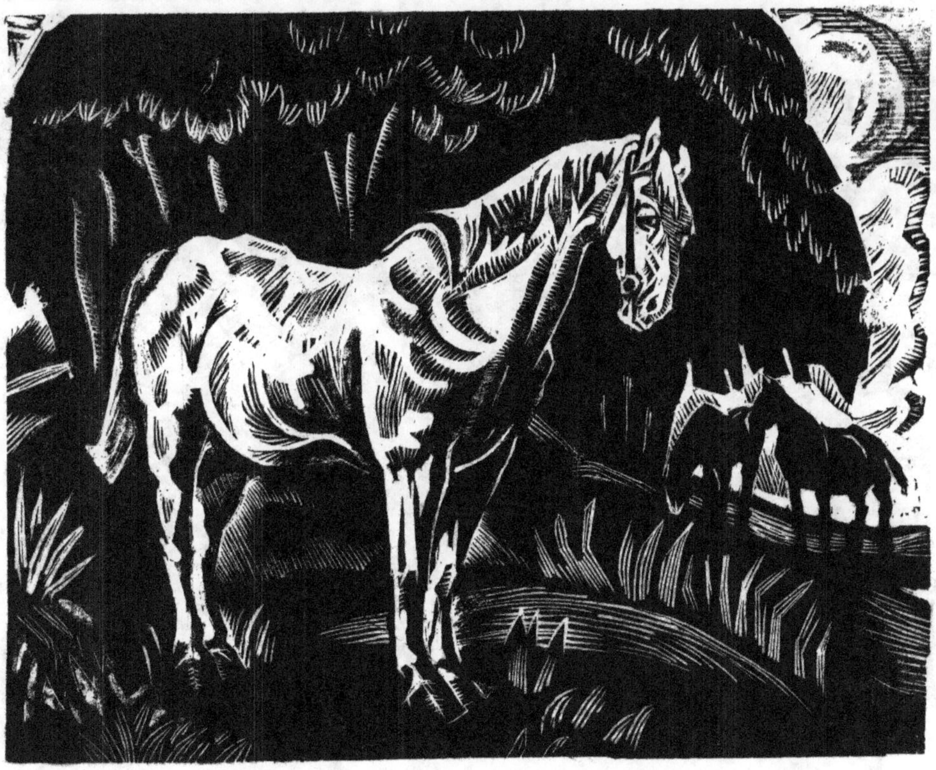

Untitled, wood engraving, 99 × 127.

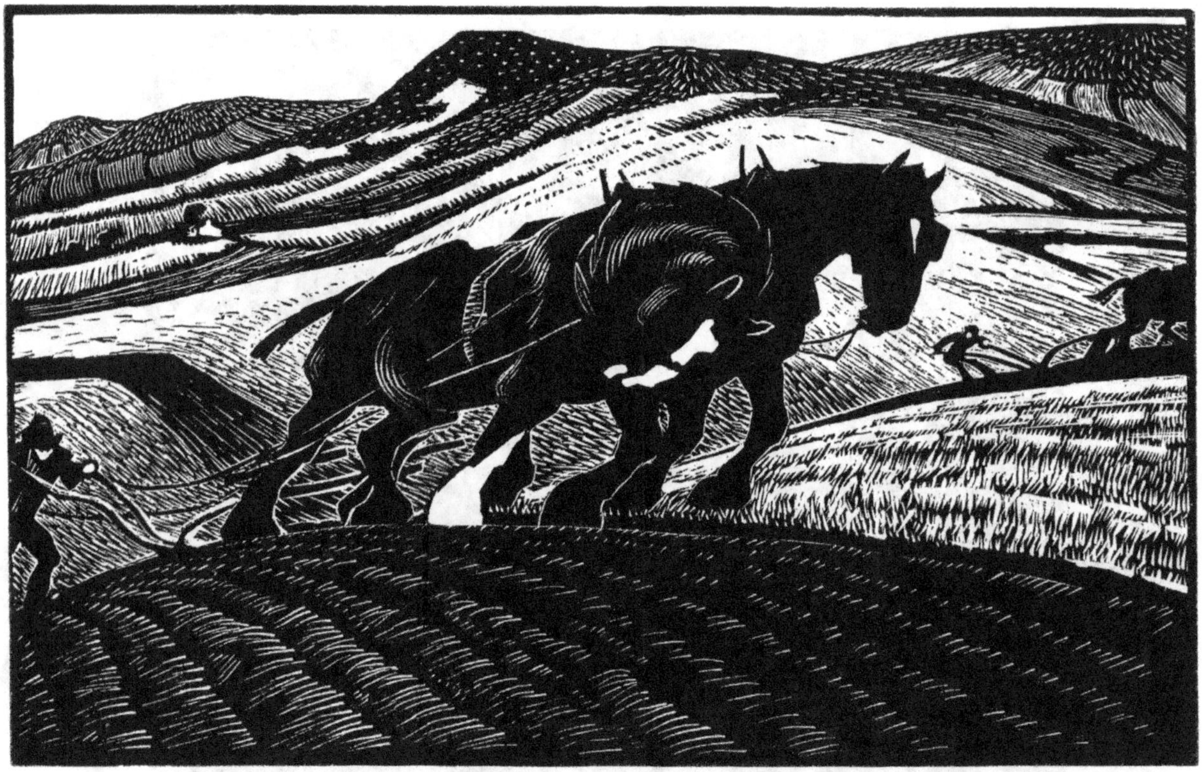

Untitled, wood engraving, 123 × 197, based on *Annalong*, 50 × 75, *County Down songs*, p. 10.
Not reproduced at actual size.

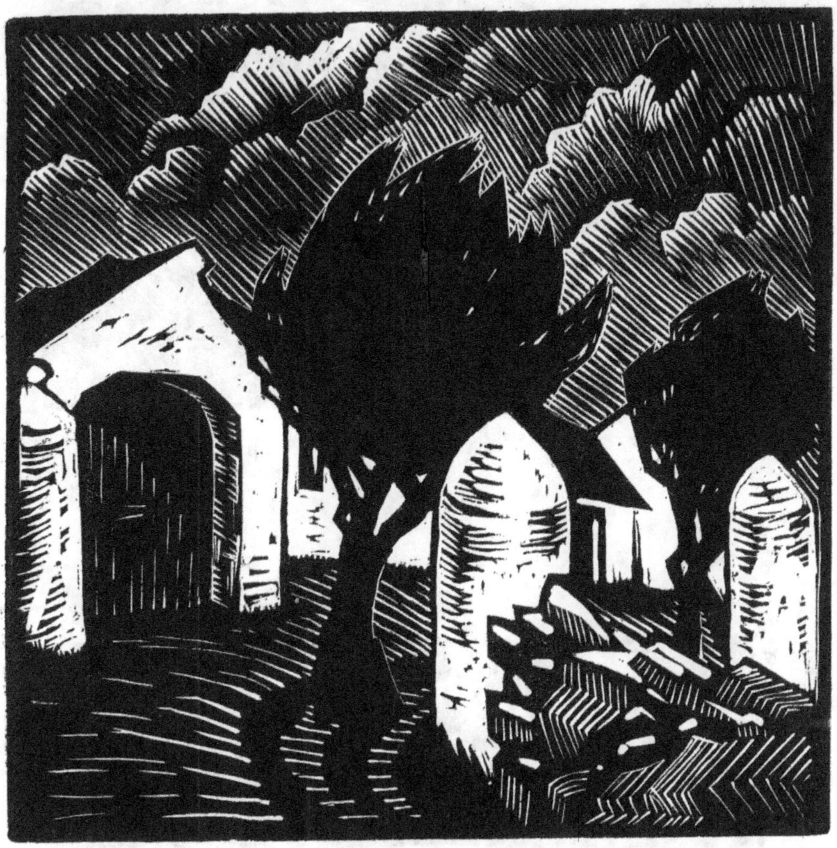

Gate posts, wood engraving
(Museum of New Zealand Te Papa Tongarewa), 109 × 114.

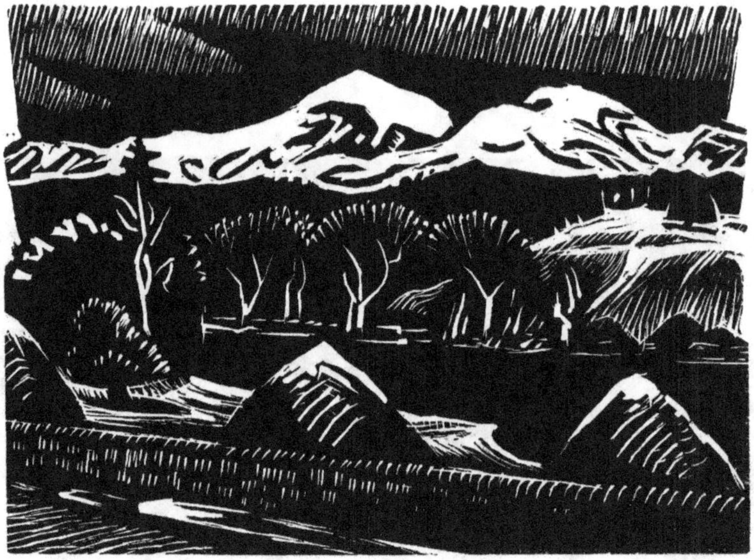

Mountains, 75 × 105, *As the sight is bent*, p. 23.

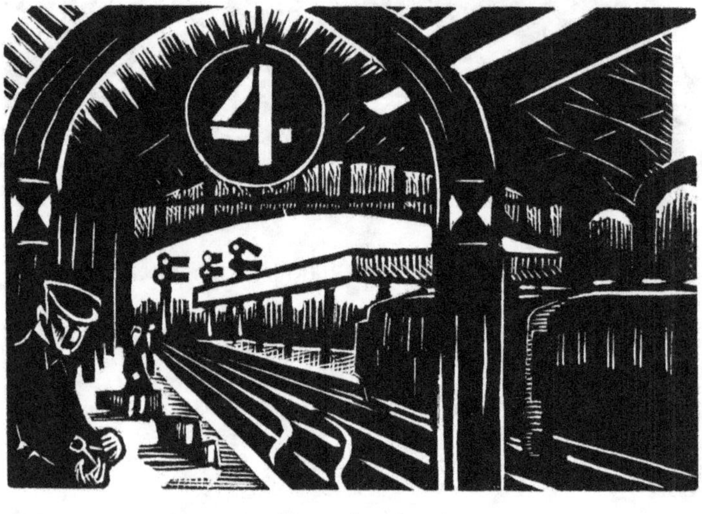

Station, 65 × 95, *As the sight is bent*, p. 41.

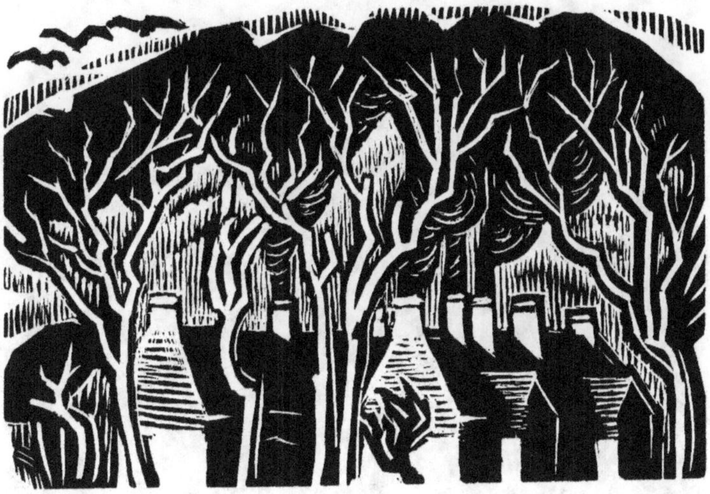

Treetops, 65 × 95, *As the sight is bent*, p. 43.

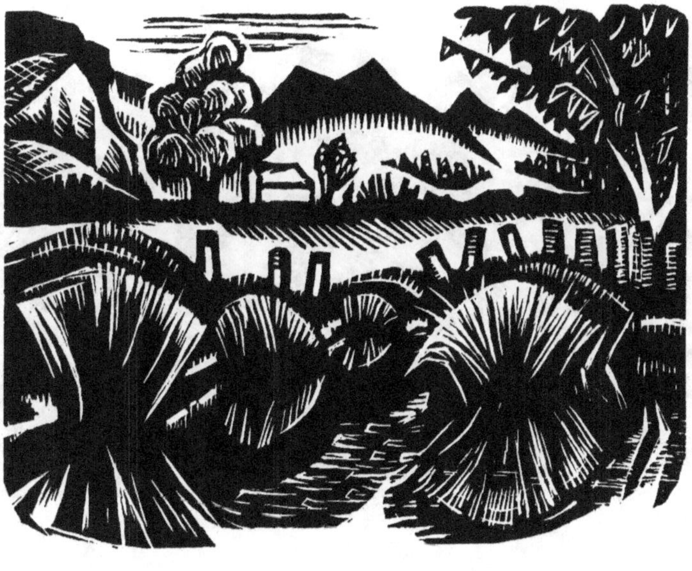

Wheat sheaves, 70 × 95, *As the sight is bent*, p. 31.

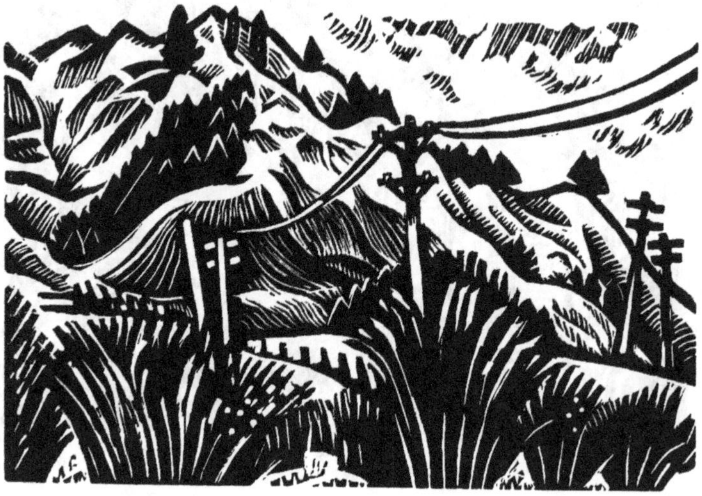

Rushes, 65 × 95, *As the sight is bent*, p. 105.

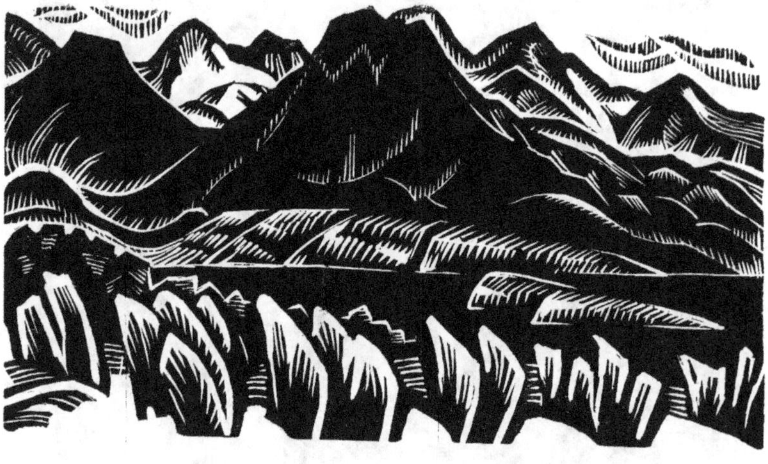

Rivers, 57.5 × 105, *As the sight is bent*, p. 49.

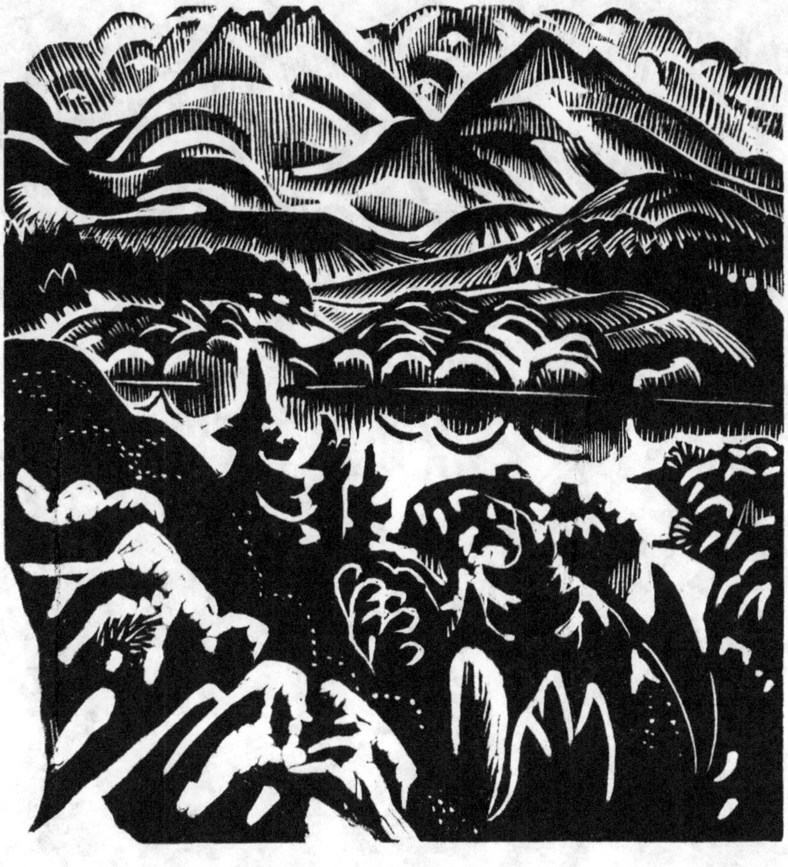

Broken mountain, 112 × 115, *As the sight is bent*, p. 37.

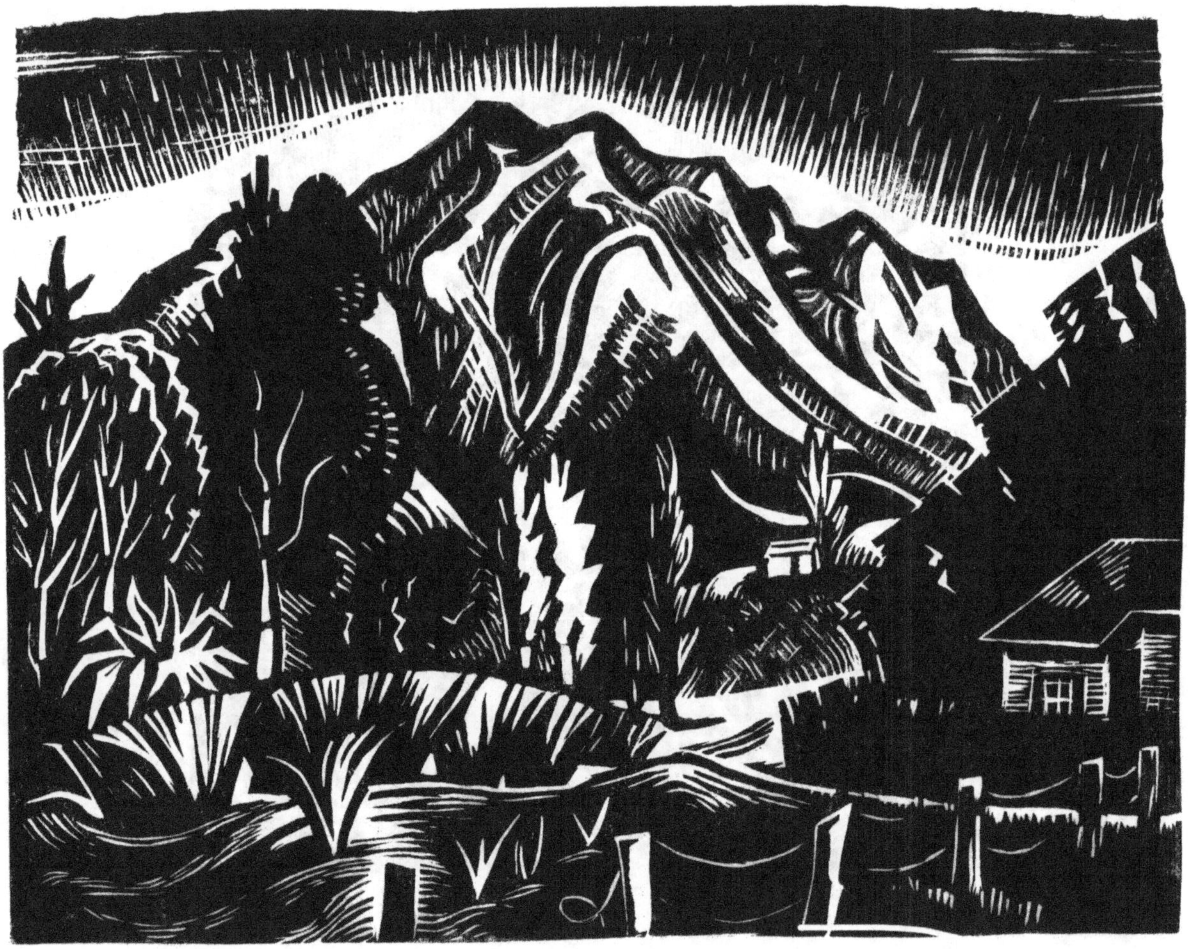

At Pohara, linocut, *c*. 1940–45 (Suter Art Gallery), 209 × 271.
Not reproduced at actual size.

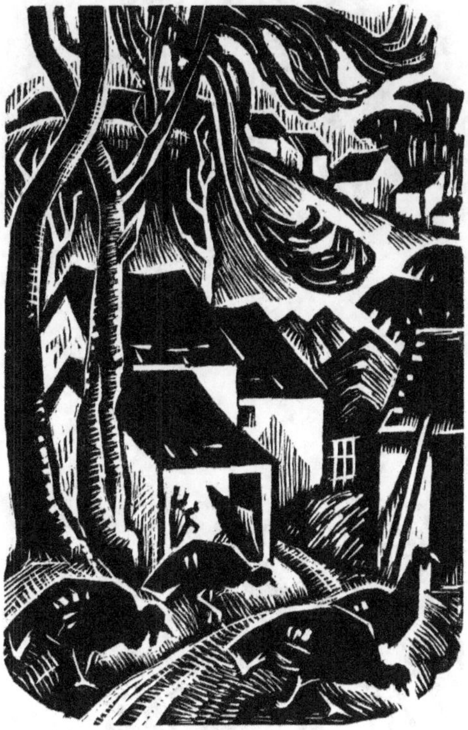

Houses, 97.5 × 65, *As the sight is bent*, p. 39.

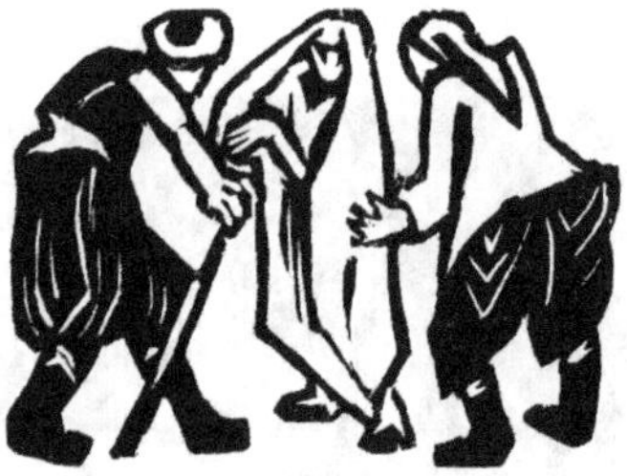

Cypriots, 30 × 45,
As the sight is bent, p. 94.

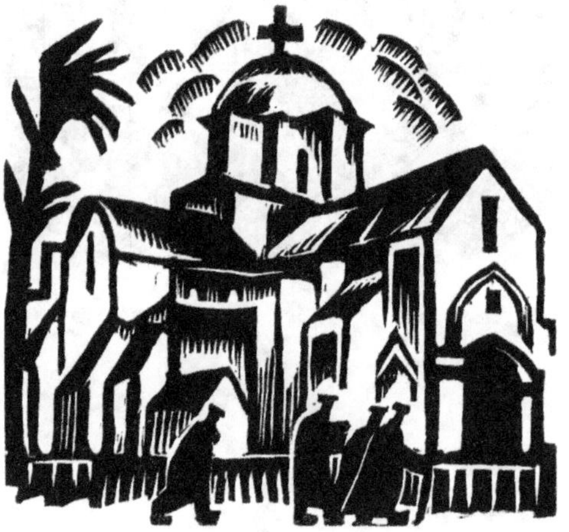

Greek church, 60 × 65,
As the sight is bent, p. 97.

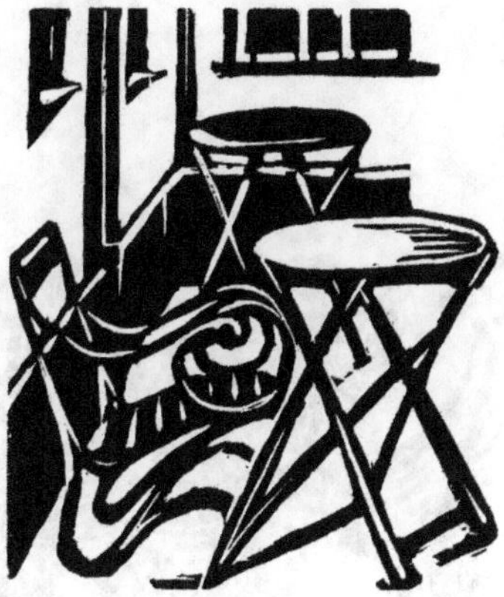

Verandah, 52.5 × 45,
As the sight is bent, p. 44.

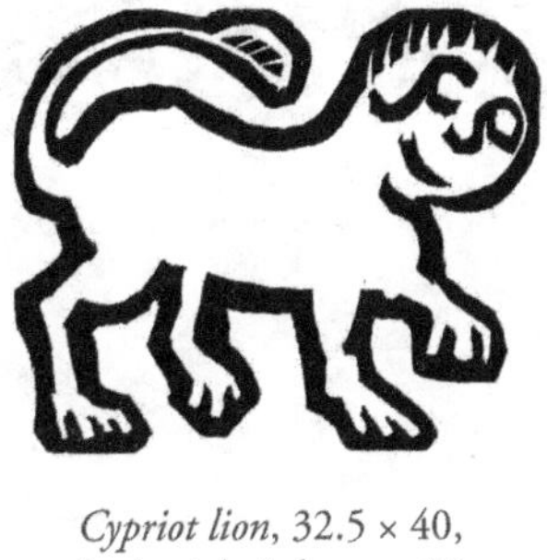

Cypriot lion, 32.5 × 40,
As the sight is bent, p. 95.

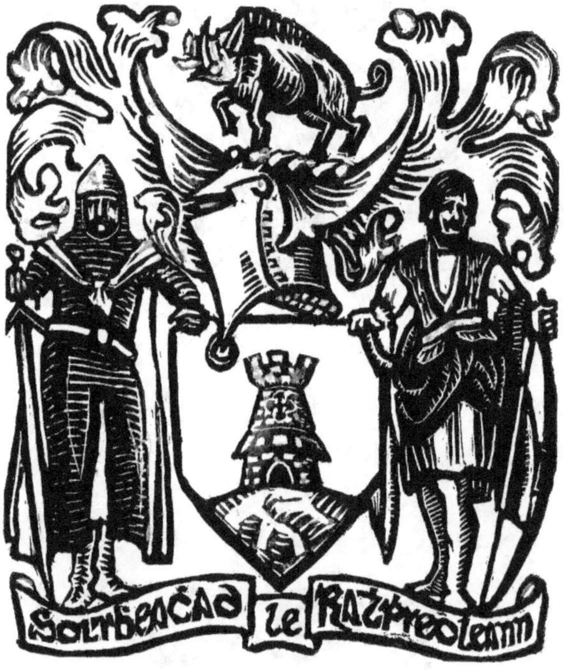

A coat of arms for a market town, wood engraving, 87 × 77.

INDEX

www.ingramcontent.com/pod-product-compliance
Lightning Source LLC
Chambersburg PA
CBHW080346030726
47598CB00009B/2648
9781913993559